Translating the Bible into Action

Translating the Bible into Action

*How the Bible can be relevant in
all languages and cultures*

Harriet Hill & Margaret Hill

Copyright ©2008 by PIQUANT EDITIONS Ltd
PO Box 83, Carlisle, CA3 9GR, UK
www.piquanteditions.com

British Library Cataloguing in Publication Data
Hill, Harriet S. (Harriet Swannie)
  Translating the Bible into action : how the Bible can be
  relevant in all languages and cultures
  1. Bible - Study and teaching 2. Church group work
  3. Language question in church 4. Multiculturalism -
  Religious aspects - Christianity
  I. Title II. Hill, Margaret
  253

ISBN: 978 1 903689 53 0

CONTENTS

Sharing Faith

Using Your Gifts

Literacy

Passing It On

PREFACE

When Jesus was born to Mary, God was translated into our human world. God doesn't require us to abandon our language and culture to relate to him; he came and made his home among us. This act of God's translation of himself continues today as the gospel is expressed in local languages and lived out in local cultures. God speaks our languages, enters our homes, sings our tunes, and brings healing to everyone and every culture that is willing to receive it. It is the nature of Christianity to express itself in the local language and culture, and in so doing it affirms the cultural and linguistic identity of all people. The result is a multi-lingual, multi-cultural church.

Too long the church has ignored its cultural and linguistic diversity. Too long it has tried to impose a universal code of thought and conduct on its members. It has not grappled adequately with the theological and practical implications of the diversity of languages and cultures in the plan of God. Some have dominated without realizing it, while others have been trodden under foot.

The church needs to encourage people to communicate with God in their own language. It needs to encourage them to integrate their Christian and cultural identities so that their worldview is transformed to reflect the values of God's kingdom. Each linguistic and cultural group has their own unique work to do in this regard.

This book has been developed to respond to this need. It has evolved over a period of fifteen years in workshops and courses with church leaders from a myriad of languages and cultures. Some have been marginalized until very recently and are just now hearing God speak to them through his word in their language for the first time. They are awed by the experience of affirmation. It tingles throughout their bodies and deep down in their souls. Good news of the best variety. This book has helped them embrace their God-given identity and interact with their new Scriptures in ways that are meaningful. Others have been in positions of power, unaware of the discrimination those from minority languages experience. This book has helped them address the diversity of languages and cultures in their churches in ways that affirm the identity and dignity of all people. It helps them minister to all of their members effectively. Since all churches speak at least one language and have at least one culture, this book is relevant to all.

We begin by identifying common barriers to Scripture engagement, and then discuss theological foundations of this translated faith. The book then explores how multilingual churches can maintain unity in Christ and celebrate the diversity of their membership. It goes on to help people use Scripture in relevant ways: identifying relevant cultural issues, preparing Bible studies and sermons, addressing human concerns, and doing meditation. It gives help on sharing faith through storying, good news encounters. It addresses sharing faith with Muslims, with children and youth, and in the home. It explores the use of music, drama, and the visual arts. It helps those needing literacy programmes and gives advice about research, marketing and how to introduce change. The materials in this book can be used in many ways, but one way that is especially effective is to use them in local Scripture engagement seminars. The final chapter in the book explains how to organize and run such seminars.

Talking about language

We refer to languages in various ways throughout this book. We use the term 'mother tongue' to refer to the first language(s) people learn when they are small children. This language is also referred to as our 'language of identity' because it shapes who we are. Most often, children learn their first language from their mother, and so it is commonly referred to as the 'mother-tongue'. In reality, children may actually learn their first language from their father, or they may learn two languages at the same time, one from their mother and another from their father.

We use the terms 'minority language' or 'local language' to refer to languages that are spoken by relatively small ethnic groups. We use the term 'majority language' to refer to languages that are spoken by the majority of people in a nation or region, such as French, English, Chinese, or Swahili. In some societies, people speak more than one majority language.

Everyone has a mother tongue. For some, it is a minority language. For others, it is a majority language. Majority language speakers, who tend to have power and wealth, often marginalize minority languages and the people who speak them. Since language and identity are often closely linked, this marginalization can affect the core of a person's being.

How to use this book

Chapters from this book can be used in weekly meetings of a church or community, or a selection of chapters can be used in a seminar that lasts several days. The materials are designed so that participants can teach what they have learned to others, so begin with those who can train others. Those passing on what they learned will learn better, and more people will benefit.

Most of the chapters in this book can be taught in an hour or two, but they can also be used over an extended period of time. For example, once a group has learned to do Bible studies, they can then work on creating a stock of them. In a seminar, it's usually possible to cover between two and three chapters per day. Schedule a series of seminars over time and cover additional chapters each time. Only those who have used what they learned in their churches should be invited to attend the follow-up seminar. Over time, you can complete the whole book. The churches will benefit as their members become well-nourished in their faith.

Whether using this book in an hour's meeting or in a week-long seminar, you'll need to select what you will be able to cover. First read all the chapters and then select those most relevant for your situation. Within the chapters you select, you will also need to decide which exercises, discussions, and assignments you can fit into the time you have available. Give participants enough new ideas to keep them interested, and enough interaction with those ideas to develop new attitudes and practices.

Stories and participatory learning

Everybody loves a *story*, so each chapter begins with a story about Pastor Simon and his imaginary adventures in the land of 'Sanatu' (see the map on page xiv). The story sets the theme for the chapter, and the discussion questions that follow get participants involved in the topic.

Each chapter has several main teaching points. These are interspersed with discussion groups and exercises because people learn best when they participate in the learning process. When teaching, observe the ten-minute rule: no one should teach for more than ten minutes without having a discussion or exercise of some sort. As much as possible, the course is designed to draw out what the participants already know. Often new ideas result from this interaction.

Some *discussions* take place in the large group. Others take place in small groups of various sorts. The kind of small group is indicated by a symbol in the margin. The table below lists the kinds of groups, their symbols, and how they function.

Type of exercise	Symbol	Directions for discussion or exercise
Stories		The story can be read aloud, either by one person or by several people taking it in turn. Alternatively one person can learn the story in advance and tell it to the group. Or participants can present a drama, based on the story.
Teaching questions		1. Ask the whole group the question(s). Give them time to think before answering. This will help you to understand what they already know and get them interested in the topic. 2. Write their responses on a board or flip chart. 3. Then look at the points listed in the book. If any are relevant to the situation but have not been mentioned, add them to the discussion.
Large group exercise		Let the whole group do the exercise together. Encourage as many people as possible to participate. This is an opportunity to 'brainstorm' and think up new solutions.

Small group discussion		1. Read over the questions or exercise with all of the participants.
		2. Divide the participants into groups of four or five. Unless a special type of group is indicated in the instructions, put people of different backgrounds together. Vary the mix of the groups over the course of the seminar.
		3. Give the small groups enough time to discuss the questions or do the exercise.
		4. Bring the groups back together. Have one spokesperson for each group share the group's conclusions with the large group. If time is limited, allow each group to say one thing rather than a summary of their discussion. Or ask them to give feedback on just one of the questions.
		5. You may want to write the findings on the board or on large sheets of paper.

Special small groups

| Church | | Divide participants into groups of four to six by the types of churches they attend, such as Catholic, Baptist, Pentecostal, Lutheran. This is indicated when discussions or exercises discuss the policies and practices of each kind of church. |
| Language | | Divide participants into groups of four to six according to the language they speak. This is indicated when the discussion or exercise deals with issues within a language community. |

Assignments are given towards the end of each chapter. These provide additional interaction to the ideas presented in the chapter. Most often, participants do these on their own in writing. This individual feedback allows the leader to see how each participant is absorbing the materials.

At the end of each chapter, some *key readings and websites* are listed. Many of the readings are at a basic level and enhance the teaching of the chapter. If the book is used for a credited course, participants should read some of the readings for each chapter. Many of the articles can be found on **http://www.scripture-engagement.org** .

ACKNOWLEDGEMENTS

This book is a written version of an oral tradition that has been passed down by many around the world over the past fifteen years. We thank all those who had a hand in shaping it. In particular, we would like to thank Rick Brown, Dave Cochran, Mary Crickmore, Bettina Gottschlich, John Lindley, Kirby O'Brien, David Payne, Michelle Petersen, David Presson, Michael Rynkiewich, Lamin Sanneh, Brian Schrag, Stephen Tucker, Andrew Walls, and Kathie Watters.

The following copyright holders have given permission for the use of photographs and/or artwork in this book: Rolf Buehler (p 188), Craig Duddles (pp 45, 202, 236, 278), Harriet Hill (pp 26, 205, 211), Margaret Hill (p 62), Ralph Hill (pp 128, 172, 173), Joyce Hyde (p 114), Rick Krowchenko (p 183), Elria Kwant (pp 3, 217), Pieter Kwant (pp 38, 90), Michael McMillan (p xiv), Kirby O'Brien (p 80), Hugh Steven (p 8) and Wycliffe Bible Translators (p 248).

Harriet Hill & Margaret Hill

WHAT WE BELIEVE . . .

1. God wants to communicate with us in a way we can understand.

2. In the past, God sent his Son—his Word made flesh—to this world to save us. Today, he communicates with us by his word, the Bible.

3. The incarnation shows us the way God wants to reach us: he comes and lives in our communities.

4. The diversity of languages and cultures is compatible with the plan of God. Our unity is based on love, not similarity.

5. Christianity can be expressed in all languages and lived out in all cultures. None is excluded; all need to be transformed by the gospel.

6. God wants the gospel to penetrate people's worldview and most often this is done best in the mother tongue.

7. In order for us fully to know our identity in Christ, we must integrate our past into what we are becoming in Christ. This includes our language and culture.

8. Churches cannot last long—nor can Christians mature in their faith—without the word of God in a language people understand.

9. Church leaders need to be sure that all members of their congregations are fed spiritually, regardless of their social class, gender, or age.

10. The more church leaders encourage the use of Scripture in appropriate languages and media, the more the members will use it.

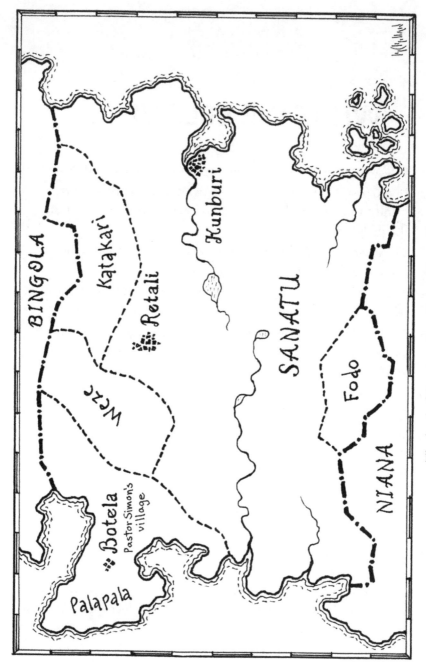

The land of Sanatu, where Pastor Simon lives

Chapter 1

BARRIERS TO ENGAGING WITH SCRIPTURE

Introduction

The vast majority of church leaders in the world would say that their faith is based on the Bible. They would also say that it is important for their church members to read and understand the Bible. But what is the reality? Few ordinary church members in any country study the Bible and apply its truths to their lives. Why is the reality so different from the ideal? This chapter looks at some of the barriers that keep people from reading and engaging with Scripture. The rest of this book proposes ways to address each barrier.

Pastor Simon's Worrying Discovery

Simon Nga is the pastor of a large church in the northern area of Sanatu. The major language there is Kisanu, the official language is English, and the local language is Palapala. The New Testament was recently published in Palapala. Each Sunday about 500 people come to the morning service. About 90 per cent speak Palapala, but the service and Bible readings are all in Kisanu or English. Some people carry a large English Bible and a few have a copy of the new Palapala New Testament with its bright green cover.

Pastor Simon is continuing his studies at a local theological college. This term he is taking a weekly course on Christian education in the church. As part of this course, he has to design a questionnaire in Palapala to study the level of Bible knowledge amongst his church members. These are some of his questions:

- Who is Jesus?
- What was the work of the twelve apostles Jesus chose?
- Why did God send a flood at the time when Noah built the ark?
- What is the Bible?
- Can you tell me one verse you have memorized from the Psalms?

Pastor Simon gave copies of the survey to 50 of his church members who had been coming to church for at least ten years. Thirty were able to write in the answers themselves. Twenty of them were not literate and so he read the questions to them and wrote down their answers.

Pastor Simon got back 41 of the questionnaires. When he added up the results, the totals horrified him. Thirty-five people had less than half of the answers right. A number of them had only one or two answers right, yet they had been sitting in his church Sunday after Sunday. Pastor Simon began to think about this. 'I've been teaching these people the Bible for years, and yet they seem to have been asleep! What should I do?' he wondered.

Soon after this, Pastor Simon received an invitation to go to a seminar for church leaders to learn to use the Palapala New Testament. He was doubtful about the idea, but since the top denominational leaders had sent the invitation, he agreed to go along. At the conference, he began to learn to read in Palapala, and he found that the Scriptures came alive for him in a new way.

'When I get back home', he thought, 'I'm going to use Palapala for the New Testament readings in the service. Maybe then people will understand the Bible better'.

 1) What are some of the barriers that prevent people from engaging with the Bible? First think of barriers that apply to engaging with the Bible in any language. Additional barriers prevent people from engaging with Scripture in minority languages and we'll address these later.

2) List the barriers on a large sheet of paper. After the lists have been made, ask one member of each group to share their list with all the participants. After all the groups have shared, talk about any of the points below that are relevant but have not been mentioned. Finish by making a composite list of all the barriers, and display it as a poster on the wall.

1. General barriers to engaging with Scripture

A. Literacy barrier

Printed Scriptures are effective when people know how to read and like to do so. But many people prefer to communicate using oral rather than written means, or they don't know how to read. Even if literacy classes were available, people may not be interested in attending them. In some cases, those who do learn to read may still prefer oral means of communication, and soon lose their new skills. In other cases, people may want to learn to read but they are hindered by poor eyesight or other problems. If Scripture is only presented in written form to people who do not know how to read or like to read, this is a serious barrier. (See Chapters 2, 16, 22, 23, and 24.)

B. Relevance barrier

People may not find the Bible to be relevant to their everyday lives. They may read or listen to the Bible for a short time because their pastor said they should, but they won't continue if they don't find that it helps them. In fact, the Bible is relevant to all aspects of our lives, but people may need help to understand it and to apply it to their lives. (See Chapters 9, 12, 13, and 17.)

C. Background Information barrier

The Bible was written for people who lived at least 2,000 years ago in cultures that were very different from ours today. The biblical authors didn't have to describe their culture in detail because their readers knew all about it. But today most of us know very little about the cultures of the Bible, and this makes it hard for us to understand the biblical author's meaning. Yet often there is little material to help people gain this background knowledge, especially in developing countries. (See Chapter10.)

D. Distribution barrier

People may want to read or listen to the Bible, but they may not be able to get a copy. This distribution barrier is so significant the British and Foreign Bible Society (one of the members of the United Bible Society) was founded as a response to it. In 1802, a poor Welsh girl named Mary Jones saved up her money for months and walked many miles to buy a Bible. When she arrived at the bookshop, she found that they were sold out. The bookshop owner decided that he would start an organization to make Bibles available to every person in a language they understand at a price they could afford. Lack of good distribution channels can be a serious barrier to the use of Scriptures. (See Chapter 27.)

E. Language barrier

People may have trouble engaging with the Bible if they read or hear it in a language they don't understand well. They may know a language well enough to buy produce at the market but not well enough to understand the Bible. Even if they understand the language, it may not be a language of their heart—a language that they use in the most intimate parts of their lives. For God's word to engage us deeply, we need to understand it and meditate on its truths in a language we understand well that touches our hearts. Otherwise, our engagement with it will be superficial and we may lose interest in Scripture. (See Chapters 3, 5, and 8.)

F. Translation barrier

Sometimes people reject translations because they do not correspond to the expectations or needs of the community.

- People may not like the style of the translation.
- The media in which Scripture is presented may not fit the community's preferences. For example, a printed translation would not be appropriate for a primarily oral community. Or Scripture in audio form will not be used if people don't have a way to play the recordings.
- A translation may be too old for people to easily understand. Translations need to be revised regularly because languages change over time and writing systems can also change. Those that were done more than 25 years ago may be difficult for people to understand.
- Reluctance to change may be a problem. People almost always reject revisions of old translations at first, because they are used to the old translations and consider them to be holy.

2. Barriers to engaging with minority-language Scripture

Certain barriers keep people from using Scripture in their mother tongue if they speak a minority language.

1) What are the specific barriers to using the available minority-language Scriptures? List them on a large piece of paper.

2) After the lists have been made, ask one member of each group to share their list with the large group. Add any of the points below that are relevant but have not been mentioned. Finish by making a composite list of all the barriers and display it as a poster on the wall.

A. Multilingualism barrier

In many places, churches are made up of speakers of many different languages. Church leaders may use a neutral language in an effort to be fair to everyone. They may fear that using the local languages will divide the church. Meanwhile, the people may not understand the deeper spiritual truths being taught because they don't understand the language being used well enough or it may not be a language of their heart. (See Chapters 6, 7, and 8.)

B. Language attitude barrier

Minority ethnic groups may consider their language to be inferior. This attitude may have developed due to pressures from the larger society. For example, in some places children were punished at school for speaking their mother tongue even when playing in the playground. Attitudes learned as a child go very deep. If people feel ashamed of their language, they will not want to use mother-tongue Scriptures. (See Chapters 3, 4, and 6.)

C. Church leader barrier

If church leaders do not encourage their congregations to use mother-tongue Scriptures, this will present a serious barrier. Church leaders may not use mother-tongue Scriptures for a variety of reasons. They may fear that they will not be able to read the mother tongue aloud properly. Or they may think that the majority language is more 'holy'. Or they may have received all their theological education in a majority language and not know how to express biblical concepts in their own language. Or they may not be from the same language group and may not have learned the local language. (See Chapters 3, 4, 5, 6, 14, and 25.)

If a church has a tradition of using Scripture in a majority language, it may present an enormous barrier to the use of the minority-language Scripture. Changing a long-established tradition is a difficult and slow process. (See Chapters 28 and 29.)

D. Community-ownership barrier

If churches feel that the translation in the minority language does not belong to them they may not use it. This can happen where a translation has been done without inviting all the churches that use the language to participate in the translation process. Some denominations may feel that they have been left out if the translation team did not include someone from their church. People who speak a different dialect than the one used in the translation may feel that they have been ignored. The lack of local ownership can be a barrier to people engaging with the minority-language Scripture. (See Chapters 2, 6, and 28.)

E. Economic barrier

Minority-language Scriptures are expensive to publish, so Bible translation agencies subsidize them so that they are affordable. But in times of extreme economic distress, even subsidized prices may be too high and the majority-language Scriptures may be cheaper. Churches may not be willing to be involved in distributing minority-language Scripture because they do not usually generate a profit. (See Chapter 27.)

F. Translation barrier

In addition to the challenges translations of the Bible into any language face, minority-language translations face some additional ones:

- Sometimes people are not interested in the first Bible books that were translated. If people's first exposure to mother-tongue Scripture is negative, they may reject it for the long term. For example, Muslims may reject the entire translation if the first book published is Luke's Gospel. The order in which materials are translated affects Scripture use.

Dialect differences may present barriers in two ways:

- The translation may not have been done in the dialect that the majority of the language group understands.
- Although people might be able to understand the dialect used in the translation, they may not want to use it for social reasons. For example, they may see the speakers of the dialect as enemies or as inferior. (See Chapter 2.)

G. Writing system barrier

The way a language is written can make it difficult to read. In general, each meaningful sound should be represented by a separate letter in the alphabet. If this isn't done, a language may be hard to read. English is a good example of a language that does not have enough letters. It has five letters for vowels, but there are 21 distinct vowel sounds. Tonal languages may need to have the tone marked on certain words or else people will stumble and have to re-read sentences.

With enough education in a language, it's possible for people to learn to read it even if it has an inadequate alphabet. However, if little education is available in a language with an inadequate alphabet, most people won't be able to learn to read it.

People may reject the way their language is written even if it is linguistically correct because it doesn't look like the majority language or simply because they don't want their language written that way. Developing a writing system that is easy to use and accepted by the people takes time, but is essential for people to read the translated Scripture.

Some languages are harder to read than others. For example, one language in East Democratic Republic of Congo has 48 separate symbols for consonants alone. This makes learning to read quite difficult, but this isn't an insurmountable barrier to the use of the Scriptures in that language. (See Chapters 25 and 26.)

1) Put the list of barriers you compiled in the first of the previous two exercises in front of the group and read it through again.

2) Ask everyone to choose four barriers they think are the most important in their area. Don't discuss solutions to these problems yet.

3) Read out each item and ask for a show of hands for those who vote for that barrier. It may be good to ask them to shut their eyes before voting, so others don't influence them.

4) Mark the barriers in order of importance to the participants.

5) Do the same thing with the second list of barriers (to engaging with mother-tongue Scriptures).

6) Put these two lists up where they can remain throughout the seminar. Be sure that the barriers considered the most important by most people are well covered during seminar teaching and discussion sessions.

Assignments

1. Design a questionnaire to test the Bible knowledge of the members of your own church. Give the questionnaire to 20 members and see how much people have understood from the sermons and Bible teaching.

2. If you have a church with members who speak the same mother tongue as well as the majority language, carry out a mini-survey to compare how well people understand Bible passages in each language.

   a) Choose two Bible passages with a similar level of difficulty—for example, Mark 10:46–52 and Mark 1:40–45.

   b) Read the first passage to six people in the majority language and ask questions to see what they have understood.

   c) Then read the second passage in the mother tongue and ask questions to see what they have understood.

d) Then does the same thing in reverse order with six more people: read the first passage in the mother tongue and the second in the majority language. Compare the results.

e) Do people understand one language better than the other? Think about what this might mean for church services and Scripture reading.

3. Another way to find out which language communicates best is to teach two subjects with a similar level of difficulty to the same group. The first week, teach in the majority language and the next week, teach in the mother tongue. Each time give them a quiz to find out how much they have understood. Compare the results.

*Readings**

Beavon, Mary. 2001. 'Promoting SU in Difficult Environments.' *Scripture in Use Today* 2:15–17.

Beine, David K. 2001. 'Views about Scripture: a Key to a Well-Used Book.' *Notes on Sociolinguistics* 6(1):5–15.

Brichoux, Felicia. 1988. 'Please Don't Speak My Language!' *Notes on Scripture in Use and Language Programs* 18:27–37.

Dye, T. Wayne. 1980. *The Bible Translation Strategy*. Dallas, TX: Wycliffe Bible Translators, pp 13–36.

Hill, Margaret. 2000. 'The Use and Lack of Use of Translated Scriptures.' *Scripture in Use Today* 1:12–16.

Landin, David. 1990. 'Some Factors which Influence Acceptance of Vernacular Scriptures.' *Notes on Scripture in Use and Language Programs* 24(6):4–22.

Payne, David L. 1988. 'On Promoting Vernacular Scriptures Where a National Language Translation Is Venerated.' *Notes on Literature in Use and Language Programs* 17:18–23.

Wilson, J. D. 1991. 'What It Takes To Reach People in Oral Cultures.' *Evangelical Missions Quarterly* 27(2):154–159.

---

* http://www.scripture-engagement.org

Chapter 2

USING APPROPRIATE SCRIPTURE PRODUCTS

Introduction

The process of translating Scripture involves many choices. Church leaders need to understand the options and issues involved in translation so that they can make wise choices about Scripture products for their communities. This chapter discusses some of the options and suggests ways of designing relevant Scripture products.

Translation Challenges in Sanatu

Pastor Simon was at a conference for all the pastors from his denomination in the northern region of their country. On the second day, representatives from Bible translation agencies gave the pastors some news about the on-going Bible translation projects in ten languages of Sanatu. The pastors listened with great interest and at the end asked many questions.

Pastor Lambo spoke first. 'Almost all the people I work with are illiterate; they are also followers of Islam. The translation team has produced a very nice Gospel of Luke with illustrations, but no one wants to buy or read it. If they'd discussed it with us, we would have asked for some Old Testament stories in audio form, and certainly no illustrations! Now what can we do?'

Pastor Mark also had a problem. 'We have a translation of the whole New Testament in our language, but it was done by a small team of people who didn't consult with us or with the Catholics. They only worked with a small denomination that has four churches. Now the Catholics are saying they want to do their own translation. What can we do?'

Then Pastor Raji shared his problem. 'We have a translation in the local language, but a lot of people don't like it. When they compare it with the English or the Kisanu translation, they find that there is a lot added into it. Now they don't trust it'.

Finally, Pastor Yeti asked about the Bible in Weze. He said, 'This translation was published in 1952. We don't speak that way anymore. When we use this translation in church, people find it hard to understand. What can we do?'

1) Divide into four groups. Have each group take one of the problems expressed by the pastors and discuss solutions.

2) Have you experienced similar problems? If so, discuss them.

1. Working with church leaders on translation programme issues

Church leaders decide which Bible translations and Scripture products are used in their churches, so it is very important to involve them in making decisions about translation projects. Since a translation is shared by all the churches in a language community, top leaders from all the major churches represented in the community should be involved. If there are no churches in the area, leaders from churches or missions that are interested in beginning ministry there should be consulted. Translators need to educate these church leaders about translation issues so that they can make informed decisions. The more those who will be using the Scripture products are involved in the decision-making, the more likely it will be that they use them when they are completed. This section looks at programme issues.

A. Choice of translators

Churches can be involved in translation projects by supplying translators and reviewers. Ideally, each of the major churches interested in having mother-tongue Scripture should propose three to five candidates that fulfil certain criteria, such as educational level, character qualities, and spiritual engagement. If possible, a Bible translation agency should hold an assessment course for these candidates. The leader of the course can assess the abilities of each participant and give the results to the church leaders. They can make the final selection based on the candidates' performance at the course as well as other factors, such as their character, availability, and so forth. The candidates who are not chosen to be translators can serve as reviewers.

B. Establishing review committees

Review committees check the initial drafts of the translation produced by the translation team. They are one of the best ways of establishing local ownership. Those organizing the translation project should invite all denominations in the area to send representatives to a training course of three to five days. At this course, participants learn basic translation principles and start reviewing some draft translation to be sure it sounds natural in the language. A number of review committees can be established in major centres of the language area.

2. Working with church leaders on translation product issues

Many decisions must be made about the kind of translation product that would be appropriate for a community. These must be considered carefully because the more Scripture products match the community's needs and expectations, the more likely they will be used.

A. Selection of media

What may seem like disinterest in Scripture may actually be disinterest in the media in which it is presented. Scriptures can be prepared in a variety of print, audio, or audio-visual media. For example, Scripture passages can be printed in short booklets, in diglot versions, in cartoon form, and so on. Audio Scriptures can include local music or drama. Films can be used, for example, the *Jesus Film*. Show church leaders examples of a variety of products to help them decide the kind of product that is appropriate for their community. Scripture engagement will increase if the media matches the community's preferences.

B. Selection of biblical passages

Certain biblical passages will be more relevant to a community than others, and it is important to start with those that attract people's attention. Possible examples are:

- passages needed for the evangelistic track of the Bible storying programme (See Chapter 16.)
- passages with high appeal to Muslim communities (See Chapter 19.)
- for liturgical churches, the gospel passages for the next liturgical year for example, if you are in Year B, translate the passages for Year C.
- Luke's Gospel: this is appropriate where there are plans to record the *Jesus Film*.

C. Selection of the kind of translation

Church leaders need to understand the different kinds of Bible translations and their goals. Over time, translators have had different ideas about what made a good translation. Long ago, people thought they should translate each word of the original text with a word in the receptor language. This is referred to as a word-for-word translation. This approach often led to awkward constructions that were difficult to read. People had to get used to this strange form of their language to understand the meaning. The King James Bible is the nearest to this type of translation in English.

Later, people understood that the meaning of the original needs to be expressed in the receptor language, regardless of whether it takes the same number of words or not. This is referred to as a "dynamic equivalence" translation. The idea was that the effect of the translation should be equivalent to that of the original, and the translation should follow the natural structures of the language. Most Bibles translated into English recently have used this translation model, with some taking more liberties to express the meaning than others.

More recently, people have realized that the author's meaning isn't found in the text alone, but in the interplay of the text with the background information that the text brings to mind. For example, when Matthew wrote that Jesus associated with tax collectors, he expected his audience to know how much Jews despised them. Giving audiences the biblical text in their language is only half of the task. If they do not have the background information that the original readers had, they will not understand all of the intended meaning. They may use their own background information and misunderstand the meaning, or they may not think of any background information and so not understand any or very little of the intended meaning.

Translators can solve this problem of background information in two ways:

1. They can keep their translation as close to the original as possible, and expect the audience to learn the background information that is different from their own. This is referred to as a 'reference translation'.

2. They can adapt the text to their audience's context. This makes the text easier for their audience to understand, but every adaptation changes the meaning in some way. This is referred to as a 'contextualized translation'.

For example, imagine translating 'Give us this day our daily bread' for an ethnic group whose staple food is rice. If there is a local word for 'bread', translators can use it and then supply the information that bread was the staple food for Jews in a footnote. Or they can translate 'Give us this day our daily rice', with the option of including a footnote explaining that the text literally said 'bread'. This would be easier for their audience to understand immediately using their own background knowledge, but it is not as close to the original meaning. Of course, for cultures that have bread as their staple food, there would be no difficulty translating the verse.

Different kinds of translations are useful for different purposes. A reference translation is best for those who want to know what the original author communicated as exactly as possible and who are willing to learn the original background information. A contextualized translation is better for those who want a translation that is easier to understand without having to learn the original context, and who are less concerned about the author's exact meaning. The kind of translation that is done needs to match the audience's needs and expectations. If it doesn't, they will not be satisfied and the translation may not be used.

1) Have you noticed any differences in translations that you have used?

2) What kind of translation do you think would be best for your church?

• • • • • •

> *The more closely Scripture products match a community's needs and expectations, the more likely they will be used.*

D. Understanding differences in translations

One thing that can look very different between translations is idioms. In an idiom, several words together mean something quite different from the meaning of the individual words. For example, in referring to a rebellious son, someone might say, 'He broke his mother's heart'. This does not mean that the son literally attacked his mother and smashed her heart with an axe, or that her heart fell into pieces like a broken glass, but that he made his mother very sad. Translators need to communicate the meaning of the idiom, not the meaning of the individual words. For example, a translation of this into Ngbaka would say, 'He caused that his mother's liver sat down'. Many idioms in the Bible come from the Hebrew culture. If these are translated literally, often they make little sense.

Many ideas that were known in biblical times may not be known by certain audiences today—for example, snow, Roman soldier's armour, the sea, or ships. Translators may have to use a descriptive phrase to translate these concepts—for example 'a large animal called a camel'. They may use a more general term—for example, flowers instead of lilies (Matthew 6:28). In certain cases, they may be able to substitute a known object for an unknown one. For example, they may substitute a leopard for a lion in 1 Peter 5:8, since the focus is on a dangerous animal.

In each of the passages below, the King James Version has retained the form of the original text rather than translating the meaning. What do the passages below mean in modern English? You may need to look at the context of each verse.

1) Mark 2:19—*And Jesus said unto them, Can the children of the bridechamber fast, while the bridegroom is with them? (KJV)*

2) Acts 18:6—*Your blood be upon your own heads; I am clean: from henceforth I will go unto the Gentiles. (KJV)*

3) Acts 2:37—*When the people heard this, they were cut to the heart . . .*

4) Matthew 3:8—*Produce fruits in keeping with repentance.*

E. Key biblical terms

While a translation project is underway, leaders from all the churches need to be involved in decisions about translating key biblical terms, such as Holy Spirit, grace, the cross, repentance, glory, eternal life, God, or angels. A Scripture engagement seminar is a good time to discuss decisions about terms like this.

The group may have to deal with a number of issues. Certain concepts may be difficult to express in the local language. Or two or more denominations may use different terms for certain biblical terms and they may not want to change.

It may take a long time, much discussion, and careful study to reach agreement, and this may block progress on the translation. Often a compromise is the only solution. For example, in a large language in the Democratic Republic of Congo, the Catholics and the Protestants had different terms for Holy Spirit. They knew they had to have one Bible for everyone to use, so they had to come to an agreement on the term used in the translation. After much discussion, their solution was to take the word for 'holy' from the Catholics and the word for 'Spirit' from the Protestants! Ten years later, no one remembered the original terms.

If a translation is already published, then it is equally important to help the church leaders understand and learn to use the terms in the translation. A booklet of key biblical terms is a useful tool. (See Chapter 7.)

1) Are any terms in your mother-tongue Scriptures still unresolved? What are they?

2) How can the discussion on these terms be moved forward?

3) Pick four biblical terms that cause problems in your language and discuss what you understand by them. When you are with others from your community, ask them what they understand by these terms.

F. Formatting options

The format of Scripture products affects whether people buy and use them. Church leaders need to help decide whether the product will be produced in print, audio format, on the web, or in a variety of these media.

If the product is to be printed, then the question of illustrations, colour of cover, layout and so forth should be decided together. The font needs to be large enough for people to read in poor light. Wide margins around the text will make it easier to read.

For audio Scripture, packaging is important. Church leaders need to decide about any music that is used. Some communities may want to use local music, while others may want to use pre-recorded music provided by recording agencies.

Think of a new translation of Scripture in your country. This might be a new translation of the Bible in a majority or minority language.

1) Have people accepted the new product?

2) If not, why did they reject it?

3. Working with church leaders on language issues

Certain language issues affect whether Scripture will be used or not. Here are some of the main areas.

A. The writing system

Basic questions about the writing system should be settled before work on the translation begins, but often it takes years of discussion before issues are fully resolved. Two areas that may need to be discussed are word boundaries and the spelling of proper names. Scripture engagement seminars may be a good place to discuss these things.

Typically, word boundary issues involve grammar—for example, whether the pronoun is written attached to the verb or separately, or whether compound words are written as one or two words. The way these words are written is a matter of opinion, but people may have very strong opinions! These things need to be discussed thoroughly.

Names need to be spelled the same way throughout Scripture, so it's important to establish rules for spelling them early on in the translation programme. There are over 1,000 proper names in the New Testament, and more than 6,000 in the Old Testament. If names—especially important names like 'Jesus'—are spelled in ways that certain churches do not accept, they may reject the translation altogether.

B. Dialect issues

The church leaders of an area need to agree about the dialect to be used in their translation. This may require many hours of discussion and possibly help from linguists. After a decision is made, church leaders from dialects other than the one selected need to promote the mother-tongue Scriptures. They can teach people to read the Scriptures aloud using the pronunciation of their own dialect. For example, if the dialect used in the translation has some words beginning with 'f', and another dialect pronounces the same words with a 'p', people in that dialect should pronounce the words with a 'p' when reading aloud. English is a very good example of one written form that serves many oral dialects.

1) Which of the above points have all the churches in your language area discussed already?

2) Which ones have been neglected so far?

3) If the translation project is still underway in your language, do you have any denominations not involved in it? What could you do to bring them into the process?

Assignments

1. Ilea is a translation project leader who wants to get the Bible translated as quickly as possible. He doesn't feel he has time to talk with church leaders about translation issues. List some reasons why he should take time to involve them.

2. Which of the subjects in this chapter do you think are the most important to cover in Scripture engagement seminars in your area? Why?

3. Translate a paragraph that is not Scripture from English into your language. You can use an information leaflet or a paragraph from a magazine or newspaper. Write down the problems you encounter.

Readings*

Beekman, John. 1980. 'Anthropology and the Translation of the New Testament Key Terms.' *Notes on Translation* 80:32–42.

Dooley, Robert A. 1989. 'Style and Acceptability: The Guaraní New Testament.' *Notes on Translation* 3 (1):49–57.

Glover, Warren. 1982. 'Diglot New Testaments-Pros and Cons.' *Notes on Scripture Use* 2:14–16.

Gutt, Ernst-August. 1988. 'From Translation to Effective Communication', *Notes on Translation* 2(1):24–40.

Hill, Harriet. 2006. *The Bible at Cultural Crossroads.* Manchester, UK: St Jerome Publishing, pp 1–12, 53–60.

Hill, Margaret. 1999. 'Assessment Courses to Choose Mother-Tongue Translators.' *Notes on Translation* 13:(4:)15–26.

Simons, Gary. 1984. 'The Lectionary Approach in Scripture Translation.' *The Bible Translator* 35(2):216–223.

Titrud, Kermit. 1994. 'Diglots in the Philippine Context.' *Notes on Literature and Language Programs* 42:23–28.

Useful websites

http://www.forum-intl.net   This is the site of the Forum of Bible Agencies International. Many of the articles listed at the end of each chapter in this book can be downloaded from the Resources—Scripture Engagement tab on this site.

http://www.biblesociety.org This is the site of the United Bible Societies.

http://www.wycliffe.net   This is the site of Wycliffe International.

---

*   http://www.scripture-engagement.org

Theological Foundations

Chapter 3

LANGUAGE IN THE PLAN OF GOD

Introduction

Christians need to have access to Scripture in a language they understand and that also speaks to their hearts. When people's mother tongue is a minority language, they may think that it is inferior to majority languages and not appropriate for communicating with God. This chapter looks at what we believe the Bible teaches about language and discusses some ways to raise the status of marginalized languages.

God speaks Palapala

Act out this skit.

Pastor Simon came back from his seminar full of new ideas about using Palapala in church services and other church meetings. At the seminar he had been amazed to discover how much better he understood Ephesians in his own language. Now he could see a way to help his congregation improve their understanding of the Bible and of their faith. He looked up who was scheduled to lead the service that Sunday and found that it was Mr Amani, so he went to visit him to discuss changing the language for the Sunday service.

Simon: Good morning! How are you and your family?

Amani: We are all fine. How are you doing, and did you return well from Retali?

Simon: Yes, everyone is well, and I had no problem on the road.

Amani: Come and sit down and drink some tea.

Simon: I've come to tell you about what I learned at the seminar and also to discuss the service for this Sunday. During the seminar, we learned to read Palapala and I found that reading the New Testament in Palapala really spoke to my heart. Almost everyone that comes to our church is a Palapala like us, so I would like us to use much more of our own language in the service, and also our New Testament readings should be from Palapala. I've brought some copies of the New Testament back with me.

Amani: Well, I find this a shocking idea! Why would we want to use Palapala to talk to God? Using Palapala in church would pollute the place! Surely we should use a respectable language like English. Anyway, you know, it's the prayers that are said in English that really work.

Simon: We learned on the seminar that all languages are the same in God's sight and that English—or Kisanu—aren't any better than Palapala. God made them all and they are all good and beautiful. Besides, God wants us to understand what he's saying. I thought I understood Ephesians, but when I heard it in Palapala, I realized that I was missing a lot of what Paul was saying.

Amani: Understand? Are we supposed to understand God's word? That would take all of the power out of it!

Simon: I know some religions teach that the less you understand, the more powerful the holy words are, but Christianity is different. God wants us to understand him and know him very well. He is powerful, but he also wants to be very close to us.

Amani: Really? Are you sure?

Simon: Yes. When Jesus came to this world as a baby, he learned to speak the language of his village. If he had been born in a Palapala village, he would have learned Palapala, not Kisanu. When someone speaks our language, we know they understand us and care about us. When I hear Scripture in Palapala, God seems to be one of us, not a foreigner.

Amani: Well, these are all new ideas to me.

What do people in your area believe is the best language to use to communicate with God?

1. Theological foundations

The use of minority-language Scriptures depends on a good understanding of how God communicates with us. In the next three chapters we will develop a theological foundation for using minority-language Scriptures. Refer to 'What We Believe...' at the beginning of this book to find these beliefs listed.

A. God wants to communicate with us in a way we can understand

We know that God wants to communicate with us because he sent his Son to this earth to live with people (John 1:14). Jesus spoke the languages of the people he lived with so that they could understand him. He also lived in their culture, and communicated in the context of that culture. For example, he spoke about vineyards and fishing and shepherds, Roman coins and Old Testament passages.

Today he communicates with us by his word, the Bible. The good news needs to be understandable to those who receive it, which means that it needs to be expressed in a language people know well and identify with. Where their culture is different from that of Jesus' day, they will also need to understand the cultural background information they are missing.

Many religions use magical rituals that ordinary people are not meant to understand. They may say prayers in a foreign language because it seems more holy. The fact that most people do not understand the prayers makes them seem powerful. Christianity is not like that. God wants to communicate with us in a way we can understand.

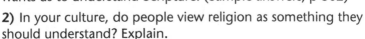

1) Find some passages in the Bible that teach us that God wants us to understand Scripture. (Sample answers, p 302)

2) In your culture, do people view religion as something they should understand? Explain.

B. The incarnation shows that God comes to us and lives with us

By using our language, Christ shows that he identifies with us. In many religions, people strive to reach God to be accepted by him. They may consider their way of life too lowly for God. But God doesn't have this attitude. Although he is completely holy, he sent his son Jesus to live among us in this world. Rather than polluting his divine nature, Jesus healed the brokenness of the people and cultures he touched. When we have Scripture in our language, God is translated into our world. He connects with who we are in our deepest identity.

1) How do people in your community feel about God speaking their mother tongue?

2) Discuss the skit you saw at the beginning of this session. Act out a continuation of it showing what Pastor Simon could say to help Amani understand that God speaks his language.

C. The diversity of languages and cultures is part of the plan of God

Collect leaves and flowers from different plants. Take time to look at them closely and then ask the following questions:

1) How is each one different?

2) What does this teach you about God's creation?

God didn't create just one kind of flower, but many. In the same way, God created a variety of languages and cultures. We know that this variety will continue to the end of this world because Revelation 7:9 says that people from every language will stand before God's throne at the end of time: *'After this I looked and there before me was a great multitude that no-one could count, from every nation, tribe, people and language, standing before the throne and in front of the Lamb.'*

The modern world relies on standardization. For example, in a factory each part of a car needs to be made identically so that all the parts fit together. Creativity is not allowed on the assembly line. People have tried to apply the way factories work to all of life. This leads them to think it is more practical for everyone to speak the same language.

God's creation is not like this. No two people or cultures are the same. God created each one in its own special way. The church is not united by making everyone the same, but by respecting the diversity of its members. Each person and group brings their praise to God in the way that only they can. If they neglect praising God in their language and using their cultural forms, the variety of praise that Revelation 7:9 speaks of will be incomplete and the church will be the poorer for it.

1) Are there ways in which people in your community are shamed for speaking their mother tongue?

2) Are there ways in which people in your community are honoured when they speak the majority language?

3) How can churches affirm the variety of languages God created?

D. No language or culture is holier than another

1) Show a King James Bible, a majority language Bible (for example Swahili), and a Bible or New Testament in a local language. Ask the group which of these Bibles is the most holy. Discuss the replies briefly without drawing any conclusions.

2) When Jesus was born, four languages were used in Israel:

- Latin was the prestigious language of the colonial authorities.
- Greek was the language of education, communication and trade.
- Aramaic was the language used in the homes of the Jews.
- Hebrew was the language of the Jewish Scriptures and religious studies.

Which language do you think Jesus usually used?

Most scholars think that Jesus usually spoke Aramaic, the language ordinary people used in every-day life. He also knew Hebrew, and probably spoke Greek, too.

If any language were better to use to speak to God, it would have been the language that Jesus used but, apart from a few isolated words and phrases, we don't even have a record of his original words. We only have translations of them.

> *God wants to communicate with us in the language we use in our every-day lives.*

On the day of Pentecost, people heard the good news in their own languages (Acts 2:5–11). They probably understood Greek, but God performed this miracle to show that he values the mother tongue, even for people who may know other languages.

In the first centuries of the church, the Bible was translated into Latin so that common people could understand it. Over time, they stopped speaking Latin, but the church continued to use the Latin Bible because they thought it was a holy, powerful language. When common people couldn't understand Scripture, the church became weak. Finally, in England in the late 1300s, John Wycliffe decided to translate the Bible into English because he wanted ordinary people to understand it. The church leaders said to him, 'How can you convey the word of God in a barbaric language like English?' When the ordinary people could understand the Bible again, the church grew.

No language is holier than another. All are capable of expressing the message of the Bible. People are always adding new concepts to their culture and finding ways of expressing them. If people lack a biblical concept, they can learn it and develop a way of expressing it in their language.

1) What language(s) do people in your community think the Bible was written in?

2) What translation(s) of the Bible do people use in your churches? Why do they use these translations? Are they able to understand them well?

3) Do you think English is a barbaric language or a language of high status? Why do you think people's views of English changed over the centuries?

4) When people can't understand Scripture, what effect does this have on their faith and their church?

2. Increasing the status of a language

If people have a low view of their language, how can it be improved?

List responses on the board. Add any of the following points that are relevant but have not been mentioned.

The following activities encourage people to feel good about using their own language.

- Teach Christians that God values all languages and cultures.
- Teach Scripture engagement courses in seminaries and other Bible institutions.
- Introduce the language into the school system.

- Associate the language with modern life, such as radio, DVDs, internet, and television. Have celebrities from the ethnic group perform in it and promote it.

- Publish in the language: New Testaments, Bibles, dictionaries, notices, and so on.

- Hold competitions using the language, for example reciting Bible memory verses, reading Scripture aloud, songs, and so on.

- Teach people to pray in their language. Help them learn useful phrases such as Lord, praise God, Our Father in heaven, heal, in Jesus' name, and so on.

1) If your mother tongue is a minority language that is marginalized, which of these ideas might you like to try to increase its status? What other ideas can you think of?

2) How can churches create an atmosphere of respect for all the languages and cultures represented in their congregations?

Assignments

1. Think of a church you know where many church members speak a minority language. Write a letter to the pastor to convince him or her that it is important to use the Scriptures in the mother tongue of the people.

2. Look up the following passages and write what they say about the use of the mother tongue: Revelation 7:9–10, Acts 2:5–11, Esther 8:9.

3. Read What We Believe ... at the beginning of this book. Underline the parts you think are the most important for your situation.

4. List five phrases in your language that would be helpful for someone from your area to learn who usually prays in another language.

Readings*

Bediako, Kwame. 1998. 'The Doctrine of Christ and the Significance of Vernacular Terminology.' *International Bulletin of Missionary Research* (July): 110–111.

McKinney, Carol. 1990. 'Which Language: Trade or Minority?' *Missiology* 18: 279–290.

Peterson, Eugene. 2006. *Eat This Book*. Grand Rapids, MI: Eerdmans.

Sanneh, Lamin. 1990. 'Gospel and Culture: Ramifying Effects of Scriptural Translation.' In *Bible Translation and the Spread of the Church*. P. Stine, ed. Leiden, Netherlands: Brill, pp 1–23.

Slocum, Marianna. 1987. 'Goal: Vernacular Scriptures in Use.' *Notes on Scripture in Use* 15:7–11.

Walls, Andrew. 1990. 'The Translation Principle in Christian History.' In *Bible Translation and the Spread of the Church*. P. Stine, ed. Leiden, the Netherlands: Brill, pp 24–39.

Useful website

http://www.worldmap.org/ World Missions Atlas Project gives the reader a flavour of the efforts being made to reach people all over the world. It shows the extent of Bible translation.

---

* http://www.scripture-engagement.org

Chapter 4

CULTURE IN THE PLAN OF GOD

Introduction

Sometimes people are told that they need to reject their culture and adopt a 'biblical' culture when they become Christians. But this isn't possible. We can't escape our culture. Whether openly or in secret, it remains a part of our life and identity. Rather than trying to escape it, we need to express our faith in the context of our culture. When we do, we're able to live out our faith genuinely and in a way that is attractive to others around us.

Samuel evangelizes in another culture

Act out this skit.

A Sanatu evangelist, Samuel, is from the south of the country. He has recently returned from being trained by a large western organization and plans to reach all the lost people in the Palapala area in one month. He has just arrived in Pastor Simon's village and he finds two men eating. Their names are Ata and Babu. They are sitting on stools under a tree, eating from one pot with their hands.

Samuel: Hello. Hello. I have come to tell you that God loves you. Yes, God, who created the whole world, loves you. He loves everyone in the whole world. He loves Africans, Americans, Chinese, everyone. Yes, God loves you. Do you accept Jesus, his Son, as your saviour?

Ata: Hello. Sit down. Eat.

Samuel: Thank you. (Scowls at the food, almost afraid of it.) Like I was saying, do you accept Jesus as your saviour?

Ata: (confused, overwhelmed, and wanting to please the visitor) Yes.

Samuel: Praise God. You're Christians now.

Ata: (Looks surprised, a bit afraid) Yes ...?

Samuel: (Suddenly realizing a problem) But why are you eating outside? Christians eat indoors. Now that you're Christians, you'll have to eat your meals inside your house. That's how Christians eat.

Ata: Inside? It's hot and dark in there. There's no room to eat. Here under the mango tree we get the breeze.

Samuel: No, Christians always eat indoors. God wants them to. And where is your cutlery?

Ata: Cutlery?

Samuel: Yes, you know, knife, fork, and spoon. Why on earth are you eating with your hands? That's primitive and pagan. Christians use cutlery when they eat. Here, use this fork.

Ata: (tries to get his food to his mouth with a fork. He's clumsy. The food drops off.)

Samuel: Let me help you. We'll have to have fork lessons in this church, I can see. (Finally gets food into Ata's mouth.) And where are your plates? You can't eat from one pot any more. Christians use plates. And they eat at a table. Here, let me show you. (He takes Ata to a table already prepared and sits him down at it. There is a plate, glass, knife, fork and spoon.) This is how Christians eat. (He models how to eat.)

Ata: (Bewildered—protests) But . . . .

Samuel: And why are you eating with your friend? Where is your wife?

Ata: My wives eat together, I eat with my friends, and the children eat over there together. I'll call my wives.

Samuel: Wives?

Ata: (Proudly) Yes, I have three wives.

Samuel: Oh la la! We'll think about that once we finish the cutlery lessons (overcome with how many problems he's encountering). Choose one, and eat your meals with her and your children at this table. You'll need to buy a plate, glass, and cutlery for each one. That's the way Christians eat.

Ata: Where am I going to find all that money? What can I do?

Samuel: I've got to go now, but I want you to know that God loves you very much. He really does. He loves you. (Rushes off.)

1) How do you think Ata and Babu felt about God when Samuel left?

2) What problems do you think Samuel had?

3) Is it possible for a person to be fully a part of their culture and fully Christian? If so, how?

1. God created us to live in a culture

God created us to live in a cultural context. A person can't live without a culture any more than a fish can live without water. Culture isn't bad; it's essential for life. Just as the variety of languages is part of God's plan, so is the variety of cultures.

1) What will happen to a fish if it leaves the water?

2) What can happen to people who try to leave their culture or are forced to do so?

2. Christianity can be lived out in any culture

Some people think that human life evolved from a simple form and is becoming more and more complex over time. People extended this thinking to cultures, with the idea that cultures evolve from simple to complex. Some thought people started as savages, evolved to being barbarians, and finally became civilized. They thought 'savages' didn't speak languages but only made animal sounds. Under the influence of this thinking, colonizers set about teaching people their own culture to help them become civilized. Some missionaries were also influenced by this thinking and tried to carry out the three C's: to Christianize, civilize, and commercialize local people.

1) Do you think this view of culture is correct?

2) Is there a superior culture?

Sometimes people apply the same kind of evolutionary thinking to the church. They think that all Christians are moving from their heathen past into one 'biblical' culture. They think that eventually all Christians around the world will look and act the same, like the early Christians. This concept is not correct. It's not possible for the simple reason that there is no one biblical culture. The cultural background of nomadic Abraham was very different from that of the Israelites at the time of the kings. In the New Testament, Jews were under a colonial power, Rome, and the culture changed again. Many of the early Christians were Greeks living in yet another culture.

When people refer to the biblical culture, which one do they mean?

The early church had to deal with the question of culture. One issue they faced was whether Greek Christians had to adopt Jewish culture to be saved. Some Jews thought that they did. For example, they thought that Greek males had to be circumcised and obey the Jewish rules about food and the Sabbath. After all, these were the cultural norms given by God in the Old Testament. When this was discussed at the church council in Jerusalem, the apostles decided that Greek believers didn't need to adopt Jewish culture to be Christian (Acts 15). At the same time, Jewish Christians were to continue in their way of life. Each lived out their faith in their cultural context.

3. The gospel transforms and redeems cultures

Some people feel that change will destroy a culture. They feel that if any part of a culture is replaced with something else, the culture will no longer function. This is true of machines, but not of cultures. Cultures change all the time as people respond to changes in their environment.

1) Did any of you become a Christian after the age of twenty?

2) When you became a Christian, did people still recognize you?

3) What was different about you?

When we become Christians, others can still recognize us, but we change as God gradually transforms us into his likeness so that we become all he created us to be. We keep our personal identity. In the same way, we keep our cultural identity as Christians but God transforms the way we live out our cultures so that they can be all that God created them to be. Christians should be recognisably Manlinke or Blackfoot or Quechua, but transformed. We should not try to forget our culture.

> *Therefore, if any one is in Christ, he is a new creation; the old has passed away, behold, the new has come* (2 Corinthians 5:17, *RSV*). How do you understand this verse?

Sometimes people think this verse means that we should reject our culture. Actually, this passage is referring to letting go of old prejudices and attitudes, the negative parts of culture. Christians need to work out how to live their Christian faith in their culture. Then their Christian and cultural identities can be integrated into one, and their witness to others within their culture will be much more genuine and appealing.

1) In the past, when the Baju of Nigeria became Christian, they were required to say the following: 'I repent: I renounce my culture. I will follow Christ'.* Do you agree with this? Why or why not?

2) Think of one custom or belief in your culture that is compatible with Christianity, but is not accepted by the church.

---

* See Carol McKinney, 1994.

4. When the gospel is expressed in our mother tongue, it penetrates our worldview

Show a net, either a real one, an illustration from a publication, one drawn on a blackboard or on overhead transparency. Then place or draw another net over it. Then tell the group, 'A language is like a net thrown over reality. Another language is another net. It is rare that the holes in the two nets fall in exactly the same places'.*

Different cultures put different 'nets' on reality. For example, some cultures have one word for both brothers and male cousins, and one word for both fathers and uncles. Others have separate words for these categories. The categories our culture uses are the glasses through which we perceive reality. When the gospel is expressed in our mother tongue, it penetrates our categories, which represent our deepest sense of reality.

---

* Translated into English from: *Nouveau Testament Interlinéaire Grec/Français.* British and Foreign Bible Society. 1993: Swindon, England.

5. Christianity is expressed differently in different cultures

1) How many of you have kissed your brother in Christ today? Why not? Do you claim to obey the Bible?

2) 1 Peter 5:14 says *'Greet one another with the kiss of love'*, and Romans 16:16 repeats this command, *'Greet one another with a holy kiss.'* Do you feel guilty for not kissing your brother today? Why not?

Actions can have different meanings in different cultures. For example,

- The left hand: In much of Africa, to give something to someone with the left hand is considered a serious insult. In England, no particular meaning is associated with the left hand.

- Looking someone in the eyes: This is a sign of respect in many cultures in the West, especially when children are being corrected by their parents. It is a sign of disrespect in many cultures in Africa and Asia.

- Standing up to speak in a meeting: This is sign of respect among the Adioukrou of Côte d'Ivoire, but it is sign of disrespect among the Kouya, also of Côte d'Ivoire.

The Bible was written for everyone, but not to everyone. Each book is addressed to a specific group of people in a specific cultural context. We are 'listening in' to words that were originally addressed to someone else. When we apply Scripture to our lives, it is the underlying principle of each passage that we should apply. Three questions help us:

- What did this mean to the people who first received the message?

- What is the underlying principle or the lesson to be learned?

- How can it be applied to our situation?

Cultures change with time so the meaning of an action does not always remain the same. This is true both of modern cultures and of biblical cultures.

1) How were people selected for leadership roles in the Old Testament?—1 Samuel 10:1.

2) How were people selected for leadership roles in the New Testament?—Acts 1:21–26.

3) What was the meaning associated with anointing someone with oil in James 5:14?

Choose two of the following passages. Try to find out what each passage meant in its original context. Discuss a) the underlying principle communicated in each one. b) Then propose a way this could be lived out in your culture. (Sample answers, pp 302–3)

1) John 13:14–15—Washing each other's feet.

2) Exodus 23:19—Don't boil a kid in its mother's milk.

3) 1 Timothy 2:8; 1 Kings 8:22—Raise your hands to pray.

4) Leviticus 19:13—Pay wages daily.

6. Christians are united by love, not by similarity

Two Christians can have different ways of living out their faith and both can be valid (Romans 14:14–16). When Christians from different cultures are together, out of love they should refrain from doing things that may offend others or cause them to lose their faith. For example, when Christians from the West visit certain places in Africa, they should be careful not to use their left hand to greet or give things to someone. Paul adopted other people's customs in order to be able to bring them to Christ (1 Corinthians 9:20–22).

What unites Christians is not that they adopt the same customs, but that they are united in love (John 17:21) and in their faith in the cross of Jesus Christ (Galatians 6:14–15).

Think of an occasion in the past when you have been with people of another culture. Have you done something in a different way out of love for those people?

Assignments

1. Identify a Western practice which is taught in your church that is confusing, offensive or has a wrong meaning in your culture.

2. Can we adopt a 'biblical Christian' culture today? Give some reasons for your answer.

Readings*

Dye, T. Wayne. 1976. 'Toward a Cross-Cultural Definition of Sin.' *Missiology* 4:27–41.

Finifrock, Monica and Kathenya, Albert. 2006. 'Swallowed in His Love: A Look at How the Mother Tongue Scriptures Shed Light on an Age-Old Rite of Passage Among the Tharaka People of Kenya.' *Scripture in Use Today* 12:3–11.

Hayward, D. 1995. 'Measuring Contextualization in Church and Missions.' *International Journal of Frontier Missions* 12(3):135–138.

McKinney, Carol. 1994. 'Conversion to Christianity: A Baju Case Study.' *Missiology* XXII(2):147–165.

Nagai, Y. 1999. 'Being Indigenous As Well As Christian: A Case of Maiwala Christians in Papua New Guinea.' *Missiology* 27(3):393–402.

Neeley. 1994. 'Creating a Farm Blessing Church Service.' *Notes on Scripture in Use* 41:36–38.

Perry, C. 1990. 'Bhai-Tika' and 'Tij Braka': A Case Study in the Contextualization of Two Nepal Festivals.' *Missiology* 18(2):177–183.

Priest, Robert J. 1994. 'Missionary Elenctics: Conscience and Culture'. *Missiology* 22(3):292–315.

Walls, Andrew. 1978. 'Africa and Christian Identity.' *Mission Focus* IV (7):11–13.

—. (1996). 'The Gospel as Prisoner and Liberator of Culture.' In *The Missionary Movement in Christian History: Studies in the Transmission of Faith*. A. F. Walls, ed. Maryknoll, NY: Orbis, pp 3–15.

—. 2002. 'African Christianity in the History of Religions.' In *The Cross-Cultural Process in Christian History*. A. F. Walls, ed. Maryknoll, NY: Orbis, pp 116–135.

---

* http://www.scripture-engagement.org

Chapter 5

MOTHER-TONGUE SCRIPTURE USE AND CHURCH GROWTH

Introduction

The rapid spread of Christianity in many parts of the world has all too often resulted in what has been called 'Christianity a mile long and an inch deep'. People may have accepted Christ as their Lord and saviour, but they may not know much about him or live in ways that honour him. The amount of Scripture churches use and the language of the Scripture they use may contribute to this situation. If people can't read or hear Scripture in a language they understand, their spiritual growth will suffer. This chapter looks at the role language plays in helping Christians grow in their faith and suggests ways to increase the amount of Scripture used in churches.

Reaching the Weze

The Weze people live near the area where Pastor Simon works. They number about 80,000 and they have been very resistant to the gospel. The only church in the area belongs to Pastor Simon's denomination. The Bible Society has started a translation project in Weze, and Genesis, Exodus and Luke are available, but few people are using them.

One week, Pastor Simon went to a regional church leaders' meeting with Yeti, the pastor of the Weze church. During the meetings, the leaders discussed reaching unreached people groups. Everyone agreed that the Weze was an unreached people group because less than two per cent of the population considered themselves Christians of any type. They discussed ways of evangelizing the Weze at great length.

Finally Pastor Yeti told a sad story. He said, 'Last year there was a big evangelistic campaign in the area, and a well-known evangelist from abroad conducted the meetings. Many people went along out of curiosity, and some came forward at the end to say that they wanted to follow Christ. The evangelist and his team gave them very nice English Bibles, but hardly anyone understood English, and most didn't know how to read. Now, one year later, a few of those people are in my church, but many lost interest after the campaign was over. I think now it will be harder to get them to come to any other evangelistic meetings'.

Yeti continued, 'My church services are in Kisanu, and I worry that at least half the congregation do not really understand what is being said. Several of the new converts have been attracted away from my church to a new cult that has just come into the area. What can I do?'

That evening Pastor Simon had a long chat with Yeti and told him about his experiences when he changed from using Kisanu to Palapala, and how everyone understood the service now. Yeti went home with a lot to think and pray about.

1) What effect has the language(s) used in your church had on the success or failure of its ministry?

2) Have you ever tried to use different languages for different parts of your church service?

1. The role of language in church growth

If mother-tongue Scriptures are to be used, church leaders need to understand their importance and model their use. Often someone in a language group needs to champion this cause and share the vision with the other church leaders.

A. Christians cannot mature in their faith unless they have access to the Bible in a language they understand

An important part of our growth as Christians comes by knowing God's word. It is our spiritual food that makes our faith grow strong. For example, when the Kasena New Testament in Ghana was published in the 1980s, people were finally able to understand God's word and the church grew both in faith and in numbers.[*]

In some places, Christians only hear a few verses of the Bible on Sunday read by the pastor in a language they barely understand. This isn't enough to make them strong in their faith, and they are much more likely to follow false teaching of sects or leave the church altogether.

Sometimes, even though people do not understand the majority language well, they like it more than their mother tongue. In this case, either they need help to learn the majority language better or they need to value their mother tongue more. To grow as Christians, they need to hear or read God's word in a language they understand well and like to use.

B. No church can last long without Scripture in a language the people understand

Missionaries who went to China in the early 1900s translated the Bible into Chinese. In 1951, the Communists chased out all the missionaries, but in the 20 years that followed, the church multiplied 500 percent! The people's faith was sustained by the Bible in their language, even through times of persecution.

By contrast, the northern part of Africa was the centre of Christianity in the first few centuries AD. The church leaders used Latin and didn't translate

---

[*] See Allison Howell, 2001.

into the local languages of Punic and Berber, even though only the very educated church members knew Latin. When Islam swept across that part of Africa from AD 600–900, the church virtually disappeared. The lack of Scriptures in the local languages played a significant role in the church's downfall. By contrast, the churches in Egypt and Ethiopia experienced many of the same pressures, but they had Scripture in their languages and have survived to this day.*

C. Church leaders must see that all members of their congregations, regardless of their social class, gender, or age, receive spiritual food in a language they understand well

Imagine a typical family that comes to your church on Sunday morning. Mr Gambu, the father, has an office job at the local hospital. His wife Mary went to school for six years but has forgotten most of what she learned there. Her mother is living with them, and speaks very little of the

---

* See C. E. Shenk, 1993.

majority language. They have six children, ranging from Caroline, who is just finishing secondary school, to little Emmanuel, who is five years old.

Imagine them walking out of the church at the end of the service. What spiritual food have they received? If the whole service and the readings were in the majority language, then Mr Gambu and the two oldest children have had a good meal, his wife has had a little snack and the grandmother and the younger children have had no spiritual food at all!

1) Which group in your church is most neglected?

2) How can they be fed spiritually?

D. The more church leaders encourage people to use the Scriptures in their mother tongue, the more the members will use them

Act out this skit.

Some church members are sitting in a room, and a young man rushes in with Scripture booklets in a local language and says how great they are. He tries to sell copies, but the people don't take much notice of him and don't buy his booklets. Then the head pastor arrives wearing a long robe and says much the same thing. Everyone promptly buys the booklets and tries to read them.

1) How can pastors help or hinder people using Scripture use in their language?

2) Why might pastors be afraid or unwilling to use the mother-tongue Scripture in church? After taking the group's responses, add any of the reasons below that have not been mentioned.

3) Finally, discuss possible solutions to the problems you have identified.

Pastors may be afraid to use their mother tongue in church for many different reasons.

- They may be afraid to read aloud in their own language in church because they can't read it fluently.

- They may feel that people will look up to them more if they use the majority language.

- They may not know how to express biblical concepts in the mother tongue.
- They may belong to a different language group from that of their congregation.
- They don't like change of any sort.

2. Increasing Scripture use in church meetings

Church leaders need to offer their members generous amounts of Scripture during their Sunday services and other weekly, monthly, or yearly meetings. Churches vary in their traditions in this regard. Liturgical churches have a fixed order of readings for the services throughout the year. In non-liturgical churches, preachers choose the Scripture passage they use each week freely. Either method can work well to provide Scripture for people.

1) How much Scripture is read or heard in the average Sunday service in your churches?

2) How much Scripture is read or heard in other meetings during the week?

3) What other ways is Scripture communicated in your church (drama, Bible stories, Scripture songs)?

4) Have each church group report back to the whole group. Help them to see the advantages and disadvantages of their present practices.

How can we help our congregations to hear more Scripture during the church service?

Assignments

1. Have some of your church members left the church or joined sects? What do you think you could do to stop this?

2. Look at the history of a church in your area. Trace its growth and the languages it used through the years.

Readings*

Howell, Allison, M. 2001. *The Religious Itinerary of a Ghanaian People: The Kasena and the Christian Gospel.* Achimota, Ghana: Africa Christian Press, pp 178–181.

Senavoe, Juliana. 2002. 'The Effects of Non-Translation of the Scriptures among the Guan of Southern Ghana-Some Preliminary Findings.' *Journal of African Christian Thought* 5(1):48–60.

Shenk, C. E. 1993. 'The Demise of the Church in North Africa and Nubia and Its Survival in Egypt and Ethiopia: A Question of Contextualization?' *Missiology* XXI (2):131–154.

Tripp, Martha D. 1984. 'A Combination of Factors Encouraging Scripture Use among the Amuesha.' *Notes on Scripture in Use* 8:15–21.

Useful Website

`http://www.cresourcei.org/lection.html`   All about lectionaries—clear explanations and some resources.

---

* http://www.scripture-engagement.org

Multilingual Churches

Chapter 6

USING SCRIPTURE IN MULTILINGUAL CHURCHES

Introduction

Using Scripture in a local language works wonderfully in communities where everyone uses that language as their mother tongue, but more and more communities and churches are multilingual. Does this mean that churches must abandon Scripture in local languages in favour of those in majority languages? This chapter addresses the issue of language use in multilingual churches.

John Mark's multilingual church

Pastor Simon was travelling again and arrived in a small Palapala village right on the edge of the language area. The Catholic catechist Lambo had asked him to visit John Mark, one of the new catechists in his area. Lambo had told Pastor Simon that John Mark was having problems in his church and could do with some help.

John Mark was very happy to see Pastor Simon and they discussed all sorts of things. Eventually they talked about the languages they used in church services and meetings. John Mark said, 'Lambo has been talking to me for months about using Palapala in church. The bishop is also telling us that the Sunday Mass should be in the language of the people. I attended a seminar last year and I know how to read it, but here we are having some big problems.

'My big question is how do we keep the unity of the church and yet feed the people spiritually in a language they understand well? As I was telling you, we already have problems with divisions within the church. There is a small but influential group of people from a neighbouring group, the Weze. They understand Palapala but if I conducted the service in it, they would feel that I was showing favouritism to my people and dividing the church. They would rather continue to use Kisanu because it's neutral for all of us. Then there is the local headmaster and a couple of other families from the south who don't understand Palapala at all. On the other hand, at least 30 people in the congregation do not understand the service when we have it in Kisanu. So what should I do?'

1) What would you say to John Mark?

2) Do you have similar issues in your area?

1. Multilingualism

How many languages do you speak?

As communities become more and more multilingual, so does the church. Church leaders need to understand multilingualism so that they can communicate the gospel effectively.

Read about Koffi and Nogbou

Koffi grew up in a small village speaking his mother tongue, Palapala. At school, he learned English. Now he uses English at his job in a government office, as well as at home. Little by little, he is forgetting Palapala.

Nogbou grew up with Koffi in the same village. Like Koffi, he learned English in school and now uses it at his work. When he finishes work and relaxes with friends or family, he prefers to use his mother tongue. He continues to speak both languages well.

1) Which case do you think is more likely to occur in your area? Why?

2) Why do you think Nogbou still uses his mother tongue at home and with friends?

A. Using different languages in different contexts

In multilingual societies, people use different languages in different settings and for different purposes. In some cases, like Koffi's, people gradually abandon one language in favour of another. In other cases, like Nogbou's, people use a majority language in formal situations, like in offices or schools, and their mother tongue in more intimate situations, such as with family and friends. This is referred to as 'diglossia', a situation in which a majority language and a mother tongue can continue to be spoken for centuries without one being lost at the expense of the other.

A quick way to find out if people are abandoning their language is to listen to the language children use at home and when they play together. If most children no longer speak their parents' language, it is in danger of dying out. Within a generation, it may no longer be the language of the ethnic group. If children continue to learn and use their parents' language, even though many people are able to speak the majority language as well, it is not in danger of dying out.

B. The two functions of language

Language has two functions:

- It allows people to communicate with others.
- It allows people to identify with a social group.

When Jesus came to earth, he spoke the language of the people he lived with. This allowed him both to communicate with them and to identify with them.

Our choice of language also shows with whom we want to identify. In the past, Bible translation organizations determined where separate translations were needed by measuring whether people in one area could understand a text recorded in another area. Now they realize that people's attitude toward a language is as important as their ability to understand it. If people want to identify with a culture, they will want to use its language. If they don't like a culture, they won't use its language.

Read James' story

James grew up in a village where his mother tongue was used all the time and most people only knew a bit of English. He was bright and learned to speak English well at school. While he was away at secondary school he became serious about his faith in Jesus and began the process of becoming a lay preacher.

The New Testament had been translated into his language, but he hadn't taken the time to learn to read it. When he returned to his village for the school holidays, the church elders asked him to preach the very first Sunday. He was delighted and prepared with great care. The congregation was made up of villagers: older men and women, and many children who were either too young for school or simply didn't go. The service was conducted in the mother tongue, but when James preached, he used English and had someone interpret his message.

1) What language would have been easiest for James' audience to understand?

2) Why do you think James preached in English?

3) Whom did James want to identify with?

4) When you hear a stranger speaking your language, how does it affect your relationship with that person?

5) In many churches, the only part of the service that is conducted in the mother tongue is the announcements. Why might this be? What does this indicate?

2. Language policy in your church

Every organization has a set of established practices about the language(s) it uses. This is known as its language policy. Sometimes language policies are stated explicitly, as in schools and offices, but sometimes they can only be observed, as in many churches or homes. Here is an example of a church language policy from a denomination in Burkina Faso.

> We will encourage the use of translations in local languages in all the churches to include:
>
> · the reading of the Bible in local languages in the church services and prayer meetings
>
> · bible studies in the local languages
>
> · reading of Scripture in local languages when visiting the sick and the elderly
>
> We will prepare Bible school students to use Scriptures in local languages by:
>
> · teaching the system the government has established to write the extra letters needed by local languages
>
> · teaching students to read and write proficiently in their own languages

Churches need to be sure that their language policy allows all their members to grow in their faith. No one should leave church spiritually hungry. Here are some principles that can help churches to address the issues of multilingualism.

- A church must recognize its multi-ethnic composition. Since ethnic differences between people can lead to tension and violence, the church may be tempted to establish its unity by ignoring such differences. Pastors who do this often use majority language Scriptures. This may bring a superficial unity, but doesn't resolve ethnic tensions which may continue below the surface. Churches cannot grow if they ignore their multi-ethnic composition. Rather than ignoring these differences, churches need to address them and meet the needs of each ethnic group within the congregation. Each group must have a way to participate in the life of the church.

- A church must value its multi-ethnic composition and lead every ethnic group to appreciate the others. This goes beyond simply tolerating one another.

- A church must recognize and rejoice in its multi-ethnic unity in Christ. Jesus speaks of our diversity in our unity when he said, 'I have other sheep that are not of this sheep pen. I must bring them also. They too will listen to my voice, and there shall be one flock and one shepherd' (John 10:16).*

The church can have a prophetic voice in the world by celebrating its diversity and demonstrating that in Christ, differences do not lead to divisions and violence. If Christians cannot love one another across ethnic boundaries, who can?

1) Church leaders often find it hard to keep the balance between creating a sense of unity between Christians from different languages and ensuring that all members are being fed spiritually in a language they understand well. In the churches of your denomination, which of these two do you think is the most neglected? Explain why you think this is the case.

2) Read James 2:1–4, 9. Make up short skits of a church that welcomes a wealthy visitor who does not speak the local language. Have some groups show a good way to welcome the visitor and meet the needs of the congregation, and other groups show a negative way that leaves most of the people without being fed spiritually. Present this to the whole group at a convenient time.

• • • • • •   *No one should leave church spiritually hungry.*

The languages used in your church reflect its language policy, even if it isn't stated explicitly. Divide into church groups and fill out the following form to discover your church's language(s) policy.

---

* See Alan Tippett, 1987.

Name of church:		
Language(s) spoken by people in the congregation:		

What languages are normally used in the following situations? If there are times when other languages are used, note these.

	Sunday service—monolingual context	Sunday service—multilingual context
Bible reading		
Liturgy		
Preaching		
Announcements		
Songs		
Bible studies		
Prayer meetings		
Youth meetings		
Sunday school		
Other		

Now discuss these questions:

1) What languages are represented in your churches?

2) Does your church meet the needs of each ethnic group represented in the congregation?

3) Does your church maintain the unity of the congregation?

4) What changes would you recommend?

5) How does your church decide where to assign pastors (priests) and evangelists?

    a. It assigns them to areas where they speak the language, when possible.

    b. It assigns them to areas without thinking about language issues.

    c. It intentionally assigns them outside the area where their language is spoken.

d. It encourages them to learn the local language if they do not already speak it.

e. Other?

6) Does your church require leaders to be able to read their mother tongue?

7) If a translation programme is underway, is the church involved in it in some way? If so, how is it involved? If not, how could it be?

8) How can your church welcome an important guest that doesn't speak the local language and still feed the rest of the congregation?

Assignment

Imagine that a leader in your church feels that using local languages in the church service will increase ethnic tension and divide the church. Write a letter to this leader telling him/her if you agree or disagree, and explain how you feel the church can maintain its unity while meeting the spiritual needs of all the members.

Readings*

Harris, A. Sue. 1997. 'Why Compete? Creating New Functions for Traditional-Language Literature Use.' *Notes on Sociolinguistics* 2(4):181–187.

Hatfield, Deborah H. and M. Paul Lewis. 1996. 'Surveying Ethnolinguistic Vitality.' *Notes on Literature in use and Language Programs* 48:34–47.

Tippett, Alan. 1987. 'The Dynamics of the Bicultural Church.' *Introduction to Missiology*. Pasadena, CA: William Carey, pp 360–370.

Useful Website

A long but good example of a language policy is that of the Catholic Church.

`http://www.vatican.va/roman_curia/congregations/ccdds/documents/rc_`
`con_ccdds_doc_20010507_liturgiam-authenticam_en.html`

---

* http://www.scripture-engagement.org

Chapter 7

HELPING INTERPRETERS PERFORM WELL

Introduction

In multilingual churches, there will always be a need for good oral interpretation. Visiting pastors who do not speak the local language want what they say to be communicated clearly and correctly. As multilingualism increases, the role of the interpreter will also increase. This chapter discusses how to help interpreters do their job well.

Interpretation gone wrong

One month, Pastor Simon was asked to make a pastoral visit to a new church in a large town. It was in the Palapala area, but this town had attracted people from all over Sanatu because it had some large plantations, a bottling factory, and a number of secondary schools. Pastor Simon arrived on a Saturday and stayed in the home of the young pastor, Thomas. He was invited to preach the next day at the main Sunday service. Thomas explained that the sermon had to be in Kisanu because many of the people in the church were from other areas and didn't understand Palapala. They had interpreters who translated the readings, the announcements, and the sermon into Palapala.

The next morning when the church service was about to begin, Pastor Simon saw Thomas running around trying to find someone. Pastor Simon asked what the problem was, and Thomas explained he was having difficulty finding interpreters. In the end he found a couple of young men who were willing to help. The service began with a couple of hymns in Kisanu, and then some short songs in Palapala using local music. Pastor Simon was amused to see how everyone seemed to wake up when they sang in Palapala!

The Scripture reading was taken from Galatians 5. A deacon read the passage aloud from the Kisanu Bible, then the interpreter stood up to interpret. 'Wait a minute!' thought Pastor Simon, 'Why aren't they using the printed New Testament in Palapala?' As the interpreter spoke, Pastor Simon became more and more agitated. They came to the passage that says, 'The acts of the sinful nature are obvious: sexual immorality, impurity and debauchery; idolatry and witchcraft'. The interpreter simply said, 'We do bad things like bad sex and other bad things', rather than listing the different sins in the passage. Later on he interpreted 'will not inherit the kingdom of God' as 'will not get lots of good things'. By this time, Pastor Simon was wondering how well his sermon would be interpreted.

When it was time for the sermon, the first thing Pastor Simon did was to read Galatians 5 in both Palapala and Kisanu. Then he tried very hard to speak in short sentences and to keep his Kisanu clear. This helped the young man interpreting to some extent, but he still didn't interpret some things correctly, especially when Pastor Simon used biblical terms like 'save', 'temple', or 'apostle'. That night, Pastor Simon and Thomas had a long discussion about the whole problem of interpretation and how Thomas could help his interpreters do a better job.

1) When do you think interpreters should be used? When should they not be used?

2) What advice would you give to Pastor Thomas about the choice, training and preparation of interpreters?

3) Share some experiences of people making mistakes when doing oral interpretation of Scripture or sermons.

1. Types of interpretation

In multilingual churches, the best way for everyone to receive spiritual nourishment from the service may be to have the main part of the service in the majority language and have the service interpreted into one or more of the local languages. If printed Scriptures are available in a language, the interpreter should read them. If the interpreter is not literate, someone else should read the passage. If no one can read the mother tongue, either the Scriptures need to be recorded so people can listen to them, or the community needs to start literacy courses.

1) What kinds of interpretation have you observed?
2) What are the advantages and disadvantages of each kind?

A. Translation sentence by sentence

Sentence-by-sentence translation is probably the most common form of interpretation. The speaker and the interpreter stand at the front of the church side-by-side. After each sentence the speaker pauses, allowing the interpreter to provide a translation. The disadvantage of this type of interpretation is that it takes up a lot of time. If the pastor preaches for 30 minutes, then with interpretation the sermon will take one hour! It takes even longer if it is interpreted into more than one language.

B. Simultaneous translation

Simultaneous translation is the most difficult sort of interpretation. While the main speaker is talking, the interpreter listens and at the same time speaks the message in the second language. This takes practice! In some situations, an interpreter whispers to a group of people at the back of the church. In other situations, the interpreter sits in a booth equipped with headphones and a microphone and those needing the translation hear it by using headphones. The disadvantage of this type of interpretation is that interpreters need to be very skilled to interpret what has just been said while listening to what is being said next.

C. Summary translation

Sometimes the sermon or other information may be followed by a summary in a second language. This may be done by the speaker or by an interpreter. The disadvantage of this type of interpretation is that the speakers of the second language will not get as much from a summary of the sermon as those who understand the full sermon. In addition, giving a summary that includes all the main points requires a fair degree of skill.

1) In your own church, which methods of interpretation have been used? Do you think any other methods should be used in certain situations?

2) Some churches have found that rather than having interpretation into two or more languages, it is better to have separate services on the Sunday morning. For example, an 8 a.m. English service with interpretation into Hausa and a 10 a.m. service in Fulani. Discuss if this would be helpful in your church.

3) How do you choose interpreters?

2. Choosing interpreters

In the story at the beginning of the chapter, Pastor Thomas was trying to find interpreters at the last minute. This does not normally produce good results. Churches should choose and train a group of interpreters so they are well prepared. Someone who wants to do this work should have the following abilities:

- A good level of understanding of both languages.
- Good verbal ability: some people are able to express themselves better than others. Often people who are known to be good storytellers have good verbal ability and a wide vocabulary. Women are often stronger in this area than men.
- A good Christian lifestyle: interpreters are seen as co-preachers with the main speaker, so it is not good to have someone who is known to be living an immoral life filling this role.
- Literacy in both languages involved in the interpretation: it is helpful if the person chosen can already read and write both languages. However, this is not as important as the first three abilities, because people can learn to read and write if they are motivated to do so.

1) What type of people usually serve as interpreters in your church?

2) Can you think of others who might become interpreters?

3) What do you think is the most important qualification of a good interpreter?

• • • • • •   *Churches should choose and train a group of interpreters.*

3. Training interpreters

Once identified, interpreters need to be trained in basic principles of interpretation and in handling concepts that are difficult or not well known. If a translation programme is underway, interpreters and reviewers can be trained together in basic translation principles using lessons from a translation manual.

A. Knowledge of basic translation principles

Interpreters need to understand the following:

- How communication works, and the important role that background information plays. (See Chapter 10.)

- That translation doesn't involve translating one word exactly for another word. They learn this best by doing exercises where they are required to express an idea in several different ways. (See Chapter 2.)

- The differences between oral and written translations. A good interpreter uses the normal oral forms of the language and does not sound like a book!

B. Difficult and unknown concepts

Translators and church leaders have put a great deal of study, thought, and discussion into the selection of the terms used in their translation. If a language already has a translation of Scripture, interpreters should use the terms that have been used in it for key concepts. A booklet listing these terms can be an enormous help to interpreters. It should give the following information for each one:

- The term in the majority language.

- The term translated into the local language.

- An explanation of its meaning in Scripture, including any useful background information.

An example of text from a booklet explaining difficult biblical concepts

Priest—*ngangga 'da Gale*

Used to describe priests in the Bible. This was a group of people that first came into being at the time of Moses. The first priest was Aaron. One of their main tasks was to sacrifice animals to God. Do not confuse this term with sango—used for modern day Catholic priests.

righteous—*wi bolo zu*

This term describes a person who is upright before God and obeys his commandments—literally a straight head.

Temple—*ga toa da Gale*

Literally this means the big house of God. This is the phrase used for the big building in Jerusalem where the priests offered sacrifices to God. The temple mentioned in Luke had been built by King Herod.

Sometimes interpreters have to translate concepts that the audience does not know. The way the interpreter translates the term depends on what the speaker said. For example, supposing that you live in a tropical climate, how would you translate 'snow'? If it is used as a figure of speech such as 'Your sins will be as white as snow', you might translate it as 'completely cleansed'. On the other hand, if a visiting speaker starts by saying, 'When I left my home country, it was snowing', you can say that it was very cold.

Do you have any helps like the example above that explains key concepts for interpreters? If not, who could prepare them?

C. Knowing the important things to communicate

Interpreters can't translate exactly what the speaker says because usually there isn't enough time to do so, and no interpreter, however good, remembers every detail of what was said. Interpreters need to recognize what is most important and only translate that.

Interpreters also need to know their audience. They may need to act as cultural mediators, providing background information that they know their audience needs. For example, if a preacher casually speaks about Solomon's wisdom without explaining who Solomon was, a good interpreter may decide to slip in a sentence quickly saying, 'Solomon was a king who received special wisdom from God after he prayed for it'.

When people have studied good interpreters, they have found that they have a speech style that is different from normal speech. Often good interpreters repeat nouns more and use pronouns less. They also use linking words more than normal. Interpreters can be encouraged to do these things to help their audience understand them more easily.

D. Opportunities for practice

The best way to train interpreters is to have them listen to good examples and then start to interpret in a non-threatening situation where they can receive feedback. New interpreters should start interpreting for a small group rather than in a church service. They should begin by translating into their own language from another language, because this is usually easier than translating into another language.

Divide into groups of three people who all speak the same two languages. Have one person give a short talk about a subject set by the seminar leader, for example, public transport in the country or how to run a Sunday school. Have the second person translate into the second language sentence by sentence. Have the third person make notes on the quality of the translation. After ten minutes, have the note-taker share his or her observations with the interpreter, and then have the group switch roles and repeat the exercise.

3. Making interpretation easier

What are some ways speakers can help interpreters?

Get feedback from the group. Add any of the points below that haven't already been stated.

Churches can do these things to help interpreters:

- Post a list in the church that lets interpreters know beforehand when it is their turn to serve.
- Meet with interpreters before the service and go over an outline of the talk. Check that they have all the Scripture portions needed.

- Show your appreciation for the interpreters. It is good to acknowledge their hard work in front of the whole church from time to time.

Speakers can do these things to help interpreters:

- Speak in short, complete sentences with simple structures.
- Wait for the interpreter to finish before starting the next sentence.
- Avoid alliteration, for example, 'I am going to talk to you about three Ss—saved, sanctified, and sent.
- Avoid any information that depends on a play on words—for example, 'Today we will look at the four 'for's found at the beginning of Romans 8'.
- Avoid cultural references that are not understood by part of the audience—for example, 'Tonight, as I looked at the big jumbo jet, ...'

Assignments

1. If you speak more than one language, observe two situations where interpreters are translating between them. Write about the positive and negative qualities of the interpreters you observe.
2. Think about a multi-lingual church that you know. When do you think it is best to divide people into ethnic groups for meetings and when should interpreters be used?
3. Take a story in English and translate it orally into another language. Make a recording of your translation. Play it back sentence by sentence and decide how you could improve.

*Reading**

Kalik, Jill. 'Spontaneous Translators: Notes and Queries.' *Scripture in Use Today* 5:32–37.

---

*   http://www.scripture-engagement.org

Chapter 8

MULTI-ETHNIC CHURCHES

Introduction

Multilingual churches are generally multi-ethnic churches because people who speak different languages usually represent different cultures. This can lead to tension because consciously or subconsciously, people tend to think their culture's way of doing things is the right way, and they tend to judge others by their own standards. Pastors in multi-ethnic churches need to help church members identify their ethnocentrism and understand one another better.

Tensions between the Mbani and the Palapala

Pastor Simon was asked by his church office to visit a church in his denomination that was about 60 miles south of his village. It was still in the area where Palapala is spoken but was very near to the southern language of Mbani. The Mbani people were quite different from the Palapala. They were cattle herders while the Palapala people were farmers. There seemed to be a serious problem between Yeli, the pastor, and some of his church members. Pastor Simon was asked to visit and see if he could help them be reconciled.

Pastor Simon had a terrible journey to get to Yeli's village. The first minibus he took broke down and the next one got stuck in the mud! By the time he arrived in Yeli's village he was very tired and dirty. When he got off the minibus, he just wanted to clean up and rest, but a group of men wanted to talk to him immediately. They whisked him off to the church compound. As soon as they had finished their greetings, the men started talking about Pastor Yeli. They complained about the use of the church farm, the collection for the poor, and the languages used in the church. Pastor Simon just listened to them and didn't try to give any answers or suggestions. He realized that they were all Mbani. After about an hour, he excused himself and went to find Pastor Yeli's house.

Pastor Yeli was also eager to talk to Pastor Simon about the troubles in the church, but he saw that Pastor Simon needed a good night's sleep first. The next day, they settled down to discuss the problem. 'It all started with a funeral', Yeli said. 'The headmaster of the local primary school died suddenly and his widow asked the church to help with the funeral arrangements. Mr Yu and Mr Gali, two of our deacons, agreed to make the arrangements. When they started doing this, Mr Ketele and Mr Rati intervened and said they were doing it all wrong. We finally agreed to a compromise, but from that point onwards we had two camps in the church. If Mr Yu suggested anything like selling the vegetables from the church garden, Mr

Ketele would be sure to tell everyone that this was a wrong thing to do and that the food should all be given to the poor. Mr Yu and Mr Gali always support my suggestions, but the other two leaders are automatically against anything I suggest. These men just can't get along with each other'.

Pastor Simon thought about the whole situation for a while and then asked, 'What language groups do these four men come from? Last night I noticed that all the men talking to me were Mbani'. Yeli replied: 'Mr Yu and Mr Gali are Palapala like us; Mr Ketele and Mr Rati are Mbani'. 'Well, I think you have an ethnic conflict here rather than an interpersonal problem', said Pastor Simon. 'Let's arrange to meet with these four men and with a couple of other mature leaders, one Palapala and one Mbani'.

1) If you were Pastor Simon, how would you lead the meeting with these men from the two groups?

2) What underlying problems between the two groups were probably causing the ethnic tension?

1. Ethnic tensions in the early church

Ethnic tensions are not new to the church. The early church was multi-ethnic and experienced ethnic tension. The seeds of this tension were sown centuries earlier when Israel was conquered by Assyria and Babylon. Many Jews were deported to other countries. There they were influenced by the Greek culture of their hosts, also known as Hellenistic culture, and began speaking Greek. The Jews who had been left in their homeland continued speaking their mother tongue, Hebrew or Aramaic. Life was difficult for them and they tended to be poor, while many of those who lived outside the homeland became wealthy. These two groups didn't get along with each other very well.

Even if Jews had lived most of their lives elsewhere, they preferred being buried in their homeland, so many of them moved back to Israel in their old age. Often the men died before their wives, and this left a lot of Greek-speaking widows in the Jerusalem church. The Jews were renowned for the excellent way they cared for their widows, but the number of widows became more than the homeland Jews could take care of. Tension developed along ethnic lines. Acts 6:1–7 tells what happened.

Read Acts 6:1–7 and discuss these questions:
1) Did the early church consider this problem important? How do we know?
2) What action did they take?
3) Were the seven men selected all ethnic Jews?
4) What was the result of their action?
5) What can we learn about dealing with ethnic tension in the church from this passage?

2. Culture and worldview

Think about these three statements:

- Every person is like all other people.
- Every person is like some other people.
- Every person is like no other person.

In what ways are all three of the above statements true?
After the discussion, mention any of the points below that did not come up.

We all:

- have bodies, and live and die like other people.
- are more similar to people from our group than to those from other groups.
- are unique as individuals.

We all learn our culture as small children, and for the rest of our lives we perceive the world through it. We consider the way that we've learned to do things and to think about life to be the normal way. When people from different cultures meet, their perceptions of what is normal are not the same. These differences can occur at various levels, such as:

- the visible level, for example, clothing styles and cooking pots

- the level of our minds, that is, the beliefs and thoughts that we can express—for example, the way we think a good wife should behave or how we think malaria is spread

- our worldview level, that is, the things we hold strongly but are often unaware of. These are much more difficult to identify. We only notice them when we are with people who think differently. For example, those who assume that people are entitled to privacy only realize that they make this assumption when they are exposed to a culture where privacy is considered anti-social.

Until we can understand people from their cultural perspective, we will interpret their behaviour according to the patterns of our own culture and misunderstand them. For example, an African attending a conference in the United States went outside in the early evening to socialize, just like he did at home. He didn't find anyone outside and concluded that Americans were not sociable. When he went into the building, he found people talking together. Then he realized that they socialize inside rather than outside.

Another example is from West Africa. At a seminar, most of the participants believed that people from a certain ethnic group ate their dead. They based this belief on the fact that the villages of this ethnic group didn't have cemeteries. When this was shared openly, the participants from the ethnic group explained that they bury their dead in their compounds, not in cemeteries. Suddenly, everyone realized that they weren't so strange after all.

1) Think of a stereotype or generalization you have of another culture. For example, Americans are noisy, or British people drink tea all the time.

2) Think about an incident you've experienced which illustrates or challenges this stereotype.

3. Reducing ethnic tension

In multi-ethnic churches, church leaders need to help their people understand each other's cultures so that they do not make negative value judgements about each other. Without this kind of understanding, the church will find it difficult to experience their unity in Christ.

To identify your own ethnocentrism, follow this process:

1. Notice when you make value judgments, that is, when you feel something is strange and can only explain it by saying something like, 'The Kisanu are stupid/slow/proud/...'

2. Analyse the situation in which you make this sort of judgment. Remember the details of the experience in slow motion. Stick to what happened. Avoid interpreting what it meant.

3. Imagine a context in which this behaviour would not be strange. Propose a possible explanation of why the person might have acted in this way.

4. Check your explanation. See if it occurs anywhere else in the culture. Talk to the person about it, if you can.

Assignments

1. Try to discover your own ethnocentrism using the method described above over a period of several days. Write down two situations in which you've sensed tension with someone from another culture. Propose an explanation for that person's behaviour and see if it is confirmed. Report back to the large group.

2. Describe some of the most common reasons for ethnic tension in your church or area. Propose ways you think the church can address these.

Readings*

Carroll, Raymonde. 1988. *Cultural Misunderstandings: The French-American Experience,* translated by C. Volk, Chicago, IL: University of Chicago.

—. 1991. *Evidences invisibes: Américains et Français au quotidien.* Paris: Seuil.

Hill, Harriet. 1995. 'The Bathroom Doors of Lamorlaye.' *Best of Ethno-info.* Nairobi, Kenya: SIL, pp 28–29.

Tippett, Alan. 1987. 'The Dynamics of the Bicultural Church'. *Introduction to Missiology.* Pasadena, CA: William Carey, pp 360–370.

---

* http://www.scripture-engagement.org

Relevant Bible Use

Chapter 9

IDENTIFYING RELEVANT ISSUES

Introduction

Sometimes people aren't interested in Scripture because they see no connection between it and their lives. They may attend church but continue to use traditional means to address the real issues of their lives. To help people connect their Christian faith with daily life, pastors need to understand the issues they are facing and help them think through how to respond appropriately with Scripture. This takes some research and reflection. In this chapter, we will explore how to do this.

A quarrel breaks out

It was the end of the Sunday morning service and groups of people were standing around chatting. Pastor Simon was greeting people and asking about those who were sick when he noticed a group of men having an intense discussion. As various other people started to join them, two of the men began yelling at each other. It looked as though they might even start a fight, so Pastor Simon felt it was time to investigate.

As he walked toward the group, he heard people shouting, 'They must go!' Others were yelling, 'No, it is not a Christian thing to do!'

After a few minutes, he understood what the dispute was all about. Traditionally, every three years Palapala boys between ten and fifteen years of age were taken into the bush for special initiation ceremonies, referred to as the gaza. While they were away, the elders taught the boys many things and circumcised them.

The local chief had recently announced that the boys would be going into the bush for the gaza the following month. The men were discussing whether or not Christian parents should send their boys. Pastor Simon soon realized that the discussion was turning into a quarrel, and he quickly suggested that the deacons and elders of the church should meet to discuss this properly the following evening. After a few final loud comments, people began to drift away.

The following evening, Pastor Simon sat down with nine men of the church. He hadn't invited the deaconesses this time so the men would talk more freely about this sensitive issue. They began by praying for God's wisdom, and then Pastor Simon said that the first thing was to share their experiences of the gaza and to understand properly what it involved. All had been to some version of the gaza, though Pastor Simon and three others had been to a shorter one for schoolboys. They all had vivid memories of being beaten and starved and of the pain they were expected to endure without crying out. They remembered some positive things as well, such as learning which plants were poisonous and which could treat illness. They also remembered the way they were made to call on various spirits and divinities to give them strength. As they discussed the gaza, they agreed that its main purpose was to turn boys into men.

After a while, Pastor Simon fetched a blackboard and put it in front of them. He said, 'Let's list the various things that happen at the gaza. We'll have one column for good things, one column for things that are definitely forbidden in the Bible, and a third column for things that are not very good but not forbidden either'.

After much discussion they had long lists. Some of the good things were: learning about plants of the forest, learning to obey your elders, bonding together as an age group, and learning to endure hardship. Some of the bad things were: calling on spirits other than God for help, learning that women were inferior and should be beaten to make them obedient, and learning how to be cruel to others. Some neutral things they listed were learning to endure pain without crying and learning how to sing falsetto!

'Now', said Pastor Simon, 'How could we help the boys of the church learn these good things and how to be good Palapala Christian men without also learning the things that are not acceptable for a Christian?'

1) What happens when important issues in life are not addressed by the church?

2) Are there any cultural issues your church has addressed successfully? Explain.

1. Identify a relevant issue

The first step in identifying the issues that are problems for people is to spend time talking with the people, listening for the needs they have. The things people are struggling with may be different from what you expect, so listen carefully with an open mind.

What cultural issues are difficult for Christians in your area?

List the answers on the board. Add any topics from the list below that are relevant but have not already been mentioned.

Areas in which Christians may encounter problems, include:

- various cultural rituals and beliefs surrounding important transitions in life, such as birth, initiation, marriage, and death
- dealing with illness, misfortune, and suffering as a Christian
- witchcraft and fear of supernatural powers and spirit beings
- marriage and divorce
- interpersonal conflict and how to resolve it
- various forms of injustice and how to respond to it

If different kinds of churches are meeting together for a Scripture engagement course, work on subjects that they can all agree on rather than addressing subjects on which they might differ, like the significance of baptism or exactly what will happen at the end of the world.

2. Study the issue without judging

After selecting an issue to address, first you need to understand it thoroughly. For example, if Christians are going to a traditional healer, you need to find out why they are doing so. Ask yourself questions like these: What needs do they have? What other solutions are available to them when they are ill or have problems? Who or what do they think causes illness? Who is going to the healer? What does the healer do exactly? What power does he use?

The various aspects of behaviour can be compared to the parts of a tree. We see the branches and leaves, but there is an equally large root system underneath the ground that supports the tree. Visible practices are like leaves. Things we believe and can explain to someone are like the branches. Beliefs, values, and attitudes that underlie our actions are like roots. We take them so much for granted that we are hardly aware of them. They are invisible even to us but sustain our practices and beliefs.

Often the church only addresses the visible practices and behaviours without addressing the root causes of an issue. They may chop off the branches of certain practices, but in no time, the stump sprouts anew and people are back to their old practices again. For example, telling people they should not engage in sexual relations outside marriage is not likely to be effective if men believe they will get ill if they don't have sex and there is a ban on sexual relations for a long period after women give birth, coupled with a ban on polygamy.

To get to the root causes, ask people why they behave as they do. For every layer of practice or thought you uncover, ask why until they have no more explanations. For example, here is a series of questions and explanations for why some people go to traditional healers.

- Why do people go to healers? (a practice, like the visible leaves)

  Because they are ill.

- Why do they think they became ill? (beliefs they can explain, like the branches)

  Because someone has cursed them.

- Why do they think someone has cursed them? (underlying beliefs, like the roots.)

  Because the person was jealous of their good fortune.

One underlying cause of going to healers, then, is the belief that jealousy causes illness. Telling people to go to a hospital rather than a traditional healer may not be effective if they believe their illness is due to jealousy.

Research the issue thoroughly. Often we are impatient and want to deal with issues before we understand them, and so we never get to the root causes. If a doctor only has a superficial understanding of a patient's condition, he may prescribe the wrong treatment and only make the patient worse rather than curing him. In the same way, we need to take time to understand an issue without making any judgement or rushing to find a solution. You may find, for example, that people go to traditional healers because they can't afford other medical treatment or are obliged to do so by their extended family members, or because they don't believe that Jesus can help them. The better you understand an issue, the better you can respond to it.

Use the mother tongue for this research, especially for key concepts, so that you know what you're referring to. Two Africans were very surprised one day after a very long discussion about demons to find that they weren't talking about the same thing at all. When speaking English, they both used the word 'demon', but one used it to refer to ancestor spirits, who were generally helpful, while the other used it to refer to malicious bush spirits. When they began using their local terms, they were finally able to understand each other.

Select a topic that would be relevant in your church. Then work through the following questions.

1) What practices are involved? That is, what can you observe?

2) What beliefs are involved? That is, what explanations do people give?

3) What are the roots that sustain the practices? Ask why, why, why, until you have uncovered root causes.

3. Determine what is true

After you understand an issue, you can begin to sort truth from error. God reveals himself through the body of Christ working together, so involve other pastors, theologians, and those who understand the language and culture well in this process. It will take time, study, and reflection to do this well. A concordance can be helpful, but be sure to study verses in their context.

Scripture is an important source of truth, but we also learn things from other sources. For example, science rather than Scripture tells us that malaria is caused by a parasite in the blood. Some topics will draw heavily on science or other sources, and others will draw primarily on Scripture.

Scripture does not directly address issues that were not known in the cultures the biblical authors were addressing. For example, the kind of unconscious soul-eating witchcraft found in many parts of Africa was not known in cultures biblical authors were addressing. The word 'witchcraft' in the Bible refers to those who used conscious magical means to accomplish their goals. For topics the Scripture does not address directly, find other passages in Scripture that address them indirectly. For example, if underlying causes of witchcraft are jealousy and the fear of spiritual attack, look for passages that speak to these issues.

1) Listed below are some beliefs underlying witchcraft from one ethnic group in Africa. Have each small group take one belief and determine how the Bible addresses it, either to affirm it, modify it, or challenge it. Give Bible references that support your claims. (Sample answers, p 303)

- If witchcraft didn't exist, the world would be perfect: only very old people would die and there would be no illness, sterility, or misfortune.
- Spirits and spiritual forces are more powerful than humans.
- Evil is stronger than good.
- Misfortune is due to others, not due to any fault of my own. For example, if I drive while I'm drunk, crash my car, and kill a passenger, it's because someone was working witchcraft on me, not because of my drunk driving.
- People need to protect themselves from spiritual attack.
- A person can become a soul-eating witch without wanting to and can do evil without knowing it.
- It is right and necessary to take vengeance against those who harm family members.

2) Determine what Scripture says about the topic you have identified earlier as relevant for your church.

4. Respond to the issue biblically

As you work with other church leaders to understand and analyse an issue, you may find that the church has condemned certain practices that are actually acceptable for Christians. For example, early missionaries condemned some musical instruments that may actually be quite acceptable to use in Christian worship today.

You may discover that some beliefs and practices need to be modified to be acceptable for Christians. For example, it is very appropriate for Christian boys to be initiated and become men, but the prayers offered during the traditional initiation ceremonies need to be directed to God, not to other divinities. You may find other practices need to be completely condemned by Christians. For example, it is not acceptable for Christians to abandon the tenth child born to a family because they think the child will bring bad luck.

Whenever a belief or practice is discouraged, it needs to be replaced with something that carries out the good functions of the original belief or practice. This is referred to as a 'functional substitute'. For example, in an area where drunkenness was a problem, one church prohibited beer at church festivals. However, rather than letting people go thirsty, or taking the festive spirit out of these events, or worse, having them drink beer in secret, the church served CocaCola instead. This made everyone happy because they associated CocaCola with parties. If the functions of a belief or practice are not satisfied in some way, people will probably continue with the old practices and beliefs undercover. Nature abhors a vacuum.

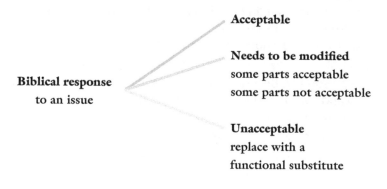

Biblical response
to an issue

Acceptable

Needs to be modified
some parts acceptable
some parts not acceptable

Unacceptable
replace with a
functional substitute

What are some functions of male initiation ceremonies?

Take answers from the group. Add any from the list below that have not already been mentioned.

Male initiation ceremonies have several functions in a culture.

- They educate the youth about cultural values.
- They provide training in sexual issues.
- They unite the age group and families.

- They make men out of boys.
- They provide entertainment.
- They provide status to elders.
- They supply income for certain people.

Discuss the questions below for the issue you are working on. Give references that support your opinions.

1) Which beliefs and practices are in agreement with Scripture?

2) Which need to be modified?

3) Which need to be removed?

4) Analyse the functions of any belief or practice that you feel needs to be removed and propose functional substitutes that are acceptable for Christians.

Assignments

1. Continue working on the issue that you have identified as important for your community. Remember to do the following:

   a. Study the problem without judging.

   b. Determine what is true.

   c. Determine an appropriate Christian response to the issue.

2. Make a list of topics for a series of Bible studies which address the root causes of your issue. Keep this to work on the Bible studies in Chapter 11.

3. Look up the word 'fear' in a concordance. List three passages you would use to make a thematic Bible study on fear.

Readings*

Beekman, John. 1959. 'Minimizing Religious Syncretism among the Chols.' *Practical Anthropology* 6(6):241–50.

---

* http://www.scripture-engagement.org

—. 1974. 'A Culturally Relevant Witness', in W. A. Smalley, ed. *Readings in Missionary Anthropology*. Pasadena, CA: William Carey, pp 132–135.

Burnett, David. 1990. 'Exploring Other Worlds,' in *Clash of Worlds*, D. Burnett, ed. East Sussex, Great Britain: Monarch, pp 25–36.

Carpenter, Mary Yeo. 1996. 'Familism and Ancestor Veneration: A Look at Chinese Funeral Rites.' *Missiology* 24(4):503–17.

Grebe, Karl and Wilfred Fon. 1995. *African Traditional Religions and Christian Counselling*. Yaoundé, Cameroun: CABTAL. Also available on *Tools of the Trade* CD. Nairobi, Kenya: SIL AFA or at **http://www.cabtal.org** under 'Resources' then 'ATR'.

Hiebert, Paul G. 1982. 'The Flaw of the Excluded Middle.' *Missiology* 10(1):35–47.

—. 1994. 'Critical Contextualization.' *Anthropological Reflections on Missiological Issues*. Grand Rapids, MI: Baker, pp 75–92.

Hill, Harriet. 1995. *The Anthro Guide*. Nairobi, Kenya: SIL Africa Area.

—. 1996. 'Witchcraft and the Gospel: Insights from Africa.' *Missiology* XXIV (3):323–344.

—. 1997. *Petit guide d'anthropologie*. Nairobi, Kenya: SIL Africa Area.

Loewen, Jacob. 1967. 'Religion, Drives, and the Place Where It Itches,' *Practical Anthropology* 4:49–72. Reprinted in Loewen, Jacob. 1975. *Culture and Human Values: Christian Intervention in Anthropological Perspective*. Pasadena: William Carey.

Ommani, John L. 2000. 'Tharaka Female Circumcision: A Case Study in the Role of the Translation Organization.' *Notes on Anthropology* 4:45–52.

Pike, Eunice. 1982. 'The Concept of Limited Good and the Spread of the Gospel.' *Notes on Scripture in Use* 2:3–7.

Steele, Mary. 2003. 'Witchcraft and Scripture Impact.' *Scripture in Use Today* 6:30–31.

Zahniser, A. 1991. 'Ritual Process and Christian Discipling: Contextualizing a Buddhist Rite of Passage.' *Missiology* 19(1):3–19.

Chapter 10

PROVIDING NECESSARY BACKGROUND INFORMATION

Introduction

People may have the Bible in their language, but they can still have trouble understanding Scripture if they don't know the background information the biblical author assumed his audience would know. For example, many readers wouldn't know why was Jesus upset when his host didn't wash his feet (Luke 7:44). In most places in the world today, guests wouldn't expect their feet to be washed. To understand why Jesus was upset, we need to know about the Jewish practice of foot-washing and hospitality. Research carried out in Côte d'Ivoire shows that when background information is supplied, people's understanding of Scripture increased dramatically.[*] In this chapter, we discuss this issue of background information and suggest ways to provide it.

Pastor Simon realizes something is missing

Pastor Simon was pleased that using Palapala in the church services was helping his members. He remembered how he had given a written Bible quiz to some of them before he started teaching in Palapala. Now he felt sure they would do much better if he gave them another test. It was nearly Easter, so he prepared a test on the

---

[*] See Harriet Hill, 2006.

passages in John on the last supper that Jesus ate with his disciples. He had people read or listen to John 13 and then asked them questions like, 'What feast were the Jews about to celebrate?' He also asked questions which required more thought, for example, 'How did Satan enter Judas?'

A good cross-section of the congregation was willing to take the test. Pastor Simon wondered if their education would make a difference to their answers so he had them record the number of years they had gone to school. Since women pass on what they learn to children, he wanted to be sure that they were understanding Scripture well, so he noted the gender of the person who took the test. Finally, he expected church leaders would understand the passage well, but he was also interested in how much lay people understood, so he kept their sheets in a separate pile.

Pastor Simon took a whole week to mark the questions and look at the results and, by the end, he was concerned. If an answer was obvious in the passage that people were reading, the vast majority of them answered correctly. He was at least happy about that, as this showed a big improvement from the days when he did all his teaching in Kisanu. He found that the more education someone had, the better they did on the test. He also discovered that church leaders had done better than other members of the church and that men had generally done better than women. None of this surprised him. His concern was that almost all the people did badly on questions that required knowing background information that was different in their culture. For example, many people had misunderstood the reference to the Jewish festival of Passover and thought that it was Easter or a harvest festival.

Pastor Simon explained all this to his wife as they ate supper together. He said, 'I thought that once we had the Bible in Palapala, everyone would understand it well. What is wrong?' His wife thought about this for a while and then suggested he go and discuss it with the bishop in the nearest town. They had become friends during the previous seminar.

The next week Pastor Simon arranged to see Bishop John. He explained the problem at some length and then waited to see what the bishop would suggest. After a long silence, Bishop John said, 'I think your basic problem is that your church members are not

Jews living in the first century AD!' After a few minutes Pastor Simon saw what the bishop was saying. As they discussed together, Pastor Simon realized that he needed to provide much more background information to help people understand the Scriptures. 'But where do I find these things?' he wondered.

Are there passages of Scripture that you find difficult to understand, even in your mother tongue? Give examples.

1. Why is background information important?

In all communication, speakers guess what the background information their audiences have, and say just enough to bring it to their minds. They don't say everything, but expect their audience to understand what they mean from what they say. For example, when Jesus said to his host in Luke 7:44, 'You did not give me any water for my feet,' Luke's first audience would have known about Jewish hospitality and how Jews honoured guests by washing their feet. They would have understood that Jesus was insulted by this breech in etiquette.

The amount of background information that people need to understand a text is far greater than the amount of information contained in the text itself. It can be compared to the part of a hippopotamus that is underwater.

When we read, or hear communication addressed to us, the intended background information comes to our mind so quickly we aren't even conscious that it wasn't stated. But the Bible was addressed to people who lived in very different cultures from ours, so when we read it, even if it's in our language, it's like reading a letter addressed to someone else. We can understand the words, but if we don't know the intended background information, we won't be able to understand what the author meant. If no background information comes to mind, we realize that we don't understand. For example, when reading Luke 7:44, audiences that don't know about Jewish foot-washing may simply wonder why Jesus would want water for his feet. In other instances, we may use the wrong background information and think we have understood, when in fact, we've misunderstood the author's meaning. For example, when Jesus gave the bread to Judas at the Last Supper, people from cultures where witchcraft can be transmitted by enchanted food may think that Jesus made Judas a witch.

At other times, we may know a concept, but by another name and so we may not realize we know what the author is talking about. For example, at a workshop in Uganda, a speaker was talking about the 'spirits' who rebelled against God at the beginning of creation. One participant didn't understand what the speaker was referring to. When someone whispered to her, 'Spirits are like divinities,' she suddenly understood. She knew all about spirits, but called them by a different name. This can happen often in translation. In these cases, helping people understand Scripture can be as simple as using the term they are familiar with.

The table below summarizes the ways background information can affect our understanding of Scripture.

	We think we know the intended background information	We don't think we know the intended background information
We know the intended background information	We use the intended background information and understand.	We don't realize that we know the background information. We don't understand, when actually we could.
We don't know the intended background information	We use wrong (or unintended) background information and think we understand, but actually we misunderstand.	No background information comes to mind and we know we don't understand.

1) Imagine the church at Ephesus. They have just received a letter from Paul, and very enthusiastically read it aloud for everyone to understand. What background information did Paul and the Ephesians share which helped them understand the letter?

After taking suggestions, add the following if not already stated: Greek culture, including worship of many gods; Greek Olympic games, including the races and the crown of leaves; Roman culture, including the armour of a Roman soldier; Knowledge of the Old Testament.

2) Read Luke 10:13–14. What is some of the background information that Luke's readers knew? If necessary, look in study

Bibles to find this information. Remember that background information is information people know before they read or hear the text. It is not an explanation of what the text means.

(After taking the groups' suggestions, add the following if not already stated: Tyre and Sidon were Gentile cities, renowned for their wickedness; Chorizan and Bethsaida were Jewish cities; Jews felt the Kingdom of God belonged to them and not to Gentiles; Jews thought God would punish Gentiles; Miracles show that a prophet is sent by God.)

• • • • • • *To understand Scripture, people need both the text and the intended background information.*

2. Identifying needed background information

Since the background information isn't in the text, how do we know what it is? We can use the same method we use in ordinary conversation. Since speakers and authors want to be understood, they make it as easy as possible for their audience to understand them, so audiences can take the first background information that comes to mind as the information the author intended. We need to identify what that was for the first audience of Scripture and then see if our audience shares it.

A. Understanding biblical cultures

Although we can't know with certainty what came to mind as the first audience heard Scripture, we can learn many things from the Bible itself and from other documents.

Knowledge of the Bible

The story of God's plan of salvation for mankind does not start at Matthew 1:1. When Matthew wrote his Gospel, he was mainly writing for Christians who were Jews. He expected them to know the Old Testament. Modern day readers also need to know the Old Testament to be able to understand the New, but many lack this knowledge.

Often people hear the Bible in bits and pieces. They may hear a Psalm, and then the story of Noah, followed by Balaam and his donkey and David and Bathsheba. This is very confusing. People need to have an overview of the main events in the Bible in chronological order. An overview like this is often referred to as a panoramic Bible when it is in printed form, or chronological Bible storying when told orally. (See Chapter 16.) It should include the key passages that are necessary for understanding God's plan of salvation.*

In your churches, do you have a way for people to get an overview of the Bible, from Genesis to Revelation? If not, what can you do about this?

Knowledge of daily life in Bible times

Biblical authors assumed that their audiences knew about the culture and society in which they lived, so they didn't tell them what they already knew. For example, Matthew didn't have to explain who Herod was, what a synagogue was, or that the Romans oppressed the Jews. Although he didn't include this information in his Gospel, it is necessary to know these things to understand it. For the passages studied in the Côte d'Ivoire research referred to at the beginning of the chapter, only 55 per cent of the background information needed to understand the passages studied could be found in other parts of the Bible. The more we know of the biblical cultures, the better we can understand the Bible. Thankfully, study Bibles, Bible dictionaries, commentaries, and other resources tell us a lot about the cultures in the different periods of the Bible.

1) When Jesus ate at the Pharisee's house in Luke 7:36ff, why was he insulted that his host didn't wash his feet and kiss him (vv 44–45)?

2) In Matthew 22:15–22, how is the Pharisee's question a trick question? What background information do you need to know to understand this? (Sample answers, p 303)

---

* People who are already familiar with the Bible but want to understand the order in which things occurred may benefit from a programme entitled *Walk Thru the Bible*. This goes through the Old Testament or the whole Bible in one day, and does so in a way that is fun and easy to follow.

Cultures Change

Like all cultures, Jewish culture changed as their living situations changed.

> What are some of the different periods in Jewish history?
>
> List them on the board. (Add any from the list below that are not mentioned.)

The periods of Jewish history can be summarized as:

- the nomadic period of Abraham
- the period of the judges
- the period of the kings
- the exile
- the post exilic period, including the rebuilding of the temple
- the inter-testamental period—including the Maccabees
- under Roman rule: 63 BC to AD 70
- under Roman rule after the destruction of the Temple in AD 70

The laws that were given in the desert at Sinai had to be adjusted when Israel settled in Canaan. The temple replaced the tabernacle, and Jerusalem became the place of worship. In the exile, when people could not come to Jerusalem each year, synagogues replaced the temple, and the law had to be adapted again to this new situation. In addition, the Israelites were influenced by many ideas in the countries where they stayed. When we read about Old Testament laws in the New Testament, we need to know how the Jews of the New Testament period interpreted these laws. We need to be sure that our audiences know this background information, too.

> 1) What Jewish practices or beliefs do you find difficult to understand?
>
> 2) What Jewish practices or beliefs do you find similar to those in your culture?

B. Understanding the receptor culture

Once you have determined the background information the original audience used to understand the meaning of a passage, you need to find out what comes to mind for your audience. Compare these two sets of background information. Notice any differences. This is the information you need to tell your audience.

Each audience is different. Your culture may share certain beliefs or practices with biblical cultures that others do not. On the other hand, there may be information your people need that others do not. You don't need to tell people things they already know, but if you don't supply information people are lacking, they won't be able to understand the text. So it's very important to find out exactly what they are missing.

Look at Luke 10:13–14 again and think about the background information you identified and ask these questions:

1) Does your audience lack any of the necessary background information?

2) Does your audience use other background information, and so misunderstand the text?

3. Providing needed background information

After identifying the background information your audience needs to understand a passage, the next step is to provide it for them.

A. The kind of background information to supply

For background information to be relevant, it needs to help people understand the passage better and it must be true. For example, read the following passage:

[9] *When considerable time had passed and the voyage was now dangerous, since even the fast was already over, Paul began to admonish them,* [10] *and said to them, 'Men, I perceive that the voyage will certainly be with damage and great loss, not only of the cargo and the ship, but also of our lives'.* [11] *But the centurion was more persuaded by the pilot and the captain of the ship than*

by what was being said by Paul. ¹² *Because the harbor was not suitable for wintering, the majority reached a decision to put out to sea from there, if somehow they could reach Phoenix, a harbor of Crete, facing southwest and northwest, and spend the winter there* (Acts 27:9–12 *NASV*).

Decide how relevant the following items of background information would be for your audience: very relevant, somewhat relevant, or not relevant at all.

- Verse 9: 'the fast' refers to the Day of Atonement, when all Jews fasted. It happened in September or October, a time when the weather made sailing very dangerous.
- Verse 9: Paul was an expert sailor.
- Verse 12: Southwest is between the compass points of South and West. Northwest is between the compass points of North and West.
- Verse 12: Phoenix is the name of a magical bird that comes back to life from death.
- Verse 12: The voyage altogether would have been about 40 kilometres.

1) Read John 13:26–27 on Satan entering Judas.

a. How would your audience understand verse 27?

b. How would it affect your audience's understanding of the text if you supplied the following background information?

In Jewish society, when a host gave a piece of the food to a guest, it was a way of showing special affection to that person.

2) Read John 13:2–17 on foot washing.

a. What would your audience understand about why Jesus was washing the disciples' feet?

b. How would it affect your audience's understanding of the text if you supplied the following background information?

In Jewish society, showing hospitality to guests started with washing their feet. This was a way of greeting them. The foot washing was done by a Gentile slave, or if there wasn't a slave, then by the women or children. A Jewish male, even if he were a slave, would not be asked to do this very menial task.

B. Ways of supplying background information

Background information can be provided in many ways in the ministry of the church: sermons, Bible studies, children's and youth ministries, films, books, and booklets.

Some Scripture products, like Bible stories, can be written or told in a way that weaves the needed background information into the text. This can be important for evangelism or sharing with people who don't know much about the Bible. Background information can also be supplied alongside the biblical text in extra-textual helps, such as introductions, footnotes, and so forth. These are not the inspired word of God, but are provided to help us understand the Bible. Research has shown that both men and women of all educational levels and ages are able to use extra-textual helps to understand the Bible better.*

What kind of helps have you noticed in Bibles?

List responses on the board. Add any from the list below that are missed.

Bible helps from which you can get background information, include:

- introductions
- section headings
- footnotes or side-notes
- illustrations
- glossaries
- concordances or topical indexes, for example, 'If you are afraid, read Matthew 10:26–31; Luke 12:22–31; . . .'
- maps

For these helps to be beneficial, people need to be taught how to use them. Here are some ideas of how to teach the use of these helps.

Introductions

Find a Bible that provides helps and read the introduction to the Gospel of Mark.

How would this help someone understand this book better?

Section headings

Read Mark 6:1–5 out loud to the group without reading the section heading.

1) What was the main point of this section?

Now read the section title.

2) How does the section title help the audience?

Footnotes or side-notes

Background information related to the interaction taking place in passages is best supplied in notes, either side-notes (in the side margins) or footnotes (at the bottom of the page). One way to teach the use of notes is to read verses with several notes and show the group how to find the note each time. Then ask them to turn to a different passage and find the footnote associated with it. The first person to find it should read it out loud.

Glossaries

Prepare a work sheet for people to fill in the definitions of words using the glossary in a Bible, such as the Good News Bible. For example:

1. Who were the Epicureans?

2. What is a Sadducee?

3. How many different king Herods are there in the Gospels?

Concordances and Topical Indexes

Prepare a worksheet to give practice in using a small concordance. For example, ask the group to find three references to the Feast of Unleavened Bread in the Bible.

A useful alternative to a concordance is a topical index which classifies references according to situations, such as marriage, divorce, illness, and so forth. If one is included at the back of your translation, make up exercises along the following lines:

1. Give two references that tell us what Christians should do when they are ill.

2. Give three references that tell us how we can know that God will forgive our sins if we confess them.

3. Give two references that would help people who are being persecuted for their faith.

Illustrations

Often people need help to learn how to read illustrations because they may not be used to seeing things represented on paper. Encourage them to study an illustration and describe what they see in detail. For example, if there is a picture of Jerusalem in your Bible, you could ask, 'What can you see outside the main part of the city? Where is the temple?' In Islamic areas, however, it might not be acceptable to have any illustrations in the Bible.

Maps

The best way to help people learn how to use maps is to begin by making a map of the local area. Help the participants learn that symbols represent things like roads or rivers. Then show a map of your country and point out your local area. Then show a map of the world and point out your country. Then find Israel on the world map and show where it is in relation to your country. If it's possible to get a large map of Bible lands, put it up in front of the group. Point out certain places and explain the symbols used. Invite people to come up and point to a town. Then discuss the biblical events that took place there.

● ● ● ● ● ●   ***For Bible helps to be beneficial, people need to be taught how to use them.***

1) Which one of these helps do you use the most? Why?

2) How can you encourage people in your church to use these helps more?

Assignments

1. Read John 4:1–26. Use study Bibles or other helps to find out what background information the text brought to mind for the original audience. Identify four biblical background facts your audience needs to be able to understand the text.

2. In Acts 13:16–41 when Paul preached in Antioch, he started by talking about the history of the Jewish people. Compare this with how he started his sermon in Acts 17:22–31 when he preached in Athens. Why do you think he presented the same gospel in such different ways?

Readings*

Africa Bible Commentary: A One-Volume Commentary Written by 70 African Scholars. 2006. Nairobi, Kenya: WordAlive Publishers / Grand Rapids, MI: Zondervan.

The CEV Learning Bible. 2000. American Bible Society.

Barnwell, Katharine. 1988. 'Training New Readers To Use Bible Helps.' *Notes on Literature in Use and Language Programs* 17:23–25.

Brown, Rick. 2002. 'Selecting and Using Scripture Portions Effectively in Frontier Missions.' *International Journal of Frontier Missions* 18 (4):10–25.

Gutt, Ernst-August. 2006. "Aspects of 'Cultural Literacy" Relevant to Bible Translation.' *Journal of Translation* 2(1):1–16.

Hill, Harriet. 2006. *The Bible at Cultural Crossroads: From Translation to Communication.* Manchester, England: St Jerome, pp 27–32, 37–52, 72–82.

Keener, C. S. 1993. *The IVP Bible Background Commentary: New Testament.* Downers Grove, IL: InterVarsity.

Zinkuratire, Victor and Angelo Colacrai, eds. 1999. *The African Bible.* Nairobi, Kenya: Pauline Publications Africa.

Useful websites

http://www.walkthru.org   The official *Walk Thru the Bible* website.

http://www.hebrew-streams.org   Explains the Hebrew background to the New Testament.

---

*   http://www.scripture-engagement.org

Chapter 11

PREPARING BIBLE STUDIES

Introduction

One of the best ways to help Christians study the Bible in depth is by organizing groups within the church to do this. The term 'Bible study' can mean very different things in different places. The type of Bible study recommended in this chapter involves group participation rather than the leader giving a sermon.

Everyone's coming to Bible study

When Pastor Simon was at Bible college, he had learned about how to lead a Bible study. He decided to organize one because even though members of his church understood Scripture better, they still didn't know the Bible very well. He announced that the next Wednesday literate people with Bibles should come for a Bible study. The time arrived, and ten people came. Some people came with an English Bible, some with the Palapala New Testament, and some with the Kisanu Bible.

Pastor Simon chose a passage from the New Testament. First, he read it aloud. Then he preached a sermon based on this passage for 45 minutes. At the end of the time, he asked for questions. A few people asked questions, but they were about things not really connected with the passage. They ended in prayer and went home.

The following week only three people came, and so Pastor Simon cancelled the Bible study because he decided people weren't interested.

A month later, Pastor Simon was invited to go to another seminar for pastors to learn more about using the New Testament in Palapala. As he learned so much at the first short seminar, he was very willing to go again. A major theme of this seminar was how to lead a Bible study.

On his return he decided to put what he had learned into practice. He announced in church that anyone who would like to understand the Bible better was welcome at a Bible study the next Wednesday. At the seminar, he had been able to buy some inexpensive copies of Mark's Gospel in Palapala. He showed them to the congregation and encouraged them to buy copies after the service to bring to the Bible study. He also told them that everyone was invited, whether they could read or not. Then he found four mature leaders in his congregation and asked them if they would be willing to lead small groups. All agreed, and they set a time to come to his house and prepare the passage together.

Wednesday arrived, and 35 people came. Pastor Simon divided them into four groups according to how well they could read. They chose the passage on John the Baptist with the theme that repentance results in changed lives. Each group had a trained leader who had been given a list of questions on the passage.

Let's visit Mr Yuh's group, made up of those who are able to read the majority language well. First he asks someone to pray. Since the group is not used to reading their own language, he reads the passage aloud, and then helps the group to read it for themselves. Then he reads the first questions from the paper he has been given, which are about the content of the passage. The group members take turns to answer, always looking back at the text to find the answers. Then they come to a general question about the passage and discuss that for a while. Finally, they come to an application question about how the passage applies to their lives. At the end, a number of the group pray about what they have learned.

Mr Thomas is leading a group of people who can't read. First, he takes the passage and reads it to them quite slowly three times.

Then he reads just a couple of verses and asks for someone to tell what they have heard in their own words. The group members help each other do this. He continues to the end of the passage and then asks if anyone can tell the whole story in his or her own words. After two or three people have done this, Mr Thomas takes the list of questions on the passage and helps the group to answer them. He also takes one verse of the passage and helps them to memorize it. At the end of their time, they pray together.

When all the groups have finished, they meet together briefly to sing and pray.

1) How is a Bible study different from a sermon?

2) Is studying the Bible commanded in Scripture? Where? (Sample answers, p 303)

3) Why might some pastors be afraid of Bible studies in which the church members participate?

4) Does your church have Bible studies? If so, do you consider them to be successful? Explain why or why not.

1. Two kinds of Bible study

Two basic kinds of Bible studies are those that are based on passages and those that are based on themes. When preparing a Bible study on a passage, select a passage that is relevant to people's daily lives. It should address root causes of problems and not just visible behaviours. For example, if people continue practicing female excision because they are afraid of being punished by the ancestors or excommunicated by the community, you might focus the Bible studies on God's protection and doing what is right in God's eyes, regardless of what people may think. (See Chapter 9.) The passage should be between ten and fifteen verses.

A thematic Bible study explores one topic, such as humility or temptation. Instead of using just one passage of Scripture, a thematic Bible study uses verses from two or three passages. The total number of verses should not exceed fifteen, and they should be taken from no more than three passages. This type of study is more difficult to do than a Bible study on one passage, as there is a danger of taking passages out of context. There is also a temptation to use too many passages, which makes the Bible study difficult to follow and remember. When working with Christians from different kinds of churches, remember to avoid subjects that churches view differently which may cause controversy.

If the participants in either kind of Bible study are not used to reading in the language used for the Bible study, it is important to choose passages that are easy for them to read. Passages they are already familiar with, such as the Christmas story, are easier to read. Topics readers are familiar with are easier to understand than those that involve things that they've never heard of, as they already know much of the background information. For example, the parable of the sower may be easy for farming people to understand; the story of Abraham and Lot may be easy for cattle herders. Generally, stories are easier to understand than passages like Romans or Ephesians where the author is trying to persuade people. As people progress in their Bible knowledge, you can choose passages that are not as well known.

If only part of the Bible is available in the language used for the Bible study, you may need to print out a supplementary sheet with extra verses from the parts of the Bible not published yet. If at all possible, ask trained translators to translate extra verses needed for a study.

2. Understanding the passage and its background

Once you select a passage, you need to understand it well. To understand a passage, you need to understand where it fits in the chapter and have an idea about how it fits in the book. Read it in different versions, if possible, and read any available commentaries, study Bible notes, or other helps. Find out who wrote the book and why it was written. As part of your preparation, read through the passage several times, as well as reading the whole chapter.

Prepare any needed background information your audience might be missing. It can be communicated in introductory remarks before people read the passage. Remember that background information is simply the things the original audience would have known from their situation before they heard the text, for example, beliefs about ritual purity or marriage customs. It is not an explanation of the text. Bible study leaders must resist the temptation to preach a sermon!

3. Preparing questions

After understanding a passage, Bible study leaders need to prepare good questions that help people discover what God is saying to them through the passage. Sometimes pastors feel that if they aren't going to be talking about the passage, they don't need to take much time to prepare, but just the opposite is true. It takes more preparation to think through how to help people to discover for themselves what the passage is teaching than to preach a sermon on it.

There are four types of questions:

Polar questions

Polar questions have a yes or no answer. For example, did Jesus go to Jerusalem? These are not a good type of question to use because participants can answer them without giving the passage much thought.

Content questions

The answers to content questions are found in the passage. Content questions help people understand what the text says. For example, 'What did Jesus do?' Give the number of the verse where the answer is found in brackets after the question.

Reflection questions

Reflection questions demand an answer that requires thinking about the passage as a whole rather than a particular verse. They make people think more deeply about the text as they search for an answer. For example, from the book of Jonah, you could ask, 'Why do you think Jonah didn't want to go to Nineveh?' These questions often begin with why.

Application questions

Application questions do not have clear answers from the text, but help people to apply the principles of the passage to their lives. For example, in a study on Jesus teaching his disciples to be servants in John 13, an application question could be, 'After reading this passage, do you think pastors should change their behaviour towards church members in any way?'

Most of the questions in a Bible study should be *content* questions, with one or two reflection questions, and one or two application questions. In thematic Bible studies, be sure to put the questions in logical order, so each one builds on the previous one. Prepare these questions in advance and test them with a small group of people to make sure they are clear. Depending on the abilities of the group and the difficulty of the passage, participants can answer five to nine questions in 30 to 45 minutes.

Mark any non-content question with an asterisk so participants will know that they need to reflect on the text to find the answer.

Model a Bible study on Mark 1:21–28. Read the passage, having people take turns reading one verse each. Then ask the following questions and have the group answer.

1) What kind of place was Jesus in? (verse 21)

2) What did he do? (verse 21)

3) When the people there heard Jesus' teaching, what did they think? (verse 22)

4) What happened in the middle of his teaching? (verses 23–24)

5) What did Jesus say to the evil spirit? (verse 25)

6) What did the people say? (verse 27)

7) What does this passage tell us about Jesus' power?

8) If we meet someone with an evil spirit, what should we do?

Make a Bible study on Luke 12:13–21.

1) Read the passage in the large group and ask for an example of a content question and a reflection question.

2) Divide the participants into language groups and have them make up questions in their language on this passage. Have them write four content questions, one reflection question and one application question.

3) Ask some of the language groups to share an English translation of their questions with the whole group.

4. Conducting a Bible study

In the story, Pastor Simon divided the 35 people who came to his Bible study into four groups so that everyone had an opportunity to answer questions. Groups shouldn't have more than 12 people in them. Meeting somewhere other than the church may help people feel more relaxed. Sitting in a circle encourages group discussion.

Each culture has norms for who can speak to whom and who can discuss things together. For example, a younger person may not be allowed to ask a question of an older person. Or older people may not be willing to discuss certain things with younger people. Or women may not be allowed to discuss things when men are present. The groups should be organized in a way that everyone feels free to participate. Pastor Simon divided those who were literate from those who were not, but in some cultures, this may not be acceptable.

During a Bible study, leaders should listen much more than talk. The group will remember much more if they can discuss the passage and discover its meaning and its application to their lives.

We remember

20 per cent of what we HEAR

30 per cent of what we SEE

70 per cent of what we DISCUSS with others

80 per cent of what we EXPERIENCE

95 per cent of what we TEACH others.[9]

If you are working with a group that has never done a Bible study of this sort before, prepare them for what will happen by giving them examples of questions and answers. This helps them understand that the answers are in the text and there is no trick or mystery to the questions.

---

* Quoted from Edgar Dale, 1969. *Audio-visual Methods in Teaching*. New York: Holt, Rinehardt, and Winston.

Some people may want to talk non-stop, while others may not talk at all. Leaders need to encourage some to speak more and others to speak less so that everyone in the group has a chance to take part.

It is your job as leader to keep the Bible study focused on the topic. If participants ask questions or make comments that are not about the subject of the study, tell them you will address these things later. End the Bible study on time. Generally, it's better to finish a bit early than to drag on until the group is bored or exhausted. People are much more likely to come back the next week if you respect the time agreed upon to finish.

1) What different types of people in your church need to meet separately for Bible studies?

2) What type of people in your church could you train as small group leaders?

3) What type of people may cause problems for the leader of a Bible study? How would you advise leaders to deal with these people?

4) What time and day is best for your community? Where is the best place to meet?

5. Oral Bible study

Many people do not read or do not like to read and prefer to learn orally. In some groups, the majority of people fall into this category. They still need Bible studies and these can be very successful. Here is one way to do an oral Bible study if the leaders are literate.

1. Provide any background information your audience might need to be able to understand the passage.

2. Read the passage through slowly or tell it three times.

3. Read or tell a couple of verses and ask someone to tell in their own words what they heard. Do this for the whole passage.

4. Ask a few people to tell back the whole passage.

5. When you are sure the group knows the content of the passage, then ask the Bible study questions you have prepared.

6. Select a memory verse and help the group to learn it.

Another way to do Bible studies orally is to use recordings of Scripture with Bible study questions. The group listens to the recording and stops it to discuss their answers to the questions. Some ministries have developed extensive programs using recorded Scripture.

Work through this thematic study on servant leadership together as an oral Bible study. Only the leader reads the Bible. Start by giving this background information:

In Jewish society, washing the feet of guests was a very important part of showing hospitality. This task was performed by Gentile slaves, or if there were none, by women or children. A Jewish man would never be expected to do it.

Read Matthew 20:25–28 and John 13:2–5, 12–17.

1) What is the normal behaviour of chiefs and leaders towards those under their authority? (Matthew 20:25)

2) How did Jesus tell the disciples to behave? (Matthew 20:26–27)

3) What service did Jesus perform for his disciples? (John 13:2–5)

4) Who normally would have done this?

5) By doing this, what lesson was Jesus trying to teach the disciples?

6) How can we apply this to the way we treat those we consider under us?

Assignments

1. The root issues you identified in Chapter 9 may need to be addressed by a series of Bible studies. Develop one Bible study on a passage that responds to at least one part of the issue.

2. Develop a thematic Bible study that responds to at least one part of the issue you identified in Chapter 9. Share this with the large group.

3. Describe one Bible study you have attended, and say what you enjoyed or how it could be improved.

*Readings**

Konkomba Team, 2002. 'Konkomba—Faith Comes By Hearing Project—What We Have Learned Team Report.' *Scripture in Use Today* 5:15–21.

Benn, Keith. 1984. 'Bible Study Cassettes: A Tool Which Churches Perceive To Be of Value in Furthering Their Goals.' *Notes on Literature in Use and Language Programs* 7:8–13.

Fee, G. D. and D. Stuart. 1982. *How to Read the Bible for All It's Worth: A Guide to Understanding the Bible.* Grand Rapids, MI: Zondervan.

—. 2002. *How To Read the Bible Book by Book: A Guided Tour.* Grand Rapids, MI: Zondervan.

Gruenig, Hanni. 2003. 'Bible Courses for Women.' *Scripture in Use Today* 6:29–31.

Houhulin, Dick. 1983. 'An Effective Bible Study Method: Bible Study Cassettes' *Notes on Literature in Use and Language Programs* 7:5–84.

Sharp, Leonard E. S. 2007. *Great Truths from God's Word.* Secunderabad, India: OM Books/Authentic.

---

*   http://www.scripture-engagement.org

Chapter 12

ADDRESSING HUMAN CONCERNS: TRAUMA HEALING

Introduction

One way to show people that the Bible is relevant to their lives is to do what is called an integrated Bible study to address their human concerns. This type of study combines material from Scripture with information from some other field to help meet a need in the community.

This chapter gives an example of such a study on trauma healing. When widespread trauma strikes a community through war, natural disaster, criminal activities, or illnesses like HIV-AIDS, biblical truths and practical counselling principles can help bring healing to those who are suffering pain in their hearts.[*]

Troubles in Sanatu

The country of Sanatu had been stable for many years but when the head of state died, it began to experience political troubles. As a result, violent crime increased significantly. The police and army

---

[*] An entire seminar can be devoted to this topic. An excellent resource is *Healing the Wounds of Trauma: How the Church Can Help*. It is listed in the readings at the end of this chapter.

seemed unable or unwilling to do much about the situation. As Pastor Simon looked to the future, he could see that the troubles were likely to increase rather than decrease and he was afraid it might lead to war. 'Is there any way I can prepare my Christian brothers and sisters for this?' he wondered.

One day the local school director, Mr Randa, came to him. Mr Randa was very distressed as he told how his family had been tied up on the road while coming back from visiting relatives. They had then been beaten and robbed of everything they possessed. Worst of all, his wife had been raped in front of their whole family. With bitterness in his voice, Mr Randa asked, 'If God loves us as you say, why did he allow this to happen to us? Was he asleep? Was he punishing us for some wrong we had done?' Pastor Simon tried to read passages from the Bible to help him, but nothing seemed to help, and Randa went away even more angry.

The next week, Pastor Simon heard that the catechist, Lambo, had been involved in a car accident and went to visit him. Pastor Simon was shocked and saddened to hear that Lambo's wife and two of his children had been killed. A drunken driver had rammed his truck into the back of the taxi they had been travelling in. Pastor Simon came to sit with Lambo in his grief, but he found that Lambo was very busy arranging the funeral and helping other family members. When Pastor Simon asked him how he was feeling, Lambo said, 'I'm a Christian so I shouldn't grieve. I know I will see them again in heaven'. Other family members were expressing their anger with the drunk driver but Lambo said, 'I'm a Christian so I have to forgive him'. Pastor Simon went away thinking that something was not quite right. He also wondered how he could learn to help people in these situations.

Have you ever tried to help people who have experienced trauma?

1) If so, what seemed to help them?

2) What didn't help them?

1. Why is there suffering in the world?

Why do you think there is suffering in the world?

Discuss the group's responses, and then bring out any of the following points that have not already been mentioned.

What the Bible tells us about the reasons for suffering:

1. Sin entered the world when Adam and Eve disobeyed God. Because of this, everyone, whether they are Christians or not, experiences the effects of this disobedience (Romans 5:12; Genesis 3:1–23).

2. Satan has rebelled against God and tries to get us to rebel as well. Satan is a liar and a murderer and he tries to get people to do his evil work in the world today (John 8:44; 1 Peter 5:8–9).

3. God gives us freedom to choose whether we will obey him or not. He made all people with the freedom to choose to do good or evil (Matthew 7:13). We can suffer because of our own bad choices or because of bad choices others have made (1 Peter 3:17–18).

2. What happens when someone is grieving?

Grieving takes time and energy. As Christians we do not grieve like those who have no hope, but it is still normal for us to be very sad or angry when someone we love dies or when we lose something important to us, like our job, our house, or an arm or leg. The Psalms show us what to do with these feelings. When the Psalmist experienced feelings of anger, abandonment, and sadness, he expressed how he felt to God in a lament, for example Psalm 3, 4, 5, 6, or 13. He cried out honestly to God and at the same time praised him for his faithfulness and love. We, too, can find healing by expressing our feelings honestly to God. If we pretend we are not affected by the loss, it will be much more difficult for us to recover.

We can think of grief as a journey that leads us through three villages.

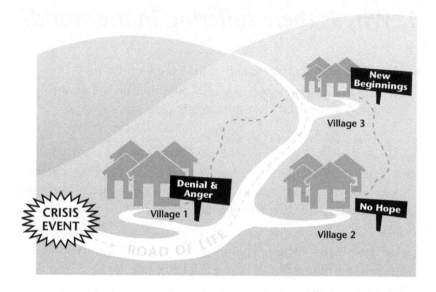

A. Village of anger and denial

Immediately after the death of a loved one, often people feel like their emotions are numb. They may find it hard to believe the person is really dead. They may also be angry either with the person who has died for leaving them, or with God for taking the person away, or with other people who they think have caused the death. This stage often lasts about a month.

B. Village of no hope

In the second village, people often feel sad and depressed for some months. They may feel that life is not worth living and have little interest in the ordinary things of life. They may feel very lonely and guilty, that it was their fault that the person died. It may feel like they have lost their identity.

C. Village of new beginnings

If people take time to be sad, to cry and feel their loss, gradually the pain becomes less and eventually they are ready to begin life anew. When people get to this village, they show signs of new life. For example, they may be interested in finding a new husband or wife, or having another child. If someone very close has died, the first two stages may take a year or more. This is normal.

D. The false bridge

Sometimes Christians feel that because they have the promises of God, they shouldn't feel pain or grief when a loved one dies or they suffer other losses. This is not biblical and it will not bring healing. People call this the false bridge because it seems to provide a straight path from the moment of loss directly to the village of new beginnings without passing through the first two villages. God made us with the need to grieve our losses. Even Jesus cried when his friend Lazarus died and he expressed painful emotions on the cross when he said, 'My God, my God, why have you abandoned me?' (Matthew 27:46).

Church leaders need to take special care to grieve their losses. Since they are busy helping others, they may feel it is inappropriate to be angry or sad. This will lead to serious problems in the long run. Going through grief honestly, like the Psalmist did, will not only bring them healing but it will also give their church members a healthy model to follow.

Have the group divide into pairs for this discussion.

1) Think of a time when someone you loved died or you lost something important to you, like your job or your house. Did you go through these villages?

2) What helped you during your time in the first two villages?

3. How can we help people who are grieving?

Sometimes we avoid people who are grieving because we don't know what to say or do. Here are some suggestions that may help:

- Help them to know that it is normal to feel sad and that they need to express this grief. If people do not allow themselves to grieve, the loss is like an unhealed wound inside them. Eventually it will cause problems. These problems could be nightmares, unresolved anger towards people, or physical problems like ulcers or headaches.

- Eventually they need to be able to bring their pain to God and ask for his healing, but this will not usually happen right away.

- Help them to write their own laments. This should include a statement of trust in God as well as expressing their pain.

1) Make up skits of a church leader visiting a woman who has just lost her husband. In one skit, the leader does everything wrong: he goes to visit her alone, preaches to her, tells her not to cry, and talks too much. In the other skit, the church leader goes with his wife or another woman, listens to the woman, helps her to grieve and offers practical help.

2) Compose a personal lament about a pain you have experienced. It may be a written text, a song, or a song with dance.

Assignments

1. List three principles in this study about grieving that were taken from Scripture and three principles that were taken from general knowledge about mental health.

2. What other kinds of integrated studies would be helpful in your context? Where would you find reliable information that you need other than biblical information? What are the main points you would like to develop?

Readings*

Finifrock, Jacob. 2004. 'What Can a Pastor Learn from a Donkey?' *Scripture in Use Today* 9:27–34.

Hill, Margaret. 2003. 'Scripture Impact and Mental Health.' *Scripture in Use Today* 7:30–31.

Hill, Margaret and Hill, Harriet, et al. 2004. *Healing the Wounds of Trauma: How the Church Can Help.* Nairobi, Kenya: Paulines Press.

Kayanga, Samuel and Josue Kakoraki. 2004. 'Local Trauma Healing Workshops.' *Scripture in Use Today* 8:34–36.

Mpandza, André and Popaud, Jean-Pierre. 2002. 'Trauma Healing Seminar in Nairobi.' *Scripture in Use Today* 5:31–32.

---

* http://www.scripture-engagement.org

Chapter 13

ADDRESSING HUMAN CONCERNS: HIV-AIDS AND THE CHURCH

Introduction

In 2007, there were 33.2 million people living with HIV-AIDS in the world. Almost seven out of every ten of these people lived in Africa. In some countries, there are whole villages where all the young adults have died of AIDS and only children and grandparents remain. In other countries, there are only a small number of people affected now, but the rate of infection is increasing rapidly. This chapter is an integrated study addressing this pandemic.*

AIDS strikes Azi and Precious

Pastor Simon's church had an active, enthusiastic youth group. One of their most dedicated leaders was a man named Azi. Pastor Simon remembered how as a young boy, Azi had always been top of the class at school. His parents were farmers without much money, and it had been a real struggle for them to send him to school. They lived frugally and paid his school bills all the way through his years

---

* An entire workshop can be devoted to this topic. An excellent resource is *Kande's Story* by Kathie Watters and Margaret Hill. It is listed in the readings at the end of this chapter.

at the teacher training college. For the last four years of his training, Azi had been studying in the regional capital, Retali.

After Azi returned home, he started teaching in the local school. He was much appreciated by the children for his enthusiastic teaching. Soon after this, he married a young girl named Precious and within a year they had their first child, a son named Joshua. Azi and Precious were committed Christians and many times they asked God to guide them so that their home would be happy and bring him glory. Soon a second baby came to join the family, a lovely little daughter they named Joy.

Everything went well for another two years. Then Azi started getting one illness after another: malaria, a deep infected sore, and a very bad cold. Each time the clinic was able to treat the various sicknesses, but he began to wonder why he was getting ill so often. After a few months, he started to lose weight and had diarrhoea almost all the time. He finally decided to go to the hospital for tests. At the hospital they examined him and did blood tests. When he returned a few hours later for the results, the doctor told him as gently as he could that the blood tests showed he was HIV positive. The doctor explained that Azi would continue to have various sicknesses because his body was losing its ability to fight off disease, and that eventually he would die of AIDS. He also encouraged Azi to tell his wife and bring her for a blood test as well.

Azi returned to the village in shock. For two weeks he didn't tell anyone what the doctor had said, but just tried to carry on as if everything was normal. His wife knew something was wrong, but she couldn't get him to tell her about it. Finally the burden of his secret was too much to bear alone and he went to talk to Pastor Simon. On hearing this news, Pastor Simon was shocked and saddened. Azi told Pastor Simon that he thought he must have caught the disease in his last year at college. All his friends there had been telling him that all men needed to sleep with women in order to prove they were men, and that if they didn't do so, they would become ill. After a while, Azi had believed this, and some nights after drinking a few beers, he had gone out with his friends and slept with some local prostitutes. After a few months of this, Azi had gone to a local church where the pastor was teaching about the need to wait for marriage to have sex and about the dangers of contracting HIV. Azi had asked God to forgive him for what he had done, and hadn't gone back to the prostitutes.

After Pastor Simon and Azi had talked for a while, Pastor Simon encouraged him to go home and tell his wife. 'She needs to go for a blood test right away', Pastor Simon said. 'If she is not HIV positive, you will need to protect her from being infected'. Azi went home, and that night he shared his news with his wife.

First she was angry with him, and then she cried and cried as she began to realize her husband was HIV positive. The next day Precious went to the hospital and found out that she, too, was HIV positive. As they lay in bed that night, they cried together as they thought of Joshua and Joy becoming orphans. All their plans for the future were shattered. That week they had both children tested and were very relieved that they were both HIV negative.

The next week as Azi was talking with Pastor Simon, he said, 'Why didn't anyone tell me about this before I went to college? I hardly thought at all about what the Bible teaches about sex and marriage. I just listened to my friends. It is too late for me, but what about the young people and the children in the church? How can we help them?' So they discussed together how to teach these things to the whole church.

Pastor Simon visited the family frequently as Azi got more and more ill. Precious also started getting various infections. People from the church prayed with the family and helped them in practical ways. Pastor Simon encouraged them to make plans about the future of their children. Azi told people openly that he was HIV positive. He tried his best to warn them about the dangers of sex before marriage and adultery. He asked Pastor Simon to use his funeral to preach about these matters. Azi and Precious talked together a lot about heaven as they became weaker, and appreciated it very much when church members came to sing and read God's word to them. Finally, within a month of each other they both died, leaving their orphaned children to be bought up by an uncle.

1) How did the church help Azi?
2) How did it fail him?

1. Facts about HIV-AIDS

The first step to overcoming HIV-AIDS is to know the facts about it. Give this quiz to the participants. When you have finished, go over the answers provided at the end of this chapter. Make sure everyone understands the medical facts connected with the transmission of the HIV virus. (Answers, pp 304–5)

1) What do the letters in the word AIDS stand for?

2) What does it mean to be HIV positive?

3) How do most people get HIV-AIDS?

4) What is the second most common way?

5) Is there a medical cure for this disease?

6) Can you get HIV-AIDS in the following ways?

    a. Hugging a person with HIV-AIDS?

    b. Sharing the same razor blade with a person who has HIV-AIDS?

    c. Using the same toilet as a person who has HIV-AIDS?

    d. Having sex with a person who has HIV-AIDS?

    e. Through an injection using a used needle?

    f. Through receiving a blood transfusion?

    g. Kissing a person with HIV-AIDS on a cheek?

    h. Drinking out of the same cup at Holy Communion?

    i. Treating the open sores of a person with HIV-AIDS?

    j. Through insect bites?

7) How can you tell if you have HIV-AIDS?

8) How can a person with HIV-AIDS live longer?

9) If a married couple finds one partner is HIV positive and one is not, how can they keep the healthy one from becoming infected?

10) What are the church's responsibilities in connection with HIV-AIDS? Name at least three.

HIV-AIDS is only transmitted through body fluids:

- *Men and women's sexual fluids*

- *Blood*

- *Breast milk*

The virus can only live outside the body for a few minutes.

2. The church's role in fighting HIV-AIDS

Local churches can play a key role in addressing HIV-AIDS. International organizations often provide medical and nutritional resources, but the local churches can provide equally important resources. They can bring people into communities of caring relationships. They can also give people moral guidance and hope for the future. If churches partner with international organizations in fighting HIV-AIDS, both groups can increase their effectiveness.

Three important areas in which churches can make a real difference are in education and prevention, caring for AIDS patients, and helping with widows and orphans.

A. Education and prevention

The most likely way for a young person to get HIV is through sexual activity, so churches need to educate young people about sex and HIV-AIDS. They need to help young people understand and accept the biblical pattern of abstinence before marriage and faithfulness within marriage. This education should be given before a child becomes sexually active, which can be a young as ten in some societies. Many Bible-based programs that address these issues are available.

Young people have a lot of energy and need to feel useful. Some churches have formed groups of three or four young people and trained them to help people with AIDS and other serious illnesses. Each group is assigned two or three families to visit on a regular basis. They establish a relationship of trust with the person who is ill and their family and give practical help.

They may also sing, pray, and read the Bible to them. Programs like this simultaneously help those who are ill and have a strong impact on the youth of the church.

1) In your community, are there already programmes teaching about HIV-AIDS and its prevention? Are your local churches involved in this?

2) Do you have a programme of HIV-AIDS prevention education for ten- to twelve-year-olds in your church? If not, what could you do to start one?

3) Do the youth in your church help to visit and look after people who are ill? If not, how could this be started?

B. Care for AIDS patients

It is not easy to care for someone who is very ill. This is made even more difficult in the case of AIDS because of the social stigma associated with the disease. Yet caring for the sick is an important ministry of the church, both to help and comfort Christians and to lead others to a real faith in Christ before they die.

Help them prepare for heaven

If the people who are ill are Christians, they will receive comfort from hearing about heaven. If they are not Christians, often they are open to hearing about how their sins can be forgiven and how they can be sure of going to heaven. Either way, we should read Scripture, pray and sing with them and their families. Let them know that they can tell God exactly how they feel. Psalm 38 shows how David expressed his feelings to God.

Help people understand HIV-AIDS and talk about the illness

Everyone needs to understand how HIV-AIDS is spread so that they can avoid getting or spreading it. People who care for AIDS patients also need to be very clear about the things that do not lead to HIV-AIDS. For example, they need to know that they will not catch it by touching someone who has it, eating with them, or taking care of their needs.

Often people who have HIV-AIDS want to hide the fact that they have it. This does not help them or their community. President Museveni of Uganda said that Africans should deal with HIV-AIDS like they deal with a lion that is stalking their village: no one would keep quiet about that!

They would warn the villagers about the danger. It takes brave people to be the first to say publicly that they have HIV-AIDS, but this is the first step in 'trapping the lion'. Their courage can help others with the virus to speak openly.

Help them to continue to be part of the community

People need other people! One of the worst parts of having HIV-AIDS is the fear of being rejected by family and friends. Churches can work to help people accept those with HIV-AIDS rather than be afraid of them. Churches can help those who have HIV-AIDS by arranging times for them to meet together and talk openly about their experiences and feelings. They can also encourage them to write a will so no one can take advantage of their children and widows.

Help them work through their grief

It comes as a tremendous shock to someone to know that they are HIV positive. The person often goes through various stages of grief such as anger, denial, depression, and finally acceptance. It may take months before they can accept their situation. A good helper will be patient with them and help them understand the grieving process. (See Chapter 12.)

Help them stay as healthy as possible

Two people who are HIV positive may have very different experiences. One may live for six years; another may live for six months. This is partly due to the overall physical well-being of the person, but the person's attitude and the care he receives also play an important role. People live longer if they continue to have something to do and are making a contribution to their families. Many jobs don't require great physical strength, like sewing clothes or raising animals. In addition, people with HIV-AIDS need to eat plenty of fruit and vegetables so that they get vitamins to fight off the disease.

People with HIV-AIDS can benefit from medication. In many countries affordable anti retro-viral drugs are becoming available as part of the government services. If patients take these drugs regularly and correctly, they can stay healthy longer. In fact, they can live a normal life for a number of years after becoming HIV positive.

1) Do people in your church admit that they have HIV-AIDS? What makes it hard for them to do so?

2) Does your church have a way to train people to visit those who are ill?

3) When you visit such people, to which of the five areas listed above do you give the least attention? How could you improve in this area?

C. Helping widows and orphans

Religion that God our Father accepts as pure and faultless is this: to look after orphans and widows in their distress and to keep oneself from being polluted by the world (James 1:27).

The church has a clear responsibility to look after the poor and needy who do not have others to care for them. As well as giving food, clothing, and shelter, a local church can help orphans and widows learn to support themselves. In many areas, churches can work with organizations that can help them set up these types of projects. Here are some projects that churches have done with success:

• Make land available to small groups of widows or orphans and give them the necessary tools and seeds to get started planting crops.

• Set up vocational schools where older children can learn trades such as carpentry, building, or sewing.

• Give a small group of three to six widows an interest-free loan to start a small business. For example, they may make clothes, furniture, jam, or snack food. They might cultivate land, set up a bakery, or breed animals. They pay back the loan after one or two years.

• Help orphans go to school by giving scholarships for tuition fees and providing text books and clothes.

1) How does your church help widows and orphans?

2) Have you thought of any other ways of helping them?

3) Imagine that in five years' time, many of the young adults in your church will have died of AIDS. How will your church and community care for the increased number of orphans?

4) If a widow is HIV positive, what advice should the church give about re-marriage?

Assignments

1. Find the most recent statistics available for the percentage of people who are HIV positive in your country.

2. Make a list of at least five organizations in your country or region that you know are working to prevent the spread of HIV-AIDS. Describe how your church denomination can work more closely with at least one of these.

3. Find any statements made by your government about HIV-AIDS. What is their policy towards making anti retro-viral drugs available?

*Readings**

Carter, Isobel. 2004. *Responding More Effectively to HIV and AIDS.* Teddington, UK: Tearfund.

Hill, Margaret and Harriet Hill, Dick Bagge, Pat Miersma. 2004. *Healing the Wounds of Trauma: How the Church Can Help.* Nairobi, Kenya: Paulines Publications, pp 62–73.

Madangatyc, Tembinkosi. 2002. *AIDS, You Don't Have To Get It!* Pretoria, South Africa: OM Books.

Raen, Konstanse. 1993. *Where is the Good Samaritan today?* United Bible Societies & Norwegian Church Aid.

Watters, Kathie and Margaret Hill. 2007. *Kande's Story* (Student Book and Facilitator's Manual). Nairobi, Kenya: Paulines Publications. In English and French.

Yamamori, Tetsunao (ed.). 2003. *The Hope Factor: Engaging the Church in the HIV/AIDS Crisis.* Monrovia, CA: World Vision.

Yamamori, Tetsunao, Bryant L. Myers, Kwame Bediako, and Larry Reed. 1996. *Serving with the Poor in Africa.* Monrovia, CA: MARC.

Dixon, Patrick. 2004. *AIDS and You.* Secunderabad, India: OM Books.

---

* http://www.scripture-engagement.org

Chapter 14

PREPARING SERMONS

Introduction

Church leaders invest a lot of time and energy in preparing sermons, but often after the service, people can't even remember what the sermon was about. In churches that don't have Scripture in a language people can understand, sermons may mainly involve translating the text into the local language. When mother-tongue Scripture becomes available, that task is already done and church leaders need to learn new ways of preaching. This chapter provides some basic ideas that can help church leaders prepare interesting sermons that communicate well.

Lambo's short sermons

One day Lambo, the Catholic catechist from the next village, came to see Pastor Simon. After they had exchanged greetings and news of their families, Lambo said, 'I have a real problem to discuss with you. As I think you know, since we went on the seminar, I am convinced that my congregation needs to hear God's word in Palapala. In fact, we have been encouraged by the bishop to hold all the service in Palapala now. But this is giving me a new problem. Up to last month, I used to read the three passages of Scriptures set for that Sunday in Kisanu and many of the people didn't really understand what the readings were about. Because of this, most of my sermon was taken up with explaining in Palapala the meaning of one of the Kisanu readings. Now everyone understands the readings so what do I talk about in the sermon? I remember learning about sermon preparation at catechist school, but that was fifteen years ago and I've forgotten what they said! My sermons are very short now, and I don't think that is good!'

If Lambo came to you, how would you help him?

1. The parts of a sermon

The two main types of sermons are preaching from a passage or preaching on a theme. A good preacher uses both kinds, but preaching well on a theme requires much more preparation. In this chapter, we look at preaching from a passage.

A sermon should have three parts:

- Introduction: start by telling your congregation the subject of your sermon in a way that makes them want to listen.
- Main part: teach on one main point. Explain it and illustrate it.
- Conclusion: end by summarizing what you have said and show the hearers how to apply what they have heard to their lives.

2. Steps in preparing a sermon

What steps are involved in preparing a sermon?

List responses on the board. (Mention any of the following points that are relevant but have not been listed.)

Study the Bible

As you study the Bible, you will get ideas for sermons. Make notes on your ideas, as you may use them at a later date.

Pray for guidance

Pray for God to guide you as you prepare. His words, not yours, are what will touch people's lives deeply. Although God can choose to speak through you if you haven't prepared, in general, the better you prepare, the better he can speak through you. Pray as though it was all up to the Holy Spirit and work as though it was all dependent on your preparation, and you will have a good sermon.

Choose a passage

You can choose passages in a number of ways. If your church uses set readings, you can use one of the passages for that Sunday. If you are preaching through a book, you can use a different section of the book each week. Or if you want to preach on a theme that is relevant for your church, you can look for the best passage on the theme. Your passage should be no longer than a chapter. It may well be shorter.

Identify the main subject of the passage

Read the passage carefully and decide on the main subject. Just as you don't eat all of the kinds of food that are available in a single day, you don't need to cover everything in a passage in one sermon.

Read the passage in various versions, if possible. Think through the meaning of the key terms in your mother tongue, even if you're preaching in another language. It is good to use commentaries and other helps to be sure that you understand the passage well. Take notes on good ideas in case you want to use them later.

Notice how the writer explained the main subject. Although some passages have three or four clear points, others consist of a single subject followed by an application. Parables are often like this. To help yourself understand the meaning, ask yourself these questions:

• What did the passage mean to the original audience?

• What does the passage mean to us today?

• How should we respond?

Think of ways to illustrate the main point of the passage

Think of illustrations to make the point clear. Use stories from your life, the lives of others, and the lives of people in the Bible. Many preachers use folk stories or proverbs. These can be very good and the congregation will listen very attentively, but be careful that they illustrate your main point and don't become the focus of the sermon. After the sermon, if people only remember the stories and not why you told them, the stories haven't served you very well.

Prepare the conclusion

If you are preaching in a church where you think most people are Christians, about 70 per cent of your conclusion should be addressed to Christians and about 30 per cent to non-Christians. It might include an action you want them to take such as a decision to believe or a decision to tell a non-Christian neighbour about Christ. It might also include an idea people can think about all week.

Prepare an introduction for the sermon

Introductions are very important. People will decide whether or not to listen to your sermon according to your introduction. It should be brief, catchy, and clear. Many people prefer to prepare this at the end after they know what the sermon will say. An introduction must do two things:

- Catch the congregation's attention. Remember that many people in the church will be thinking about all sorts of things when you begin your sermon. You need to attract their attention with a question, proverb, or a personal experience.

- Give them an idea what you are going to talk about so that they can easily follow your ideas. Be sure to tell them clearly where you are going, and then go there. Don't get lost along the way.

······   *A sermon should have one main point.*

In groups of four or five, read Mark 4:35–41 through twice. Then fill out the following sheet, discussing each point together.

> 1. What is the main point of this passage?
>
>
>
> 2. How is this teaching expressed? List some points for the passage. Use as many or as few lines as you need.
>
> a)
>
> b)
>
> c)
>
> d)
>
> 3. What is a good illustration of this main teaching?
>
>
>
>
> 4. Write notes for the conclusion. Include an application for both Christians and non-Christians.
>
>
>
>
> 5. Now think about the introduction. Write down your opening sentence.

1) Think about three sermons you have heard or preached in the last few months.

- What language was the sermon preached in?
- What language were the Scriptures read in?
- What was the subject of each sermon?

2) Which kind of sermon is most frequently preached in your church?

- A translation of the majority language Scriptures with some extra explanations.
- A sermon on a passage, going through it verse-by-verse.
- A sermon on a theme.

3) What improvements would you like to see in the sermons in your church?

Assignment

1. Select a passage and make a sermon outline for it, as you did for Mark 4:35–41.

Useful websites

http://www.langhampartnership.org   The Langham Trust is dedicated to help local pastors know how to preach. This site is full of resources, announcements of seminars, and other helps.

http://www.scripture-engagement.org   This website is provided by the Scripture Engagement development group of the Forum of Bible Agencies International (FOBAI). You can search in the right-hand 'Search this site' box for articles on preaching related topics.

Chapter 15

MEDITATING ON GOD'S WORD

Introduction

In the Christian context, meditation has been defined as 'a prayerful reading and pondering of the Scriptures'. It is a time when we let God speak to us through his word. In this chapter, we will explore how Christians can engage with Scripture and grow closer to God through meditation.

Pastor Simon gets quiet

Pastor Simon was invited to another Scripture engagement seminar in a town some distance to the north. He was somewhat worried about the travel arrangements, so the first thing he did was to find out which other church leaders were going from his area. He found out that he would be travelling with three other church leaders: Lambo, the catechist from the local Catholic church, John, a pastor of a Pentecostal church, and a Lutheran pastor who lived a bit further to the south. They all met as planned and went together in a minibus to the place where the seminar was being held.

That evening, they arrived safely at their destination and settled in. The next morning the seminar began. After the opening, one of the first sessions was about meditation. The participants heard about the need to listen to God as well as to talk to him. The next morning, instead of the usual devotional time of singing, Bible reading, and a short talk, one of the church leaders led them in a meditation on a Bible passage. The following morning, everyone was given a passage for meditation and told to find a quiet place and encouraged to be still and listen to God for 25 minutes. This seemed like a long time to Pastor Simon, longer than he had ever waited in silence before God. Part of him became impatient, but he sat quietly. As he did, he sensed the wonder of God's love in a new and real way. When the group came back together, some people shared what they had learned.

In the minibus going home, the four church leaders were squeezed together on the back seat. They discussed the seminar for most of the journey. John, the Pentecostal pastor, said, 'For me, the most extraordinary thing about this seminar was being told to sit in silence and meditate on a Bible passage. I'd never tried anything like that before. To start with I thought it was a strange idea, but once I really experienced it for myself, I knew this was something people in my church need to learn. Now I see that there are many different ways of worshipping God, and they are not all connected with loud noises!' They agreed this was something to teach people when they got home.

1) Have you ever tried to get quiet inside and let God speak to you through a passage of Scripture? If so, how was this experience for you?

2) Do you find it easier to hear God speak when you are alone, or when you are with a group of Christians? Why do you think that is?

1. What is biblical meditation?

Think of someone who is a good friend of yours. Will you get to know your friend if all you do is talk and never listen to what he or she wants to say to you?

Bible studies give us a foundation of Bible knowledge which can keep us from being led astray, but we also need to let God speak to us personally through his word. Meditation involves reading a short passage of Scripture slowly, thinking about it deeply, and listening to what God has to say. Normally, people meditate alone, but meditation can also be done in a group.

> *We need to be silent and let God speak to us personally through his word.*

2. What does the Bible say about meditation?

Read these passages aloud, and then discuss what each verse says about meditation.

Psalm 77:12   I will think about all that you have done;
               I will meditate on all your mighty acts (*GNB*).

Psalm 119:99   I understand more than all my teachers,
               because I meditate on your instructions (*GNB*).

Joshua 1:8   Do not let this Book of the Law depart from your mouth;
               meditate on it day and night, so that you may be careful to
               do everything written in it. Then you will be prosperous
               and successful (*NIV-UK*).

Philippians 4:8 In conclusion, my friends, fill your minds with those things
                 that are good and that deserve praise: things that are true,
                 noble, right, pure, lovely, and honourable (*GNB*). ('Fill
                 your minds' here has the same sense as meditate.)

In many non-Western societies, activities are normally done by groups of people. Because of this, people may find the idea of meditating on God's word alone to be a strange idea. Can you think of ways to make meditation easier for them?

3. Practical suggestions for meditating

Before beginning to read a passage, tell God all the things that are worrying you, and imagine putting them into his hands and leaving them there. Get quiet on the inside as well as on the outside. You may need to confess sins before beginning and know that he has forgiven you.

If you are reading a passage that tells the story of an event, imagine that you are there watching the action or are one of the characters. For example, in the story of the prodigal son (Luke 15), you could imagine you are the prodigal son, his brother, his father, his mother, or someone observing the whole thing.

One phrase or sentence in the passage may stand out for you. Stay with that thought and let God speak to you through it. Don't be in a hurry to move on. Linger in God's presence. You may want to memorize it so that you can go on thinking about it during the day. Our minds are quick to absorb a lot of information, but our hearts take time to let even one simple idea sink in deeply. It's when an idea sinks in deeply that it changes our lives.

Don't get discouraged if you don't sense God's presence or voice. The discipline of getting quiet and waiting on God will have effects, though you might not recognize them until later. You may simply enjoy a time being with God with no particular message, or he may speak to you through the passage later in the day.

People who can't read can meditate, too. If the leader reads a short passage aloud two or three times, then the members of the group who cannot read will be able to think about the passage and let God speak to them through it.

1) Invite the participants to sit or lie down in a comfortable position and shut their eyes to prepare for the Bible story.

2) Set the scene for the story of the calling of Matthew.

Matthew was a tax collector and no one liked tax collectors. The Jews considered them traitors and the Romans saw them as cheats. One day Matthew left his house to go to his office. As he went down the street, not even the children would greet him. They ran away as they saw him coming. He arrived in his office and settled down to arrange his papers and count his money.

3) Read Mark 2:13–17 sentence by sentence, leaving a long pause after each one so that the participants can imagine themselves in the scene.

4) When you have finished reading the passage, allow a few minutes of silence.

5) Ask anyone who wishes to share what they experienced with the group to do so.

1) In groups of four to six, meditate on John 15:1–8 using the following steps:

- One person prays to ask God to speak through his word to everyone.
- Members of the group take turns reading the passage until it has been read through at least twice.
- Everyone remains quiet, thinks about the passage, and listens to God.
- After ten to fifteen minutes, people in the group share what God has said to them.
- The group prays together about what has been shared.

2) Report back to the large group. Ask each group to share one thing they have learned.

Assignments

1. How is meditation different from a Bible study?

2. Write down three Old Testament passages that you would like to use for meditation.

3. Meditate on a passage. If God speaks to you during this time, write down what he has said. This may be something you want to share with others, but not necessarily.

4. Write your reflections on how meditation has helped you and how you find it challenging.

*Readings**

Demarest, Bruce. 1999. *Satisfy Your Soul: Restoring the Heart of Christian Spirituality*. Colorado Springs, CO: NavPress.

Nouwen, Henri. 1993. *The Return of the Prodigal Son: a Story of Homecoming*. NY: Image.

Silf, Margaret. 1999. *Inner Compass: an Invitation to Ignatian Spirituality*. Chicago, IL: Jesuit Way.

---

* http://www.scripture-engagement.org

Sharing Faith

Chapter 16

BIBLE STORYING

Introduction

People don't have to learn to read before they can understand the Bible and grow in their faith. In this chapter, we discuss an oral method of engaging with Scripture, Bible storying. This involves telling a series of key Bible stories starting with creation and going through to the resurrection. This method is particularly helpful in reaching unevangelized people, but it also helps Christians have a clearer understanding of God's plan of salvation and grow in their faith.[*]

The Katakari want to know more!

Ngiri Baya was an evangelist sent by his denomination to work amongst the Katakari people. Traditionally, they followed another world religion and had been very resistant to Christianity, but since the Katakari Bible became available, a small number of people had become Christians. Ngiri found one small Protestant church and one small Catholic Church in a region of about 500,000 people. As soon as he could, Ngiri settled down to learn the language.

Ngiri got to know the two groups of Christians. They told him how they had tried to persuade Katakari people to join literacy classes

---

[*] This chapter is a brief introduction to storying. If you feel it would be an important means for engaging with Scripture in your area, you may want to hold an entire workshop or series of workshops on this subject.

with very little success. They also told him how previous attempts at evangelism had been unsuccessful. Ngiri was very discouraged and wondered how in the world to start his work. Just then he received an invitation to attend a seminar on Bible Storying, which he happily accepted, though he had little idea what he was going to learn.

At the seminar, the leaders started by explaining that Bible storying was an oral approach that involved telling Bible stories in chronological order to a group of people over a period of time. Ngiri learned how to prepare a set of stories. Then he practised telling the stories he had read in the Bible, trying to be as accurate as possible. He learned how to ask the group questions about stories that helped them discover lessons from them. He had lots of fun preparing dramas and songs based on these stories. When he played Noah in a drama, he built his boat with great enthusiasm!

At the end of the seminar, Ngiri had learned to tell four stories really well. He was ready to prepare a set of stories that he thought would help the Katakari understand the overall plan of the Bible from the creation of the world to the beginnings of the early church. The Katakari traditionally bred animals, so he included stories from the Bible about sheep and goats. Since he had the Bible in Katakari, he was confident he could prepare the rest of the stories with the help of a Katakari speaker.

When Ngiri returned home, both the Protestant and the Catholic Churches asked him to tell them what he had learned. He decided that the best way to do this was to tell a story and then help them to learn it. He also had the group discuss what they liked about the story and what they found hard to understand. The Christians were very enthusiastic about Bible storying, and soon Ngiri had a small group of people who wanted to go with him to tell stories in a village that didn't have a church.

They set off the following week and after getting permission from the chief of the village, they gathered together a group of men, women, children and even all the village dogs! Ngiri told the story of how God created man and woman, and then he asked some questions to help his audience understand what they had heard. Then his group sang a song they had composed about how God created Adam and Eve using traditional Katakari music. By the end, the audience was joining in the chorus and a couple of the women were dancing! The villagers told Ngiri and others to come back soon and tell the next story.

Ngiri and the members of his group settled into a pattern. Each Monday, Ngiri spent most of the day preparing the next two stories. He read them a number of times from the Bible and then, because his mother tongue was not Katakari, he worked with a mother-tongue Katakari speaker to develop the best way of telling the stories. On Tuesday, he went over the stories again with his group. Then they prepared either a drama or a song for each story. On Wednesday afternoon and Saturday morning they went out to the village to tell the stories. After the first few weeks, Ngiri had other members of his team tell the stories. He always asked the audience to repeat the stories they had already heard, and he asked them questions to bring out the important parts of the story.

After about six weeks, Ngiri's group had told twelve stories and were approaching the stories about Jesus that showed God was planning to send a Messiah. The week they planned to tell about the death and resurrection of Jesus, all the Christians met to pray that the Katakari would accept Jesus as the sacrifice for their sins. As they came to the end of the account of how Jesus rose from the dead, many of the village people did just that.

1) How is Bible storying different from preaching?

2) Why do you think this approach would be successful amongst unreached people groups?

1. Preparing an individual story to tell

It takes time to prepare a story. It is much easier to prepare if the passage is already translated into the language you are using. If you do, here are some steps to follow.

A. Learn the structure of the story

1. Read the story through at least twice. Use different versions or languages, if possible.

2. Divide the story into sections. For example, in the case of the fall in Genesis 3.

- Section 1: The snake talks to Eve, Eve and Adam take the fruit and eat it. They realize they are naked and make clothes from leaves.

- Section 2: God comes to them and they hide. God talks with Adam and Eve.

- Section 3: God states the punishment that will come to the snake, Eve, and Adam.

- Section 4: God makes clothes for them from skins and sends them out of the garden.

It can be helpful to draw small stick pictures to remind you of the order of the events in the story.

B. Imagine the story while reading it aloud

Part of preparation involves finding ways to bring the story alive so the audience can experience what happens. Imagine you are in the story. Is the story taking place in a house or by a lake? Use all your senses. Smell the smells of the scene. See the sights in your mind. Hear the sounds. Taste the flavours, and so forth. You may find that acting out the story is helpful, as it gets your body involved as well as your mind. It may help you realize things in the story you never noticed before.

Read the story aloud again with expression, or listen to a recording of it as you imagine you are in the scene. This will help you remember the details.

C. Identify any background information your audience will need

Look in study Bibles or other helps to be sure you understand the background information that would have come to mind for the original audience. Then think of your audience and the background information that might come to mind for them. They may be missing some of the intended background information or use some from their culture that leads them to misunderstand the author's meaning. For example, in the story of the Passover, unleavened bread may need to be explained, or the sacrificial system, or the relationship between the Egyptians and the Israelites. In the story about the four men taking their paralytic friend to Jesus, people may need to be told that Jewish houses had flat roofs with tiles that could be removed. Some of this information can be given before starting the story, some may be woven into the story, and other things may be addressed in the discussion afterwards. Illustrations can be helpful to show things people have never seen before. (See Chapter 10.)

D. Practise telling the story

Now it's time to practice telling the story so you are comfortable with it. Close your Bible, put any notes you may have made away, and try telling the story in your own words. Leave out any details that distract from the main teaching of the story. For example, in the story of blind Bartimaeus, you don't need to say he is the son of Timaeus, unless genealogies are important in your culture. In the story of Noah, the exact size of the boat is not important, but it is important that people understand that it was large. Be sure you don't leave out any details that are needed to bring out the main teaching of the story. Don't add extra details simply to embellish a story, like exactly how drunk the prodigal son became. Let the story speak for itself.

Every language has different ways of telling different kinds of stories, some for true stories, some for folk stories, some for telling people what to do, and so forth. For example, if you hear a story in English that begins with 'Once upon a time' and ends with 'and they lived happily ever after' you know that it is a fairy story and not true. Find the correct way of telling each story from the Bible. It will probably not be the same for the story of Noah and for a parable.

Keep telling the story to your family and friends until you are confident you can tell it well. Watch their reactions to see if they are able to understand and find it interesting. Then record it in some way, for example, on a computer, an MP3 player, or a cassette player.

Finally, play the recording of your story for a consultant to have it checked for accuracy and style. If the consultant doesn't speak the language, translate the story back into a language your consultant speaks. If the consultant suggests making changes in the story, record the new version of the story. Always keep a good recorded version of each story to refer back to and to share with others.

In small language groups, prepare to tell a story using the process just described. Each person should try telling the story. If you have Genesis in your language, tell the story of the fall from Genesis 3. If Genesis is not yet available, then prepare to tell another story, for example, the calming of the storm in Mark 4:35–41.

2. Preparing to discuss the story with the audience

After the story has been told, the next step is to ask the audience questions to help them understand the important points. One good way to begin is to ask the audience to re-tell the story. You could go around the circle and ask each person to add a couple of sentences to the story. Another way to begin the discussion is to ask the group to act out the story.

Then ask more reflective questions. Use questions that help you achieve your purpose in telling the story. For example, if the story is part of the evangelistic track, then the overall aim is that people realize that sin separates us from God and that they accept Christ's death as the sacrifice for their sin. Some questions that help the audience think about these issues are

* What does this story tell us about God?
* What does this story tell us about human beings?
* What does this story teach us about sin?

More general questions might be

* What did you like about this story?
* What did you find difficult or troubling about this story?

The discussion period is not a time to preach or teach, but rather to lead the group to reflect on the story themselves. This is more difficult than it may seem and you may need practice, especially if you are used to preaching or lecturing.

Allow the group to answer freely without correction. However, only observations from the story are valid, so ask those who give answers to say which part of the story supports their answer. If the group doesn't understand everything at first, don't worry. As they hear more stories, they will gradually understand more.

Use culturally appropriate means of conducting the discussion. In some cultures, questions may mainly be used to insult, scold, and mock a person, and commands may be more appropriate in the discussion time. For example, rather than asking a question, it may be more appropriate to say, 'Tell me what Adam and Eve were not allowed to do in the garden.'

For each story, think of local beliefs that might come to people's mind. Some parts of the story may be similar to local beliefs and reaffirm them. For example, a story might reinforce the idea that sacrifices are necessary. Other parts of the story may challenge local beliefs. For example, the story of Jesus healing the Gadarene demoniac may challenge the local belief that a mad man can never be cured by anyone.

Some local beliefs may cause people to misunderstand the story. For example, in the story of the storm on the lake, local beliefs may cause people to think that the disciples had sinned in some way and so were responsible for the storm. Some stories may seem to reaffirm local beliefs at first, but then challenge them. For example, a group whose highest divinity is the serpent found the story of the fall similar to stories in their culture at first, but then had their belief challenged when the serpent was punished by God. Bring out local beliefs that affect how people might understand the story in the discussion.

● ● ● ● ● ●   *Let people discover what the stories teach!*

Practise discussing the story of the fall in small groups. Have one person lead for five minutes, and then switch roles. If the leaders begin to preach or teach, the rest of the group should correct them.

3. Choosing the story set

Storytellers select a set of stories that are appropriate for their situation. They consider four main things when choosing their story set: the cultural background and needs of the audience, the main message of the Bible, the chronological link between stories, and the aim of the storytelling.

A. The cultural background and needs of the audience

No two people groups are identical. Each group has natural bridges that serve as points of contact between their world view and the Bible. Each group also has barriers that may prevent them coming to Christ. For example, for many non-Christians in North America or England, you might find the following bridges and barriers:

Bridges

- People are open to new ideas.
- The Judeo-Christian heritage still has influence on the culture.
- Because of the lack of community, many people are lonely and unsatisfied.

Barriers

- People are mainly interested in material prosperity.
- There is very little sense of a spiritual world.
- Many people are independent and feel they are self-sufficient.

1) Draw up lists of bridges and barriers for your ethnic group.

2) Share the results with the whole group. See if any of the groups share any bridges and barriers.

Take one bridge and one barrier that have been chosen by most of the groups. Find a Bible story that addresses them. For example, the story of the tower of Babel would address the issue of people thinking they are in control of their destiny.

B. The main message of the Bible

Every story set must have the five essential stories listed below. All the other stories chosen should be fit in around these five in a chronological fashion. The five essentials are:

- the creation of man and woman
- the fall
- the birth of Jesus
- the crucifixion of Jesus
- the resurrection of Jesus

After deciding on a series of stories, check to see that it covers the main beliefs of the Christian faith. One way to do this is to compare your story set with the Apostles' Creed (below), since it expresses these beliefs.

I believe in God, the Father almighty, creator of heaven and earth.

I believe in Jesus Christ, God's only Son, our Lord, who was conceived by the Holy Spirit, born of the Virgin Mary, suffered under Pontius Pilate, was crucified, died, and was buried; he descended into hell.

On the third day he rose again; he ascended into heaven, he is seated at the right hand of the Father, and he will come again to judge the living and the dead.

I believe in the Holy Spirit, the holy catholic church, the communion of saints, the forgiveness of sins, the resurrection of the body, and the life everlasting.

C. The chronological link between stories

Stories should flow from one to the next. Where there is an obvious gap in time between stories or a change of focus, a transition is needed. For example, if the story after the fall is the story of Elijah on Mount Carmel, the story teller needs to say something like this at the beginning of the Elijah story:

Adam and Eve had children and they in turn had children until there were many people in the world. Some of these people obeyed God, some were disobedient. God sent prophets (those who spoke his word) to warn people about the wrong things they were doing. One of those prophets was named Elijah, and one day. . . .

D. The aim of the storytelling

The aim of the storytelling may be evangelistic, or it may be to disciple new Christians, or to help new church leaders grow. An evangelistic story set helps people understand what went wrong in the Garden of Eden and the need for sacrifice, so they understand their need for Christ's sacrifice. A discipleship story set shows how God has worked with his people over time. A topical story set addresses a relevant issue. For example, a set of stories might be developed to help new Christians who are facing persecution from their community.

Here are a few examples of story sets of twelve to fifteen stories that can be used to explore which stories and themes work well in your community. These are only examples, and each language group will need to make up their own set. More stories can be added until you have a more complete panorama of the Bible. The new stories should be inserted in their place in chronological order.

Sacrifice Theme:	Jesus as Victor over Satan Theme:
Creation	Creation of people (Genesis 2)
Fall	Fall (Genesis 3)
Cain and Abel	Elijah and the prophets of Baal (or Balaam) (I Kings 18:16–46)
Abraham and the sacrifice of Isaac	Zechariah (Zechariah 1:1, 2:10–11, 3:1–9, 11:4–13)
Passover	Birth of Jesus (Matthew 1:18–25)
Day of Atonement (Leviticus 16)	Parable of wheat and tares (Matthew 13:24–30)
Suffering Servant (Isaiah 52–53)	Healing of demon-possessed boy (Mark 9; or some other relevant story of Jesus casting out of a demon)
Birth of Jesus	Parable of the strong man (Luke 11:14–22,37–40,53–54)
Baptism of Jesus (Behold the Lamb of God)	Jesus' betrayal (Luke 19:47–48; John 12:27–31; Luke 22:2–6; Matthew 26:15; Luke 22:39, 47, 52–54, 71; Matthew 27:1–7)
Two or three stories of ministry of Jesus, his teaching, and conflict with religious leaders	Jesus' crucifixion (Luke 23:1–3,13–24; Matthew 27:27–31; Luke 23:32–53)
Jesus' crucifixion	Jesus' resurrection and ascension (Luke 24:1–12, 36–49; Acts 1:8–11; Mark 16:19; Ephesians 1:20–21; Colossians 1:13; Hebrews 2:14–15)
Jesus' resurrection	Simon the sorcerer (Acts 8:4–25 or some other relevant story of spirit world interaction in Acts, for example the Jewish sorcerer Acts 13:4–12; the slave-girl fortune-teller Acts 16; Sons of Sceva Acts 19:8–20)

Paul in Corinth and Ephesus
(including 1 Corinthians 5:7)

A better sacrifice (Hebrews
9:6–14)

Design a set of twelve to fifteen stories for your ethnic group.
Start with the five essential ones, and build around them. State
why you have added each one.

4. Conducting the storying session

Here is the usual way to have a storying session:

1. Review the previous story you told the group by asking questions
   about it or by asking a couple of people to tell the story.

2. Tell the new story. If suitable pictures or videos are available, use
   them. (See Chapter 24.)

3. Ask the audience to tell the story back to you and discuss it.

4. Prepare a song or drama based on the story and perform it for the
   group. (See Chapters 22 and 23.)

Reread the story at the beginning of this chapter, noting how
Ngiri moved through this process.

5. If the Scripture passages have not
been translated

Providing Scripture in oral form to people who prefer oral communication
puts the Bible within their reach. But it is equally important to give the
Scripture to them in the language that they know best. If there is no
mother-tongue translation of the Scripture passages, try to arrange for a
trained translation team to translate them, or ask people with expertise in

storying in languages without a translation of Scripture to help you craft the stories.

If there is only a New Testament in the language, it will contain many terms needed for Old Testament stories, for example, terms for sin, spirit, angel, and so forth. Find and use them in your stories.

Translating stories is easier than translating Scripture passages because storytellers can leave out details that don't contribute to the main point. Often the most difficult challenges of translation are in these details. For example, finding a way to express 'gopher wood' in a local language may be quite difficult, but in a story, you can simply say 'wood'. Another factor that makes translating stories easier than translating Scripture is that it often begins with the Old Testament which has less abstract terms than the New. Regardless of the number of difficult terms, however, each one needs to be worked through carefully so that the correct meaning is expressed in a way that people can understand it.

Make a list of all the terms in the story of the fall in Genesis 3:1–9 that would be difficult to express in your language. Put brackets around terms that will not be necessary to include in the story, like 'fig' leaves.

6. Stories in other media

Stories can be told live, but they can also be recorded or delivered in written form. This is especially useful in situations where people are not free to come to a story group due to social pressure or illness, but are very interested in hearing recordings of the stories. If stories are recorded with actors taking different parts, it makes them livelier than having one person do all the parts. Groups can listen to the stories and then discuss them. Bible stories can also be distributed in printed form. These are especially useful in family devotions, Sunday schools, and as reading material in literacy programmes. Some church leaders may use a series of Bible stories as a series of sermons over a two- or three-month period.

Assignments

1. Can you think of ways that you could use storying in your church?

2. Why is it that all denominations and churches can use Bible storying?

3. If you have internet access, go to
http://www.chronologicalbiblestorying.com make notes on one article you choose from that site.

4. In addition to telling stories orally in small groups, what other ways of delivering the stories would be appropriate in your context?

Readings[*]

Brown, Rick. 2004. 'How to Make Oral Communication More Effective.' *International Journal of Frontier Missions* 21:4:173–178 (also at **http://www. ijfm.org**).

Bull, Celia. 2003. 'Chronological Storying—A Case History.' *Scripture in Use Today* 6:2–7.

Jarrett, Kevin. 1989. 'Gaining a Hearing for the Gospel: Oral Communication in an Oral Society.' *Notes on Literature in Use and Language Programs* 21:3–9.

Useful websites

http://www.onestory.org Read about OneStory, a multi-agency partnership that trains people for crafting stories across languages and cultures.

http://www.faithcomesbyhearing.com Hosanna, Faith Comes by Hearing records Scripture and organizes listening groups in language groups of all sizes around the world.

http://globalrecordings.net Gospel Recordings Network, also known as Global Recordings Network, has free downloads of Bible stories and basic Bible teaching in many languages.

http://www.oralstrategies.com Keep abreast of the latest developments in oral strategies in ministry at this site.

---

[*] http://www.scripture-engagement.org

Chapter 17

PREPARING FOR GOOD NEWS ENCOUNTERS

Introduction

One of the reasons we read the Bible is so that we can apply biblical principles to problems in our lives. Bible studies are one way to do this, but we can also apply biblical principles in casual conversations or when people come to us for counsel. We need to know the Bible well enough to be ready to use it appropriately when situations like this arise.

Mr Mba comes for help

People came to Pastor Simon's house to ask for help with all sorts of problems all the time. One day Pastor Simon was helping his wife Sarah with some planting at the back of their house when a couple from the church arrived, Mr Mba and his wife Grace. Pastor Simon saw straight away that Mr Mba was very angry and that Grace was very frightened. After the initial greetings, they sat down and Mr Mba told them that he wanted to divorce his wife. He explained all the things his wife had done wrong at great length and very loudly. He also said that she was disobeying the Bible, which said that she should do everything he asked her to do. Grace sat there with her head bowed and didn't say a word.

After a long time Mr Mba finally stopped talking and gave Pastor Simon a chance to speak. First, Pastor Simon asked Grace if she would like to say anything but she shook her head, still looking down at the ground. Then Pastor Simon started to counsel them. They were speaking Palapala, of course. As they talked, Pastor Simon asked his wife to bring his English Bible out from the house. He found the passage where Jesus speaks about divorce in Mark 10. He read it aloud in English (which Mr Mba didn't speak) and then translated it into Palapala, but it seemed like Mr Mba wasn't listening to him at all.

After a while, Sarah took Grace into the house so that she could talk with her alone. After a couple of hours, the Mbas left but nothing was resolved.

Pastor Simon and Sarah sat down together and talked about what had happened. Pastor Simon said, 'I should have been able to tell Mr Mba what the Bible says in Palapala, then he might have listened. Also, I know there are other passages that could help him, like 'husbands, love your wives', but on the spur of the moment, I couldn't think where they were in the Bible'. Sarah replied, 'Yes, I wanted to comfort Grace with some verses from the Psalms that have helped me many times, but it was hard to explain them in Palapala. We need to be ready for situations like this'.

1) In small groups, list some of the types of problems that a pastor has to deal with frequently. Here are two examples:
- two Christians in your church who will not talk to one another
- a Christian who is afraid because he thinks someone has cursed him

2) Report back to the large group. Make one composite list of all the problems suggested.

3) Ask the participants to vote for the four problems they see as the most common for their communities and for individuals.

4) List the four most common problems in order with the most common one first.

1. Understand people's situations

When someone is sharing a problem it's very important to listen to them attentively until you understand their situation and feel their pain. Reciting Scripture verses to someone before you understand their situation may seem simplistic and lacking in love. If their pain is severe, it may take a long time before they feel they have been heard and are ready to hear you share God's word.

When a person is ready, a Scripture passage can help them hear God speaking to them about their situation. This can be thought of as a good news 'encounter', when they encounter how the good news applies to their daily life. There is often no time to prepare for these opportunities, so we need to prepare ourselves by becoming aware of common problems and Scriptures that speak to them.

1) Have you ever felt annoyed when someone quoted Scripture at you? Why?

2) In what situations may it be unhelpful to quote Scripture?

• • • • • •   *Christians need to be prepared for good news encounters.*

2. Be prepared

It's important to know Scriptures that will address the most common problems in your area. Having a list of passages for situations, such as the one below, can be very helpful.

When you are afraid:	Matthew 10:26–31; Luke 12:22–31; John 14:1–3; Hebrews 13:5–7; 1 Peter 5:7
When you are ill:	Matthew 8:14–16; Luke 5:12–15; Luke 7:1–10; James 5:13–16

| When you are sad: | 2 Corinthians 6:3–10; 2 Corinthians 8:9; James 1:2–4,12; 1 Peter 1:3–7; 1 Peter 4:12–16 |
| When a Christian dies: | John 11:25–26; John 14:1–3; 1 Corinthians 15:20–26, 42–57; 2 Corinthians 5:1–8 |

Select verses that will help people know where to go in the Bible to find the help they need. For example, youth may need a special set of verses to encourage them to live godly lives. Where materialism is a problem, verses about true riches may be in order. Where people fear spiritual attack, a set of verses about Christ's power and protection may be helpful. When studying the verses that you think address problems, be sure to read them in their context so that you use them in the way the biblical author intended.

Prepare a sheet or booklet with relevant topics and Scripture passages. This can be included at the back of a New Testament or Bible at the time of publication.

1. Have each group read the first problem listed below and find a Scripture passage that addresses it.

a. Two Christians in your church will not talk to one another.

b. A Christian is afraid because he thinks someone has cursed him.

c. Someone thinks that every time he goes to an evangelistic meeting he must become a Christian all over again.

d. A Christian needs a certain document urgently. The official will only sign it in return for a bribe.

e. Someone says she is going to heaven because she is baptized.

f. A Christian is planning to take one of the church deacons to court over a field boundary dispute.

g. A Christian couple that cannot live together in peace and want to get a divorce.

h. A young Christian thinks that it is impossible to stay pure before marriage.

2) When a group finds a verse that would help counsel someone with that problem, let them show it to the leader. If the leader agrees it is an appropriate verse, then they can go on to the next problem.

3) Congratulate the first group that finishes the whole list.

3. Memorize key verses

What are some reasons for memorizing key Scripture passages?

Make a list of reasons on the board. Add any of the following reasons not mentioned by the group.

Memorizing Scripture helps you:

- to be able to help people with relevant Scripture when they have problems.

- to be able to answer non-Christian's questions during an ordinary conversation with them.

- to meditate on God's word when you are doing something else, like working in your fields or travelling on a bus, or when you are too ill to read the Bible.

- to meditate on God's word when you don't have a Bible, for example, in prison or if you are fleeing a war zone.

- to allow God's word to soak into your mind, so that it influences everything you think and do.

- to help people who cannot read know God's word.

- to fight against Satan and keep you from sinning (Matthew 4:1–11; Psalm 119:11).

- God tells us to do so (Joshua 1:8).

Memorizing Scripture is important for all Christians. Children are especially good at it. If they do this when they are young, it can guide them through their adolescent years and into adulthood. At Scripture engagement seminars, participants can memorize two or three verses, and then be given more verses to learn on their own by the end of the seminar. During a three-day seminar, some participants have memorized up to ten verses. They can share these Scripture verses with people when they return home.

To begin, find short, easy, relevant memory verses. Make any adjustments necessary for the verse to stand on its own. For example, 'I am the bread of life' should be changed to 'Jesus said, "I am the bread of life."' If the verse is very long, you may wish to choose part of it and mark it as 'a' or 'b', for example, John 6:35a. A number of organizations have prepared standard sets of basic memory verses which are available in places such as Christian bookshops, the local branch of Navigators, or on the internet.

Two factors are important when memorizing Scripture in a local language:

- The verses must already be translated into the language and checked by a consultant.

- The verse(s) must be memorisable in the language. A verse that is nine words long in English might become 20 words long in the local language. If the first verse that people try to memorize in their language is too complicated, they may think the Bible memorization is too hard for them.

> **What has helped you memorize Scripture?**
> (If the following points are not mentioned, add them.)

There are many ways in which to memorize Scripture.

- Turn verses into a song and sing it.
- Learn verses together with other people.
- Review verses frequently after learning them.
- Learn verses that are relevant to life.
- Repeat the verse aloud and then write it down.
- Write the verses to be learned on cards and place them around the house or church.
- Learn a whole chapter section by section, adding each new verse onto the learned section.
- Hold competitions.
- Learn a series of verses for evangelism.
- Memorize verses for a drama.

One of the easiest ways of memorizing Scripture is to make it into a song. (See Chapter 22.) Theme verses from Bible studies or sermons may also be easy to memorize and will reinforce the teaching people have received. If people enjoy competition, prizes for the people who can repeat the most verses accurately can motivate some people to memorize lots of verses.

In your church denomination, do people have the habit of memorizing Scripture?

1) If so, how do they do it?

2) If not, how could you encourage them to begin?

Assignments

1. Think of one problem you have experienced in the last year or a problem that someone has brought to you for counsel. List four passages that would help.

2. Choose ten verses that would help a new Christian to learn how to grow in their faith in Christ.

3. Choose five verses that are easy to memorize in your mother tongue and are relevant to a local problem.

4. Divide into groups of three. Have one person in the group share a problem that he or she is experiencing. The second person listens attentively, trying to understand the problem. At this stage, he or she should not give any advice, but only try to understand. The third person observes how well the second person listened and understood the problem. After five minutes, take a few minutes for each person to discuss how he or she felt.

   a. Did the person sharing feel understood or misunderstood?

   b. Did the person listening find it difficult to not give advice or preach?

   c. What did the observer notice?

   Now change roles.

   After five minutes, change roles again.

   In the large group, discuss your observations.

Readings*

Barnwell, Katharine, and Richard C. Blight. 1996. 'How to Prepare a Glossary and a Topical Index: Preliminary version.' *Translator's Workplace CD-ROM*. Dallas, TX: SIL.

Brown, Rick. 2004. 'Choosing Relevant Scriptures.' *Scripture in Use Today* 8:7–9.

Dye, Wayne. 1985. *The Bible Translation Strategy: An Analysis of its Spiritual Impact*. Dallas, TX: Wycliffe Bible Translators, pp 39–61.

---

* http://www.scripture-engagement.org

Chapter 18

ENGAGING PEOPLE WITH SCRIPTURE IN EVANGELISM

Introduction

When we share Scripture with Christians, our aim is to help them grow in their faith. When we share Scripture with non-Christians, our aim is to lead them to accept Jesus as their saviour. As the evangelist John said at the end of his gospel, 'I have written these things so that you may believe that Jesus is the Messiah, the Son of God, and that by believing in him you will have life' (20:31). Evangelism involves communicating the message of the Bible to those we want to reach for Christ, and this is best done in the heart language of the hearer. This chapter focuses on developing skills in leading non-believers to Christ.

Catching fish

In the area around Pastor Simon's village, there were five other small villages which had very few Christians. For some time, Pastor Simon had been thinking and praying about the people in those villages who didn't come to church and wondering how to lead them to faith in Christ.

Like many places, there had been an evangelistic campaign a couple of years earlier, but it had only reached a certain part of the population. Some people were completely uninterested in the meetings. Others had come forward to receive Christ and the evangelist went home feeling satisfied, but not much changed in their lives.

Pastor Simon was thinking about Ngiri Baya's success using Bible stories among the Katakari, when another evangelist from his denomination came from the capital to visit the area. Pastor Simon thought the evangelist would want to run an evangelistic campaign like he had done before, so it was surprising when he asked, 'When you go hunting or fishing, you know what animal or fish you are trying to catch. We first need to know more about the non-Christians in this area. Who are they? What do they believe? What is important to them?'

The evangelist and Pastor Simon prepared some questions, and then visited people in the five villages to see how people would answer them. Some of their questions were:

• What do you know about Jesus?
• When we pass from this life as we all will some day, where do you think we will go?
• What do you worry about?
• Are you afraid of anything?

After they had listened to people in many different compounds, they sat down to put all the results together. They found there were basically two different beliefs about God. There were the people who believed in the divinities and a God who was far away. These people did not consider themselves Christian. They consulted the traditional healer every time anything went wrong. They felt the church had nothing to do with them except occasionally they might go there for a funeral or a wedding service.

The second group of people considered themselves to be Christians. They went to church, especially at times of festivals like Christmas, and might have gone forward once at an evangelistic campaign to receive Christ into their lives. But their Christianity was very much on the surface and didn't change much in their lifestyle or worldview. If there was real trouble in the family or serious illness, they went quietly to the traditional healer to find out who had cursed them.

Pastor Simon and the evangelist didn't find any followers of other major world religions in the area.

The people in both of these groups had similar fears and worries. These included fear of poverty, AIDS, and spiritual attack, worry about family members, and concern about what happened after they died. Pastor Simon and the evangelist prayed together for a long time and then began to discuss the best way to reach these people. Since most people were affected by HIV-AIDS in some way, they decided to start by addressing that. They prepared a booklet in Palapala that explained the disease from both a Christian and a medical point of view. It also taught people how to share the good news of salvation in Jesus Christ with those who have HIV-AIDS. They went to the chiefs of the villages and offered to hold seminars using the booklet. Four of the five chiefs accepted their offer with great interest, and dates were set.

1) What are some advantages to finding out what people think and need before beginning to evangelize them?

2) In your own home area, would you find the same two groups of people Pastor Simon found in these villages? Would you also find other categories of people?

1. Using the mother tongue in evangelism

In 1932, a man named Cameron Townsend was evangelizing in Guatemala, a country in Central America. As part of his ministry, he sold Bibles in Spanish to the people. One day an Indian from the hills asked him for a Bible in his local language. Cameron didn't have one. The man asked, 'If your God is so great, why doesn't he speak my language?' Cameron took up the challenge of translating the New Testament into this man's language, and went on to found Wycliffe Bible Translators and SIL. The aim of these organizations is to make God's word available to all people in a language they understand well so that they can know Christ and grow in their faith in him.

Why do you think people may be more open to Christ when they hear about him in their mother tongue?

2. Explaining how to know Christ as saviour

As we engage in good news encounters, we need to recognize that people's most basic need is to know Christ as their saviour, regardless of their immediate problem. We can't assume that if someone goes to church, even for many years, that they have this new life in Christ. Even church leaders can know all about Christ without ever knowing him personally. If we have any doubt about whether people know Christ, we can look for appropriate ways to offer them opportunity to take this step.

We need to be able to explain the way of salvation in a way that is relevant to them in their cultural context. Explanations of salvation developed in the West often focus on whether people go to heaven or hell when they die. This may not be the most pressing concern for people of other cultures. For example, missionary John Beekman found that the Chol Indians of Mexico were much more concerned about this present life and protecting themselves from the attack of malicious spirit beings. He presented the gospel by stressing Christ's power over evil spirits and nature here and now. This was good news for the Chol, and they responded in great numbers.

1) The Yanamamo of Venezuela believe that God exists and that he is powerful and good, but they believe that he does not like them. They believe they are under the power of spirits which provoke them to attack and kill one another, making life very difficult. How would you share Christ with a Yanamamo?

2) Below is the way one group in Democratic Republic of Congo (DRC) from a traditional religion began their explanation of God's plan of salvation. What things have they brought out that might be important for their audience?

In the beginning of the world, God made people to be like him. He put them in the Garden of Eden that had all good things in it. God loved the man and woman he had made very much. God came to the people, he talked with them, and he walked with them in the garden. So you can see how much God loved them (Genesis 1–3). But although God showed his love to these people, they disobeyed his words and did wrong. Even though they turned away from God, God didn't turn away from them. God made a way so that people could return to him.

1) The following verses are often considered basic for leading someone to give their life to Christ. Decide if they would be the most appropriate verses to share with people from your culture. If not, suggest other verses and explain the main point you want to communicate by each one. At the end of your discussion you should have a list with no more than ten of the most important Scripture verses for people from your culture that bring out four or five main points. The list should be short enough for people to memorize.

- God loves us. John 3:16.
- People are separated from God by sin. Romans 3:23.
- Jesus is the only bridge that people can pass over to get to God. Romans 5:8; 1 Corinthians 15:3–5; John 14:6.
- Trust that Jesus can save you. John 1:12; Revelation 3:20.

2) People who don't know Christ may not feel comfortable praying to receive him as their saviour. You can encourage them to talk to God just like they talk to other people, but it is often helpful to have a prayer of confession ready that people can say. Here's an example of one from the Democratic Republic of the Congo (DRC):

Lord Jesus, I thank you because you died on the cross because I am a sinner. I trust you, and I ask you to come into my life and be the chief over all I do. Thank you because you forgive all my sins, and you give me life that never ends. Please direct my life and help me that all I do should please you.

Now compose a prayer in your language that would be meaningful for a person from your culture to say if they were ready to accept Christ into their lives.

3. Connecting felt needs to salvation

Once we know how to explain the way of salvation, we need to be able to connect it with people's felt needs. The same basic information about salvation can be presented in different ways for different situations.

You have the chance to explain the gospel to the following people from your culture. After listening to them, which Scripture passages would you use?

- A man has never been to church and thinks God is far away and uninterested in people.
- A woman goes to church occasionally and thinks she will go to heaven because she does more good things than bad.
- A woman wishes to become a Christian after an evangelistic meeting.
- A follower of traditional religion is in great fear of the spirits.
- A man has just come out of prison after committing a crime and feels very ashamed.

Assignments

1. Think of an average village pastor, catechist, or a church member of your denomination. What sort of non-Christians does he meet day by day? Mainly Muslims? Pagans? Nominal Christians? If you are not sure, ask a selection of church leaders in the area.

2. What kind of training would be most appropriate in your church to teach people how to lead non-Christians to Christ?

Readings*

Beekman, John. 1974. 'A Culturally Relevant Witness.' In W. A. Smalley, ed. *Readings in Missionary Anthropology.* Pasadena, CA: William Carey, pp 132–135.

Brown, Rick. 2002. 'Working Together To Advance the Kingdom of God: An Integrated Strategy for the Total Team.' *Scripture in Use Today* 5:3–9.

* http://www.scripture-engagement.org

Chapter 19

HOW MUSLIMS USE THE BIBLE

Introduction

To translate the Bible into action in Muslim communities, Christians need to understand how Muslims think and especially how they view the Bible. This can help Christians to interact with Muslims in a respectful and relevant way. This chapter explores these issues.

Yusufu's story—Part 1

In the far northeast of Sanatu, there was an area where many people were followers of Islam. One young man there, Yusuf, is twenty years old. After the third year of secondary school, he left school and now works as a guard at a bank. All of Yusuf's friends and family belong to a Muslim community which considers Christianity to be a corrupt religion. Yusuf had read a little about Christianity at school, but the only thing he remembered was the descriptions of the Crusades, when Christians killed many people in the Middle East.

Yusuf works with a small group of men who know each other well. One day Yusuf heard that his mother was very ill in their home village and he wanted to go home and see her. He worried about it all day, but only one of the other guards listened to his worries.

His name was Ali, and he was a follower of Jesus. Ali even lent him a little money to help him pay for the transport to his village. Yusuf went home and soon after he arrived, his mother died. All the family mourned together.

When Yusuf returned to work, he began to spend time with Ali. Whenever he told Ali about some problem, Ali responded with a relevant story from the Bible that he had learned from audio recordings of Scripture.

Yusuf found Ali to be a kind man who truly loved God and this attracted him to hear more. But he was concerned that the Bible might be corrupted and teach the worship of multiple gods. So one day Ali brought a Bible to work with him and opened it at Mark 12:28–30. There Jesus said that the greatest commandment was to remember that 'the Lord our God, the Lord is one', and that 'you should love the Lord your God with all your heart, all your soul, all your mind, and all your strength'. Yusuf was relieved that the Bible clearly taught the worship of one God. He asked Ali if he could borrow some of his Scripture recordings to listen to at home.

As Yusuf listened to the Old Testament passages about various prophets, he realized that all people are sinful, even the prophets. He also realized that God is reliable and so good and holy that he cannot put up with sin at all. He also saw that God loves people and provided sacrifices to cleanse them from their sins.

Ali showed Yusuf a passage in the Qur'an, 3:45–55, that describes how unique and important Jesus is. Yusuf was surprised and wanted to learn more about Jesus. So Ali lent him a recording of the Gospel of Matthew. Yusuf began listening to it at home, and whenever they had time at work, they discussed what he had heard.

Yusuf was deeply impressed by what Jesus taught in the Sermon on the Mount and realized that it must have come from God. He wished the people in his community would follow this teaching and behave like that. It seemed that they simply weren't able to no matter how much they tried.

Yusuf was shocked when he listened to Matthew 11:20–26 where Jesus said that the people who saw his miracles and didn't repent and believe in him would be condemned on the day of judgment. This frightened Yusuf. He had always said that he believed in the

Prophet Jesus, but did he really believe? Did he need to repent and become a follower of Jesus like Ali? He knew he deserved to be rejected from paradise and sent to hell because of his sins, but now he thought that if he believed in Jesus, he may be saved from this.

When Ali told him that God revealed himself to ordinary people who had child-like faith, he was even more shocked. He had always thought you needed to be very educated to hear from God. Then Yusuf listened to Matthew 11:27, 'My Father has entrusted everything to me. No one truly knows the Son except the Father, and no one truly knows the Father except the Son and those to whom the Son chooses to reveal him' (NLT). In Yusuf's culture, rich families made the eldest son responsible for the servants and for allowing visitors to see the father, so all this made sense to him. As he thought about this verse, he realized that Jesus was claiming to be the only mediator between God and man, and that he had the authority to reveal the truth about God. Yusuf had known from the Qur'an that Jesus had done wonderful miracles that no other prophet ever did and that Jesus had never sinned, but now he realized that Jesus is Lord of all and the way to God. He was more powerful than any prophet.

Then Yusuf heard Matthew 11:28–29, 'Come to me, all of you who are weary and carry heavy burdens, and I will give you rest. Take my yoke upon you. Let me teach you, because I am humble and gentle at heart, and you will find rest for your souls' (NLT). Yusuf thought, 'Rest for your souls! This is what people pray for at funerals! Peace! This is what people wish on each other in their greetings'. All his life, Yusuf had been afraid of many things: punishment in hell, shame, witchcraft, evil. Jesus was offering him rest from all these fears.

Yusuf and Ali continued for some months to listen to Scripture tapes and discuss them. He realized that the Old Testament prophets told about Jesus' coming. He understood that Jesus had died in his place as punishment for his sins, and had risen from death and ascended to heaven where he reigns as Lord of all and as saviour of those who believe in him.

Yusuf prayed that God would show him what to do. Then one night he had a dream. In this dream, Jesus stood by his bed and said, 'I love you. Why don't you follow me?' When Yusuf woke up, he knew that he wanted to become a follower of Jesus. He went to find

Ali and they prayed together. Yusuf gave his life to Jesus Christ and his heart was filled with joy.

Yusuf didn't tell his family or friends about this right away. He wanted to prepare them first. He started by being kind to them, just like Ali had been to him. Gradually, he was able to listen to the Scripture recordings with them and discuss them. After some months, he dared to tell them about his dream. The family discussed it and agreed that Yusuf should obey the call of Jesus to follow him. They said they would support him, as long as he didn't shame them by ignoring their customs and dishonouring their prophet like some Christians had done.

Eventually Yusuf became part of a group of Muslims that met in Ali's home to pray and to study the Scriptures together.

1) Why do you think Yusuf began listening to portions of the Bible?

2) What were the main factors that led Yusuf to believe in Jesus Christ as his saviour?

3) Why do you think Yusuf waited so long before telling his family about his dream?

4) Yusuf's family accepted his testimony about Jesus, the Messiah, but they asked him to honour their customs and their prophet. What do you think Yusuf should do?

5) Do you know people like Yusuf? What things were most important for them in their journey to Christ?

1. Muslims and the Bible

Muslims are taught to believe in God, the day of judgement, angels, prophets, and Scriptures. The four main books of their Scriptures are the first five books of the Bible (which they call the Taurat), the Psalms (Zabûr), the New Testament (Injîl), and the Qur'an. In practice, most Muslims have only ever read the Qur'an, but many of the people in the Bible are mentioned in the Qur'an as prophets, and Muslims want to know more about them. The mains prophets are Adam, Enoch, Noah, Job, Lot,

Abraham, Ishmael, Isaac, Jacob, Joseph, Moses, Aaron, David, Solomon, Elijah, Elisha, Jonah, Ezekiel, Zechariah, John the Baptist, and especially Jesus, the Messiah. So unlike most non-Christians, Muslims know about prophets and divinely inspired Scriptures, and they believe that they are important.

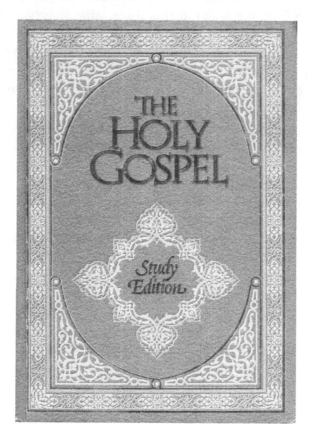

Several things discourage Muslims from reading the Bible, however. One is the Muslim belief that Jews and Christians have distorted these books. They fear that the Injíl has been altered to teach people to worship many gods: Allah, Mary, and Jesus. They also fear the curse the Qu'ran pronounces on anyone who claims that someone is a 'son of God'. They regard it as an insult to God to suggest that Jesus is the offspring of a sexual union between God and Mary.

If translations use names and terms different from those used by Muslims, this can cause further problems. For example, some translations use 'Yezu

Kristo' for Jesus where the Muslims in that language community have always used the form 'Isa al Masih' (Jesus, the Messiah). Some translations use a form like 'Yuhannes' for John the Baptist where the Muslims know him by the name 'Yahya'. Many translations use a term for the Holy Spirit that Muslims use for the angel Gabriel, or a term for intercessory prayer that Muslims use only for their ritual prayer. Although Muslims call Jesus 'the Messiah' and 'the Word of God', they don't know what these terms mean in the New Testament. There are many other terms in Scripture they might misunderstand, so they need help from a tutor or friend, or an explanation in the introduction or glossary of Scripture publications.

Another problem Muslims have with Christians is that they are suspicious of people who distribute Scripture. They feel someone who is interested in the Bible should pick up a copy or a tape for themselves, rather than be handed it. In addition to being less offensive, this could avoid legal problems. They also prefer to study it with others, either other Muslims or with a Christian who is able to answer questions about it.

Finally, they feel that since Scripture is holy, it shouldn't have illustrations on the cover or inside. The cover itself should be elegant, not black, and not made of paper. The text of Scripture should be on off-white paper surrounded by a frame, and the introductions, footnotes, section headings, and cross-references should be outside the frame.*

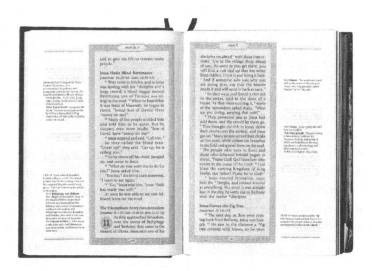

---

* See *The Holy Gospel* published by the Australian Bible Society and other Bible societies as a good example of a Muslim-friendly format.

2. Studying the Scriptures together

Muslim believers around the world live out their faith in Jesus Christ in different ways. Many stay within their culture and community. Continue reading Yusuf's story.

Yusufu's story—Part 2

One day Yusuf met a Christian named John, who was from a different part of the country. Yusuf invited him to his house for tea. Unlike the Christians who ran the bars in Yusuf's town, John was a deeply religious man who knew the Bible well. They talked about the Pharisees, Sadducees, Herodians and Zealots, what these groups believed, and why they rejected the saviour that God sent to them. Then they tried to think of similar characteristics in their own lives that might be hindering their walk with God. John told Yusuf that if he continued to observe the fasts and feasts, as his family had asked, he would be like the Pharisees. Then John said, 'A group of people come to my house every Sunday to study the Bible. Would you like to join us?' Yusuf smiled.

On Sunday, Yusuf went to John's house. When he walked inside he immediately felt uncomfortable because he was the only one wearing a long robe and cap. The women were sitting with men, and that made him uncomfortable, too, especially since these women weren't wearing clothes that covered their arms, legs and hair. He tried to be very careful to not defile himself by looking at them. They were preparing to pray and read the Bible, but Yusuf was surprised that he was the only one who had removed his shoes. Worse yet, some of them had set their Bibles on the ground. Some even had set it near their feet! On the wall there was an image of Jesus, and Yusuf wondered if this was the idol his friends had told him Christians worshipped. The whole atmosphere didn't seem reverent to him. The group sang a song in English and another in his mother tongue, but the melodies were foreign and sounded odd to Yusuf. Then John read a short passage of Scripture and talked for a while. At the end of the meeting, Yusuf said to himself, 'I'm never coming back here'.

On Wednesday, Yusuf and his brother went to Ali's house to study the Scriptures with a group of men who gathered there once a week. The women met on different days and were led by Ali's wife, Maryam. Ali welcomed Yusuf and his brother. They removed their shoes at the door, washed their hands and feet, and sat cross-legged in a circle with the others on clean mats. After they prayed, Ali opened the Scripture chest, took out the Injîl, and set it on a special stand. He read two chapters aloud, and prayed that God would give them light. Then they meditated quietly for a few minutes on what they had heard, looking to the Holy Spirit to help them understand its applications to their lives and thoughts. Different ones talked about the passage in turn, saying what it taught them about God, about their duty to one another, and about how they should live.

Ali read a key verse from the passage several times and everyone repeated it until they had it memorized. After that they talked about other passages that they had read during the week, difficulties that they had faced, victories that they had won, and things that they wanted prayer for. Then they prayed together about their problems and gave thanks to God for his blessings and love. Then they drank tea and talked with one another as friends. Yusuf and his brother felt like they were among the family of God.

1) How did Ali show respect for Yusuf and his culture?

2) What could John have done to show more courtesy and respect?

3) How did the two meetings differ in the way they treated and studied the Scriptures?

4) What are some Muslim customs about handling Scripture that are important to respect?

5) If a Muslim asked you why he should study the Bible, what would you say?

6) If a Muslim asked you how to study the Bible, what would you say?

3. Accepting cultural differences

The apostle Paul said, 'I have become all things to all men so that by all possible means I might save some' (1 Corinthians 9:19–23). Sometimes we do things as Christians which make it likely that Muslims will reject our message. As much as possible, we should adopt the cultural practices of those with whom we work. Many cultural practices are neither good nor bad, for instance, wearing a cap, but are simply an expression of the identity of that group.

Many things about the way traditional Christians worship God are offensive to Muslims or make them feel uncomfortable. To experience how this feels, do the following exercise as a large group. (It is not meant to be a model for a new church!)

1) Sing a well-known Christian chorus together.

2) Then change the mood by asking everyone to remove their shoes and line up in a row about four feet away from the person next to them. The women should line up in a separate row in the back, at a bit of a distance from the men. Find out which direction Jerusalem is and have them all face that direction.

3) Have them sit cross-legged in a circle and pray the Lord's Prayer with their palms facing upwards as if to receive the Lord's blessings.

4) Have them pray in the same fashion for the seminar or for any current requests.

5) Then ask the group,

    a. How did you feel when we sang the Christian chorus?

    b. How did you feel when we prayed?

    c. Was it all right to pray in this way?

As much as possible, we should adopt the cultural practices of those with whom we work.

Below are some questions that a Muslim who is following Christ might ask. Have each small group discuss one of them. Then have them share their response with the large group, giving Scripture verses to support their views.

1) I'm used to wearing my long robes and my embroidered caps. Does the Injîl (the New Testament) allow this?

2) I don't want to eat pork or drink alcoholic beverages. It would make me feel polluted, and my witness would be compromised. Does the Injîl allow me to abstain?

3) Ramadan is coming. I would like to use this as an opportunity to fast and pray in Jesus' name. Does the Injîl allow this?

4) I would like to continue saying my prayers, confessing that Jesus is the Lord and saviour. Does the Injîl allow this?

5) In the evenings I like to go to the mosque to pray and to talk to others about the Lord Jesus, the Taurat, and the Injîl. Does the Injîl allow this?

Assignments

But in your hearts set apart Christ as Lord. Always be prepared to give an answer to everyone who asks you to give the reason for the hope that you have. But do this with gentleness and respect (1 Peter 3:15).

1. If a Muslim asks you about the Bible or Jesus, how can you use Scripture and testimonies to 'give the reason for the hope that you have'?

2. How does 'giving a reason for the hope that you have' differ from arguing or trying to convince someone?

3. How can you show gentleness and respect for the customs and religion of another person?

4. If you have contact with Muslims, think of two questions they've asked you and Scripture references that would be appropriate to share with them.

Readings[*]

(All articles in the *International Journal of Frontier Missions* are available at
http://www.ijfm.org)

Accad, Fouad. 1997. *Building Bridges*. Colorado Springs, CL: Navpress.

Brown, Rick. 2002. 'Presenting the Deity of Christ from the Bible.' *International Journal of Frontier Missions* 19(1):20–27.

—. 2002. 'Selecting and Using Scripture Portions Effectively in Frontier Missions.' *International Journal of Frontier Missions* 19(2):10–25.

—. 2005. 'Explaining the Biblical Term 'Son(s) of God' in Muslim Contexts.' *International Journal of Frontier Missions* 22(3):91–96.

—. 2007. 'Why Muslims Are Repelled by the Term "Son of God"?' *Evangelical Missions Quarterly* 43(4):422–429.

Love, Fran and Jeleta Eckheart. 2000. *Longing To Call Them Sisters*. Pasadena, CA: William Carey.

Massey, Joshua. 2000. 'God's Amazing Diversity in Drawing Muslims to Christ.' *International Journal of Frontier Missions* 17(1):5–14.

Nealson, J. 2007. *Baghdad Believer*. Minneapolis, MN: Mill City Press.

Williams, Brad. 2006. 'The Emmaus-Medina Intertextual Connection: Contextualizing the Presentation of God's Word.' *International Journal of Frontier Missions* 23(2):67–72.

Woodberry, Dudley. 2007. 'To the Muslim I Became a Muslim?' International Journal of Frontier Missions 24(1):23–28.

---

[*] http://www.scripture-engagement.org

Chapter 20

ENGAGING CHILDREN AND YOUTH WITH SCRIPTURE

Introduction

At a Scripture engagement seminar in West Africa, participants were asked to compare the amounts of effort that were put into different ministries of the church. The ministry that received the least attention was working with children. This is often the case, in spite of the fact that more than 50 per cent of the population of many southern hemisphere countries is under the age of eighteen. This chapter shows the importance of children's ministries and how to develop appropriate materials and programmes.

No room for children

Pastor Simon's church congregation was growing larger! Each Sunday morning more and more people seemed to crowd into the building. Many came because they appreciated worshipping God in their own language. One day Pastor Simon called a meeting of the deacons, and one of the main items to discuss was what to do about the lack of space in the church on Sunday mornings. They discussed the possibility of building a larger church, or adding another section on to the existing church, or starting daughter churches in outlying areas where people came from. They agreed to think and pray about all these possible solutions, but they knew it would not solve the immediate problem for the coming Sunday.

Then Mr Yuh said, 'There is a simple solution which we can carry out right away. We need to ask someone to look after the children during the service, and then we can clear all the children under the age of about fourteen years out of the church. Then we'll have lots of room for the adults'. Everyone agreed that this was a brilliant idea. Pastor Simon didn't think about it again until Saturday. Then he quickly found a couple of women and asked them to take charge of the children during the service and teach them something.

So the next Sunday, as the families arrived, all the children were told to go outside. By the time the service began, about 100 children and teenagers were milling around outside the church. One of the deacons came out and told the two women to take them further from the church where they wouldn't disturb the service. They did this and then started the children singing a simple repetitive chorus in English. They sung this over and over again, and then chose another easy song. After a while, one of the women tried to read a Bible story in English to them all, but the small children cried and wandered around and the teenagers chatted to each other, so after a while they went back to singing again until the main service was over.

1) What was the attitude of Pastor Simon and the deacons towards the children in their church? How do we know this?

2) What could be done to help the children learn something during the church service, either in the church or outside?

1. The importance of children's and youth ministries

Why is it important to help the children come to Christ and grow as Christians?

(Bring out any of the following points if they are not been mentioned.)

Children are small persons, but they are important for the church.

- Children are the leaders and members of the church of the future.
- Children come to Christ more easily than adults who already have their ideas fixed.
- Children can have Scripture influence their lives during their formative years. This will affect them all their lives.
- Children are part of the family of God and no part of the family should be ignored.
- Children can often reach other children for Christ.
- Parents may be brought to Christ through their children.

> What types of children's ministries are active in your churches now? Have the small groups report back to the large group.
>
> Add ministries from the following list that have not been mentioned.

Typical ministries that a church may run to cater specifically for the needs of children are:

- Sunday school
- children's week day clubs
- camps
- youth meetings
- youth choirs

2. Running children's meetings

Several things could help Pastor Simon improve his children's and youth ministry.

A. Use appropriate language

Sometimes people use Sunday schools and other children's meetings to teach children the majority language. Alternatively, where children are not speaking their ethnic language, churches sometimes use this time to try to teach it to them. Neither of these approaches will help the children spiritually.

The main aim of these meetings should be to bring children to Christ and help them grow as Christians. Because of this, the language chosen should be the one the children understand the best. An easy way to test which language is the best for communication is to listen to the language children use when they are playing outside. That is the language that should be used in children's meetings. In the case of small children, this is almost always their mother tongue. If the children speak different mother tongues, it may be possible to divide them up into language groups for the main teaching time, and then join together for other activities when a common language is used.

B. Divide into age groups

It is unrealistic to expect one person to teach anything meaningful to a group ranging in age from three years to fourteen! Children of different ages have different needs and varied capacities to listen. All the children could meet together to sing or watch a drama but they should be divided into age groups when they are being taught a Bible story. At the very least, the children should be divided by age into three groups: those from three to six years old, from seven to eleven years old, and those who are over eleven. If there are a lot of children involved, more age divisions may be helpful. With older children, it may also be helpful to have groups for those who can read and for those who cannot.

C. Use Scripture

Since the Bible is the foundation of our faith, children should hear Bible stories and memorize verses from a very early age while they are still eager to listen. The best way to do this varies with the age of the child. When the children are young, the best approach is for teachers to tell them Bible stories while holding a Bible to show where the story came from. In the case of older children (eleven years of age or older), teachers can read the Scripture passage, explain it, and ask the children questions. If a number of the children can read, they can take turns reading the Bible aloud.

Children of all ages can memorize Bible verses. (See Chapter 17.) Once they learn a verse, it will stay with them all their life, and God may well use it to speak to them years later. Children often enjoy competitions to see who can say the most memory verses or can answer the most questions on Bible knowledge correctly. Churches can hold these competitions, first within their church and then with other churches.

In some youth organizations, young people win badges or certificates for learning certain practical skills, such as caring for small children. If the organization does not already have a Bible knowledge badge, it could introduce one that involves knowing the books of the Bible in order and memorizing certain verses. Another badge could be given for knowing how to read and write the mother tongue properly.

Children also enjoy singing, so sing with them, especially Scripture songs. Youth choirs may be the only meeting that young people attend apart from the Sunday service. If that is the case, introduce a short Bible study for choir members before they begin practising. Choirs can make up new Scripture songs and publish the best in a songbook or record them. (See Chapter 22.)

Even if a children's or youth meeting is for games, singing, or fellowship, end it with a Scripture reading, a short meditation, and a prayer.

D. Train the teachers

Would you ask someone to build a piece of furniture without teaching him how to do it? Certainly not. Teaching children is a skill that needs to be learned like any other skill. Some people have more natural ability than others in this, and the church should begin with them and help them improve their skills. One of the church leaders should meet with the Sunday school teachers each week to help them prepare the lesson and to pray together.

Churches can also arrange periodic teacher training seminars for Sunday school teachers on a Saturday or for several sessions in the evening. They can use a suitable book, filmstrip or video, or invite an expert to come and help the church. At the end, they can give a certificate to those who pass a final test. If the certificates are presented to the teachers publicly in church, accompanied with prayer for them in their important work, it will help them feel valued by the church members.

1) In your church, do people consider working with children to be important? What shows this? If not, how could this be changed?

2) In the existing meetings for children and youth, do the leaders read Scripture or tell Bible stories? If so, in what languages? Are there areas that you would like to change?

3) Is there any sort of training for those who teach children? If not, what could be done about it?

3. Designing Sunday school lessons

Many good Sunday school books are available in major languages. If teachers use one to teach the lesson in a local language, they need to prepare beforehand. They should read through the lesson a number of times, practise reading the Scripture passage in the local language, and prepare any visual aids the book suggests. As they do this, they should think about how to say things in their language. If only the New Testament is available in a local language, they should use books of lessons based on it.

If teachers don't have a book of Sunday school lessons, they can learn how to prepare lessons themselves. It's easy to take a theme from the Bible and choose a series of Scripture passages to use over a two- or three-month period. A good lesson is always based on a Scripture passage. Some possible themes are:

- miracles that Jesus did
- people that Jesus met
- parables that Jesus told
- things that happened on Paul's missionary journeys
- the story of Joseph
- the story of Daniel

Here is a plan for making lessons for children younger than 12.

A. The theme and passage

First, decide the Bible passage you will use. Then decide what the main point of the story is, and how you can apply it to the children in your class.

> *A good lesson is always based on a Scripture passage.*

B. Introduction

Try to begin the lesson with something that will attract the attention of the children and make them want to listen. You might bring an object to show them. For example, if you were teaching about the miracle when Jesus stilled the storm, you might show them a pillow, and ask, 'Do you think Jesus ever used one of these?'

C. Main part of the lesson

When you are teaching little children, tell the story in your own words, simplifying as needed. When you are teaching older children, you can read the story aloud a few verses at a time and explain it as you go along. Or you can tell the story in your own words and then read some of it from the Bible.

D. Questions

Find out if the children really understand the story by asking questions. Some questions may have a one-word answer the children can find in the story, for example, 'Where did Jesus go?' Others, such as 'Why did the disciples wake Jesus up?' may require longer answers. Others such as 'Why do you think the disciples had so little trust in Jesus?' may require the children to reflect on the answer. Avoid questions that have an answer of yes or no, because these kinds of questions don't make the children think about the story very much. From time to time, you may want to have a competition between two teams to see which one gets the most answers right.

E. Application

It is important that the children know what the story has to do with their lives. For example, the storm on the lake teaches us to call on Jesus when we are afraid. Discuss real life situations with the class and pray with the children. Encourage children to pray; they can pray aloud as well as adults.

F. Memory verse

Each week have the children learn a memory verse and review the verse from the previous week. At the end of the month review with them all the verses learned that month, without adding any new ones.

G. Activity

Children learn better if they can do something practical like drawing or making something like simple puppets. These are the instructions for making puppets out of papier-mâché:

1. To make the head, take some clay and mould it into the shape of a person's head.

2. Exaggerate some of the features, such as giving a man a long nose or ears that stick out.

3. Then mix some glue or flour and water. Soak some strips of paper in it and cover the whole head with the wet strips of paper.

4. After the head has dried completely, make a hole at the bottom and remove the clay. Now you have the head of the puppet. You can put your finger in the hole to move it around when you use it.

5. Paint the head and glue on string as hair.

6. Attach some old clothes to the bottom of the head and you have the puppet.

The children can use the puppets to act out the story. Actors stand or kneel behind a high table with a cloth over it to hide them. They put their hands in the puppets and move them around to act out the drama while they say their character's lines in a dramatic way.

Dramas of any sort help children understand a story. If you don't use puppets, you can ask the children to act out the story themselves after they hear it, or you can have an older group present a drama to younger children. (See Chapter 23.)

1) Divide into groups of six. Have each group pretend to teach a different age of children.

2) Read the story of the storm on the lake (Mark 4:35–41). Give everyone fifteen minutes to prepare to teach their story.

3) One person in each group starts to teach. After ten minutes, tell the groups to change teachers. This continues until everyone has had a chance to teach a part of the lesson. The people in the group who are not teaching should behave like children of the age of their group. For example, if the group is supposed to be six-year-olds and the teacher talks for a long time, they should wriggle and play around!

4) At the end, discuss in groups how the teaching went and how it could be improved.

4. Using Scriptures in schools

Church leaders may be able to teach Scripture in local schools, or churches may have teachers in their congregations who would like to do so. Many organizations prepare children's materials in local languages that could be used in schools; the organizations include Lion Hudsons, United Bible Societies, Scripture Union, Walk through the Bible for Children, and Gospel Light. Contact a local Bible agency, a mission working specifically among children, or the internet to find out what is possible in your area.

Teach Scripture in the early classes in the mother tongue so that they are properly understood. If teachers are not used to reading in this language, hold a course to help them learn to read and write it.

If your local schools allow pastors to speak to the children once a week, they should use Scripture in the appropriate language(s). The pastor's example will encourage the teachers and students to learn to read Scripture for themselves.

1) How do you think the Scriptures could be used more in children's and youth meetings during the week? What about clubs or camps in the holidays?

2) Is the Christian faith taught in your local primary and/or secondary schools? If so, what is taught? Do church leaders have any input into what is taught?

3) Do you think that the most appropriate language(s) is being used in all these situations where children are being taught? If not, who could change the situation?

Assignments

1. Imagine that a deacon in your home church says to you, 'Why are you wasting time teaching children? You have to wait until they are about fifteen years of age before they will understand anything'. Write down what you would say to him.

2. Make an outline for a lesson on Genesis 3 for seven- to eleven-year-olds.

Readings*

Bradley, Karen. 2007. 'Can You Believe God Doesn't Even Have a Grandma?' *Scripture in Use Today* 13:4–8.

—. 2007. 'Some More Scripture Use Resources for Children.' *Scripture in Use Today* 14:21–23.

Matthews, Heidi. 2003. 'Seminars for Sunday School Teachers.' *Scripture in Use Today* 7:18–19.

Reeck, Roger and Marilyn. 2001. 'Scripture Use for Young People—from Mexico.' *Scripture in Use Today* 2:13–15.

Strachan, Wendy. 2007. 'Opening Up the Bible with Children.' *Catalyst* 2:2–6.

---

* http://www.scripture-engagement.org

Chapter 21

FAMILY PRAYERS

Introduction

This chapter explores the importance of family prayers and shows how all the members of the family can benefit from them. It also discusses the language to use for family prayers. 'Family' in this chapter means all the people who are living in the same house or compound.

Falling asleep in family prayers

One day Pastor Simon travelled to another town to see some of his extended family. While he was there, he stayed with one of his cousins, Josiah, and his wife, Caroline. Josiah and Caroline had six children, ranging in age from three to sixteen. One of Caroline's sisters and two children of Josiah's brother were also living with them.

The first evening Pastor Simon was there, he was very happy to see Josiah calling his family together to pray before they went to bed. But one hour later, he was not so sure he was glad they had family prayers! First they sang a song together and then Josiah read part of Ephesians from a very literal English Bible. Then he preached a sermon in Palapala about how children should obey their parents. He talked and talked and soon the younger children were asleep and the older children were whispering to each other. Finally he stopped talking and they all went to bed. His wife, Caroline, had not said a word and the children had only been involved in singing a short song at the beginning.

1) If you were one of the children in Josiah's home, do you think you would look forward to family prayers? Why or why not?

2) What do you think Josiah could do differently to involve all of his family?

1. The importance of family prayers

Why are family prayers important?

After taking feedback, add any of the points below which have not been mentioned.

Family prayers are important in Christian homes for many reasons.

- It is the responsibility of Christian parents to teach their children about God (Ephesians 6:4; Deuteronomy 6:4–7).

- Family prayers show children that their parents care about them and are interested in their spiritual life. This is especially important for children of pastors, who may feel their parents are only interested in the people in the church.

- Family prayers teach children to pray aloud.

- Family prayers teach children that the Bible is important and true.

- Family prayers help the family to live together in peace. If there are problems between family members, it may provide a time to discuss them and find solutions.

2. Contents of family prayers

What activities might be included in family prayers?

Family prayers are for the whole family! Discuss together possible activities that involve different members of the family. Add any of the points mentioned below that have not been stated.

A. Bible reading and reflection

Each member of the family who can read should take turns reading the passage for the day. Children as young as eight can read a short section if they have help preparing to read it aloud. After the passage is read, the father or mother can ask questions to find out if the children have understood the passage. Then parents should share only one thought about the passage. If there are small children in the family, the whole Bible teaching time should not be longer than ten minutes.

Children under eight have difficulty understanding passages directly from the Bible. They sometimes find Bible stories designed for children or a children's Bible a great help. If these are not available, it is better to tell a Bible story rather than reading it aloud. If you have both younger and older children, tell the Bible story freely for the little ones, then read it from the Bible for the older ones.

Bible reading should be in the language the family understands best and normally uses to talk to each other. This is a time to help your children really believe and understand about God deep down in their hearts.

B. Singing together

Singing Christian songs together can be fun, but don't let this take up a large part of the family prayer time. Families that are musical could create new songs or practice a song to sing for the congregation during a church service.

C. Praying

Sometimes people think that small children cannot pray. This is not true! As soon as children can talk to people, they can talk to God. They may have a simple trust in God that is good for adults to copy! Have a time when everyone in the family prays a very short prayer, thanking God for something that has happened that day or asking God about something that is going to happen.

D. Sharing joys and worries

Family prayers are a good time for everyone to share what they are feeling about things that are going on. For example, an eight-year-old may say he is scared of a big child at school who hit him, while an older girl may tell how happy she is to get a good mark on her school test. The mother may tell about a friend who is ill and needs their prayers, and the father may tell them about his concern that the rain hasn't come yet. After sharing, they can pray together.

Family prayers are particularly important if there are problems in the family or in the area, like robberies, riots, or war. It is much healthier for children to have the chance to share their worries at the end of the day than to go to bed and worry about them in silence. Parents need to listen to their children rather than just telling them what to do or what to believe.

E. Special activities

Include some special activities once a week or month to help make your family prayers more interesting. Possibilities include

- Learn memory verses as a family. One per week is enough. Large families can have competitions to see who can remember the most at the end of the year. Older children can write the memory verses out on cards and put them up on walls.

- Have older children write down things the family has prayed for, such as a new house, a friend for a lonely child, or books for school. When the request is answered, they can write down the date.

- Let an older child lead the family prayers once a week.

- Act out the story you have read. Each person in the family should be a character. This can be fun to do and it helps the children to learn the story well. (See Chapter 23.)

1) Describe your own family prayers. Does everyone in the family take part?

2) Which of the ideas described here would be good to try with your family?

3) When and where are best for your family to meet for family prayers?

4) How can you continue to have your family prayer time when you have visitors staying with you?

• • • • • • *Family prayers should interest everyone in the family.*

3. Selecting the Scripture passage

Have a system for selecting the Scripture passage to read each night. You can do this in several ways.

- Use a list of readings prepared by your church or another organization or one that is available in a local Christian bookstore. If your church selects passages that have not yet been translated into your mother tongue, encourage them to use those that are.

- Read one of the gospels a paragraph at a time, from beginning to end. Leave out parts that may be too hard for the children to understand or that would not interest them, like lists of names.

- Choose a relevant topic and make a list of Scriptures that address it. A topical index can help in making lists like this. Read one or two references each day. Some topics may last a whole week.

- Choose some of the Bible stories listed in Chapter 16.

1) Choose one Bible passage that would be good to use in family prayers, for example, Matthew 7:24–29 or Luke 15:3–7.

2) Give participants fifteen minutes to prepare a family prayer session based on the passage.

3) Then in small groups discuss what you have planned.

4) Afterwards, have the groups share their best ideas with the whole group.

4. Overcoming barriers to family prayers

What are some barriers to family prayers?

1) List the responses on the board in a column.

2) Then in a second column, list possible solutions, as shown in the table below.

Barrier	Possible Solutions
Many visitors are present.	Involve the visitors in the family prayers. Ask the visitors to wait until the prayer time is over.
The parents don't feel capable to lead the family prayers.	The church can provide resources and training. Parents can work together.
The children of the family are still very small.	Keep the family prayers short. Use Bible stories rather than the Bible.
Family members are too busy.	Keep family prayers short. Make it a discipline to have them. Find a different time in the day to meet together.

Assignments

1. Do you think it is important to have family prayers? Why or why not?

2. Do you think that most families in your church pray together each day? If so, do they use Scriptures in the language they use normally in their homes?

3. How can you encourage church members to have family prayers regularly?

4. Does a book of Bible stories exist in your language? If not, how could one be made?

5. Do you have any lists of Scripture readings that could be used for family prayers? If so, what are they?

Using Your Gifts

Chapter 22

ENGAGING PEOPLE WITH SCRIPTURE THROUGH MUSIC

Introduction

Music plays an important role in Christian life. It gives us a way to express our emotions and our thoughts in praise and worship. People of all ages enjoy singing, playing a musical instrument, or just listening to their favourite music. This chapter looks at the role of music in Scripture and how Christians can use many different forms of music, including their own local music.

Singing from the heart

One Saturday, Pastor Simon needed to go to Retali for a meeting with people at the denominational office. While he was there, he decided to visit a friend he had met at the last seminar for church leaders. His friend Pastor Zoki was very happy to see him and they talked nearly all night. On Sunday morning, Pastor Simon was happy to go to his friend's church. As this was a big church with people from at least three different language groups, Pastor Simon found it interesting to see how they managed to have some things in Kisumu, but also readings from the Bible in the three local languages.

The part of the service that struck him the most, though, was the music. He'd never heard anything like it! The congregational singing was animated and people really seemed to be worshipping God. The choir songs fascinated him. They were in a great variety of styles, some with local traditional instruments and some with electric guitars!

Later on that Sunday afternoon, as Pastor Zoki and Pastor Simon sat outside the house chatting, they compared their two churches, both the positive things and the problems. Then they talked about music. Pastor Simon said, 'In my church, we sing from a hymn book that we've used for a good number of years. Most of the songs are translations from Western hymns. Although there are about three hundred songs in the book, the song leaders only use about twenty of them, because they are the ones the congregation have memorized. Now that we are using Palapala for the services, we also sing a few songs in our language, but they are mainly translations from the Kisumu which are translations from English! The result is that people sing very slowly with very little life, and I wonder how much they actually understand the words. The choirs are livelier, but sometimes their words don't make much sense to the congregation. Some of the songs actually teach bad theology! The music in your church is completely different! What happened?'

Zoki said, 'Well, it really all started with the Catholic church on the other side of town. You remember Father John who came to the last seminar? We went together to a funeral and his choir was there to sing. I was fascinated by the way they sang through the story of the raising of Lazarus from the dead, using a music style that was used traditionally at funerals. Everyone listened to the song with great attention, and after that I was asked to read the passage aloud from John 11.

'After the funeral, we got the chance to send some of our musicians on a special seminar to help churches use their own ethnic music, and you've seen the result. Not only are people worshipping better in the services, but the music has attracted others to come to church. We've made some cassettes of Scripture songs, and even the neighbouring women who never come to church listen to them. Now they are asking more about Jesus. There has been another advantage. We've been trying for some time to get church people to memorize Scripture but have not had much success with the adults. Since we started using Scripture songs, people are remembering lots more Scripture verses.'

1) Why do you think the music in Pastor Zoki's church had such a powerful effect on people?

2) Do you have Scripture songs in your language that use local music forms? If not, what could you do about it?

1. Music is used in many ways

1) What are some ways music is used in your culture?

2) What are some ways music is used in the Bible? Give references.

Add any of the points below that have not been mentioned.

Music can:

- express many different emotions, including joy, fear, anger, and repentance (Psalms).
- teach by reminding people of God's actions (Exodus 15)
- accompany dance (1 Chronicles 15).
- celebrate cultural festivals (2 Chronicles 35:15).
- fight spiritual warfare (1 Samuel 16:23; 2 Chronicles 20:21–23; Psalm 149; Isaiah 30:31–32; Acts 16:25).
- celebrate victory in war, for example of Moses and Miriam (Exodus 15).
- animate processions (2 Samuel 6).
- praise 'big men' (1 Samuel 18:7).
- worship (Revelation 5; 2 Chronicles 5).
- mourn (Matthew 9:23).
- encourage and strengthen people (1 Corinthians 14:26).

1) In a column, list all of the ways your church uses music (for offertory, processions, and so forth).

2) In a second column, list the language(s) the songs are usually sung in.

3) In the third column, list the type of music that is used (traditional tunes, borrowed music, Western music).

4) Share the results with the whole group.

2. Reclaiming music for God's glory

Just as individuals must bring themselves to Christ to be redeemed, people must bring their culture's music to Christ so that it can be redeemed and become all that God intended it to be.

We need to bring our whole selves to Christ.

Ask someone to read Mark 12:30:

Love the Lord your God with all your heart and with all your soul and with all your mind and with all your strength.

We don't want to take God's word only into our heads, but into every part of our being. Using songs from our own culture can help do this.

Often music has been stolen by Satan.

Ask someone to read 2 Corinthians 10:5:

We demolish arguments and every pretension that sets itself up against the knowledge of God, and we take captive every thought to make it obedient to Christ.

We are commanded to take every thought and every part of our culture captive to make it obedient to Christ. Developing Christian ethnic music reclaims for Christ what Satan has stolen.

Sing a new song.

Ask someone to read Psalm 96:1:

Sing to the Lord a new song; sing to the LORD, all the earth.

God wants us to sing new songs to him, using musical forms that already exist. Old songs and borrowed songs are not bad, but each culture should also be composing new songs, flowing from the unique musical resources that God has given them.

3. Reclaiming musical instruments for God's glory

Bita reclaims his balaphone for God's glory

Bita was a very well known player of a West African instrument called a balaphone. He played in night clubs and made a lot of money. One day he went to a special evangelistic meeting and became a Christian. Soon he started attending a church. Many people there had seen him on television and knew he was an expert balaphone player so they asked him to play in church. At first he refused, because he felt the balaphone was tied up with the sinful things he had done before he became a Christian.

Then one day he had an idea. He talked to the pastor of the church and they agreed on a plan. The next Sunday he took his balaphone to church and the pastor invited him to bring the instrument up to the front of the church. Then the pastor prayed to consecrate this balaphone for the work of God. He poured some oil on it to show that now it was set aside for God. From then on Bita often played his balaphone in church to praise God. Everyone was encouraged.

Do you think Bita did the right thing? Why or why not?

Have each group read one of the following passages and answer the question below: 1 Chronicles 15:16–29; Daniel 3:5; Psalm 150; Isaiah 5:12.

1) Does the passage describe a pagan or godly event?

2) What instruments did the people use at this event?

3) Were any instruments used for both pagan and godly events? Were traditional instruments used for pagan worship also used to worship God?

4) What instruments are used traditionally in your area? What kind of events are they used for?

5) What instruments are used in your churches? Could more traditional instruments be used?

4. Our heart music

Our musical language is buried deep inside us from our childhood and is the music of our hearts. It touches our emotions in a powerful way. It is a channel through which the Holy Spirit speaks to us deeply. Often when a church uses local music in services, people are moved.

1) How can you introduce newly composed Scripture songs into the different types of Christian meetings inside and outside the church building?

2) Who are the best singers, musicians, and performers of local music in the villages and cities you know?

3) If they are Christians, pray for them, and encourage them to compose new Scripture songs.

4) If they are not Christians, pray that God call them to himself, so that they can use their gifts to praise him.

Our heart music is a channel through which the Holy Spirit speaks to us deeply.

Assignment

Divide into language groups to compose new songs.

1. Pray and ask the Holy Spirit for inspiration.

2. Think of a need in your community that you would like God to speak to through song. Find one or more verses in the Bible that apply to this need.

3. Write down the verse(s) and divide it into poetic lines. Each line should have no more words than can easily be sung in one breath. The punctuation marks in the Bible will often guide you in making a paragraph into a set of poetic lines. If there is a chorus which is repeated, choose an important point of the Scripture passage for it.

4. Choose a type of music that will best communicate the theme of the passage, for example, a love song or a harvesting song. You can take a tune you know already or you can make up a new tune.

5. Put words to the music. You may want to use only part of a Scripture verse or repeat some of the words or phrases. You can make small changes to the words, like leaving out the word 'and' or adding in the word 'then', but the main words in the verse should not be changed. If you have changed the words of the passage, check them with a pastor or another wise leader who knows the Bible to make sure that they faithfully communicate the meaning of the passage.

6. Sing your song for the group. Ask them for feedback.

Readings[*]

King, Roberta R. 1999. *A Time to Sing: A Manual for the African Church.* Evangel Publishing House: Nairobi, Kenya.

Neeley, Paul. 1994. 'Social Factors in the Acceptance or Rejection of Indigenous Hymns.' *Notes on Literature in Use and Language Programs* 42:29–33.

Olson, Bruce. E. 1978. 'Night of the Tiger.' In *Bruchko*. Altamonte Springs, Florida: Creation House, pp 147–153.

Saurman, Mary E. 1993. 'Music: A Bridge to Literacy.' *Notes on Literacy* 19(3):34–42.

---

[*] http://www.scripture-engagement.org

Schrag, Brian and Paul Neeley, eds. 2004. *All The World Will Worship: Helps for Developing Indigenous Hymns.* Duncanville, Texas: Ethnodoxology Publications.

Scott, Joyce. 2000. *Tuning in to a Different Song: Using a Music Bridge to Cross Cultural Barriers.* University of Pretoria: The Institute for Missiological and Ecumenical Research.

Chapter 23

ENGAGING PEOPLE WITH SCRIPTURE THROUGH DRAMA

Introduction

Drama can be a very important tool to help people engage with Scripture. It can take many different forms and can be presented in many ways. This chapter helps people get new ideas about how to use drama in their churches.*

A Christmas drama gone astray

It was Christmas Eve. Pastor Simon's church always had a service on Christmas Eve that went on into the early hours of Christmas morning. One part of it was almost always a drama of the Christmas story performed by the youth. This year they had not prepared much because they had been practising for an important football match.

They started the drama and Pastor Simon was glad to see that this year they were talking in their mother tongue, Palapala. In the past, they had performed in English, which meant that many people had not been able to understand it. They started the drama at the

---

* This is only an introduction to the subject of drama. If you want to develop this ministry in your church or on the radio, you may want to have an entire workshop or series of workshops devoted to developing dramas.

point at which Caesar Augustus imposed a census on everyone in the Roman Empire. This part took thirty minutes and as each person came to have his name written down, the soldiers joked with them and demanded small bribes. The part when Joseph and Mary arrived in Bethlehem and the baby was born was over very quickly. After that, the shepherds came and amused everyone by bringing their rather unwilling dogs with them! The kings came next and, finally, Herod's soldiers took about forty minutes to kill all the babies, doing it with great enthusiasm.

After the service, Pastor Simon went home with his excited children. They were talking about the drama, but the parts they remembered and talked about were the census, the shepherds' dogs and particularly the part when the babies were killed. As he heard them talking about these things, he began to think, 'Is this type of drama really communicating the message of the Bible, or was it giving rather strange ideas about which parts of the story were important?'

1) What is the purpose of drama in the church?

2) How could Pastor Simon help the youth improve their drama presentation next year?

1. Drama and Scripture Engagement

What kinds of drama have you seen used by the church?

List the kinds of drama on the board. Add any that are not mentioned from the list below.

Many kinds of dramas can be used in church, for example:

- dramas performed for an audience or dramas performed by a group as a learning experience

- dramas involving voices only, voices and acting, or acting only (mime)

- dramas on Bible passages or themes

- dramas using lots of props and those that use none
- dramas that introduce the subject of a sermon or speech, and those that give the main teaching
- dramas done in person or recorded on radio or film
- dramas done indoors or outdoors

The Bible is full of examples of drama. For example, each year the Israelites had a special Passover meal when they celebrated their deliverance from slavery in Egypt. This included a small drama.

The youngest child asked four questions which the parents always answered in the same way:

- Why is this night different from all other nights?

  Because on other nights we eat matzo and bread, but on this night we eat only matzo.

- Why on all other nights do we eat many herbs and on this night only bitter herbs?

  To recall the bitter lives of our ancestors, who were slaves in Egypt.

- Why on all other nights do we dip our food only once, and twice on this night?

  It is our custom to dip on other nights. We dip a second time to remember that our ancestors dipped a leafy branch to smear lambs' blood on their doorposts.

- Why on all other nights do we sit up to eat, but recline on this night?

  Because free people reclined in ancient times, and our ancestors became free on this night.

Then the child goes outside to see if Elijah is coming that year or not.

There are many other examples of dramas in the Bible. God told Isaiah to go around naked to show how the nations would be stripped of their power (Isaiah 20). He told Hosea to marry a prostitute as an illustration of his marriage to unfaithful Israel (Hosea 1 and 3). He told Ezekiel to act out God's message to Israel in a number of dramatic ways (Ezekiel 4, 5, 6, 12). In Acts 21:11, Agabus acts out a warning to Paul. If God told the prophets to communicate through dramatic means, we certainly can use drama, too.

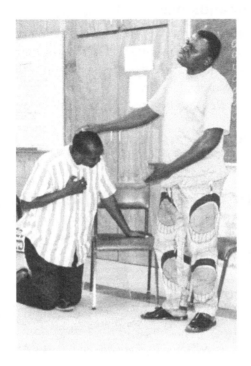

1) If people say that it is wrong to use drama in church, how would you respond?

2) What other dramas can you think of that appear in the Bible?

2. Basic questions for any drama

Before preparing a drama, it's good to answer a number of questions.

A. What is your goal?

Dramas can be used to evangelise, to build up believers in their faith, or to help a group understand a Scripture passage better and engage with it. Agree on the goal you hope to accomplish through your drama so that you are sure to get your main point across.

B. Who is your audience?

Think of your audience as you prepare your drama. What are their interests and needs? What do they already know about the world and about the Bible? What theme or Scripture passage would be relevant to them? Once you've chosen a Scripture passage, identify any necessary background information your audience may need and decide how to supply it to them.

C. How will you deliver the drama?

The way you prepare the drama will depend on how it is to be delivered. Think about where you'll perform it. Will it be delivered in person? On the radio? By film? However a drama is delivered, it is important that it finishes in the allotted time. If it goes on longer than people expect, you may not be asked to do another one.

Dramas generally take more time than expected to perform. The shorter the drama, the more carefully you need to prepare it. A pastor once said, 'It takes me no time at all to prepare a one-hour sermon, a couple of hours to prepare a half-hour sermon, and a whole day to prepare a ten-minute sermon'. It takes more preparation to do a short drama, but the quality improves as the less important lines are cut out.

If you need sound effects, you can make them using ordinary household items. For example, small stones falling on a piece of aluminium roofing can sound like a heavy rain storm.

If you want to record the dramas, you'll need recording equipment. Many computers are able to make good quality recordings which are easy to edit. (See Appendix 4.)

D. How will you get feedback?

Before you perform a drama in public, perform it for someone who has good judgement. Ask the person to answer these questions.

1. What do you think the main message of the drama is?

2. Is there anything offensive in the drama? If so, what?

3. Can the drama be improved in any way?

4. Preparing a drama based on a theme

A drama can be based on a theme that illustrates a truth from the Bible and shows its relevance to daily life. An example would be a series of dramas illustrating the fruits of the Spirit. The fruit of gentleness could be illustrated by a story of a group of Christians where one person in the group showed gentleness towards a handicapped person, but another one is rough with a mentally ill man.

Here is another example of a drama on the theme of forgiveness.

> A woman tells her son to take an expensive meat sauce she has cooked to his father, who is selling in the market. On his way, his neighbour's daughter bumps into him and the food is spilled on the ground. The dish breaks. His mother refuses to forgive the neighbours even though they reimburse the loss. Later, her son is trying to hit a bird in a tree with a slingshot. The rock misses and hits the neighbour's daughter in the eye. She is wounded. The family who refused to forgive now needs forgiveness from the people they had refused to forgive. They pay the neighbour's hospital bills, but there are still ill feelings between the two families.
>
> One of the fathers calls an elder to intervene. He brings the two families together and tells them the parable of the unforgiving servant (Matthew 18:23–34). The two families apologize to each other and forgive each other. The concluding scene shows the children of both families playing together, the two women going to the market together, or the two men chatting together. A neighbour asks one of the women why she is singing so happily and she explains that it is because the other woman has forgiven her.*

Theme-based dramas are more challenging to develop, but they also allow for more creativity. Each story needs to have the following:

- A main character who has a problem: the main character should have a problem and change in some significant way by the end of the story.

- Scripture applied to the problem: one of the characters tells a Bible story that shows the solution to the problem. During the drama, the

---

* See Appendix 3 for more examples of dramas on themes.

characters should ask the same questions as the audience would be likely to ask, and answer these questions in a way that the audience would find satisfying.

- An application: the concluding scene should show how Scripture could be put into practice to make a difference in the life of at least one character. Alternatively, it could show the consequences of not putting Scripture into practice. This is the main point, so allow enough time for it. Don't spend twenty-eight minutes on a problem and one minute on a solution.

Dramas on themes require more time to develop. Use this process.

1. Decide on the theme you want to address. The first themes to be treated should be values that the culture has in common with the Bible, but ones that people struggle with. For example, use themes like neighbours getting along with one another, gratitude, or forgiveness. Later, go on to biblical themes that question cultural values.

2. Develop the script.

   a) Describe the problem exactly, using the following questions as a guide: Who? What? When? Where?

   b) Describe the cultural and biblical views on the topic. Select one or more Scripture passages that address the theme. Be sure you understand the passage well.

   c) Brainstorm, that is, let everyone come up with ideas. All ideas are good as starting points. Silly ideas can lead to brilliant ones, so don't silence any ideas at this stage.

   d) Select the best story line. Develop the main character's problem, the biblical solution, and the application. A character may become a Christian but this does not need to happen in every drama. A Christian may learn how the Bible can help him or her in a way he or she didn't know before. A character may refuse to change, and this is all right as long as another character shows a better example.

   e) Develop the introduction and the ending.

   f) Add song and dance as appropriate.

   g) Leave out any material that could cause misunderstandings or offence. For example, if you're doing a programme about abortion, know that there will most likely be women who have had abortions in the audience. Be sure your message is sensitive to all who are likely to see it.

3. Assign roles.

4. Rehearse repeatedly and get feedback.

1) Prepare a drama on a theme, using the process above.

2) Present your drama to the whole group.

5. Preparing radio drama programmes

Around the world, both rich and poor people listen to the radio. It's a very powerful means of communication because it reaches people who may never enter a church or meet a Christian.

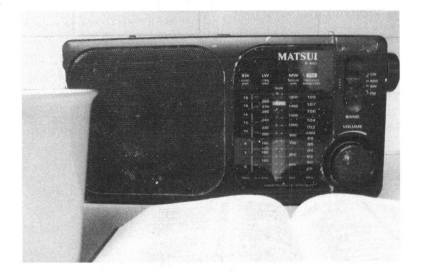

FM stations are usually local and have good reception. Often their rates for broadcast time are affordable, and they may even give free airtime for religious programmes. Short-wave radio broadcasts over a much larger area, but the reception is poorer so voices and sound effects need to be very clear. Short-wave stations also charges higher fees than FM stations.

Dramas prepared for radio need to be a specified length: no more, no less. Some radio stations want programmes that are exactly fourteen minutes long; others want them to be exactly twenty-nine minutes. Find out the length of programmes on the radio station where you plan to air your drama. Prepare a set of dramas, perhaps a dozen or so, for airing over a three-month period.

Since a radio audience doesn't see the actors, they can read their scripts rather than memorizing them, but this has its own challenges. The actors need to read their parts with expression but without sounding like they're reading. They need to 'put their face in their voice'. They should imagine they are addressing a household rather than a stadium full of people they don't know. Since the audience can't see the action, it is especially important to use sound effects.

Radio listeners form a relationship with the announcer, so greetings and leave-takings are very important. Each programme should open in a way that people can recognize it as one of the series. At the end of the programme, just before saying goodbye, the announcer needs to let the audience know when they can hear the next episode and give them some idea about the content.

For recordings of Scripture, use different voices for different characters in the story and include music between passages. People find it difficult to pay attention to continuous Scripture reading by one person and lose interest rapidly.

1) Write a one-minute radio programme to advertise Scripture in your mother tongue.

2) Record it, if possible.

3) Perform or play it for the group.

Assignments

1. What are the advantages of using drama in evangelism?

2. What are the dangers of youth groups preparing dramas? How can these dangers be avoided?

3. Listen to a radio programme and think about how it was designed. Identify what you think was good and what was not good.

4. If you have internet access, go to: **http://www.ibs.org** Go to the radio section of their home page. There are three one-minute programs there that you can listen to!

*Readings**

Banale, Apep. 2003. 'Using the Luke Video Script for Dramas.' *Scripture in Use Today* 6:9–11.

Bernardi, Philip. 1992. *Improvisation Starters: A Collection of 900 Improvisation Situations for the Theater.* Cincinnati, Ohio: F&W Publications, Inc.

Federwitz, Alvina. 2005. 'Morality Play Writers' Workshops.' *READ* 40(1):23–76.

Kaai, Anneke. 2008. *Seeing a New Song: The Psalms Connection.* Nairobi, Kenya: Wordalive.

Kindell, Gloria. 1996. 'Ethnopoetics: Finding Poetry.' *Notes on Literature in Use and Language Programs* 50:31–46.

La Rivière, Leen. 2005. *Creative—and Christian! Biblical Principles.* Carlisle, UK: Piquant Editions.

Passerello, Carole and Marilyn G. Henne. 1989. 'Dramatized Scripture To Promote Scripture-in-Use: Three Case Studies from the Central America Branch.' *Notes on Literature in Use and Language Programs* 21:24–30.

Peterson, Michelle. 2004. 'How God Has Expanded Jula Radio Theater.' *Scripture in Use Today* 9:17–19.

Prettol, Joyce. 1989. 'Drama Productions for Scriptures in Use.' *Notes on Literature in Use and Language Programs* 22:21–24.

Siewert, Alison. 2003. *Drama Team Handbook.* Downers' Grove, Illinois: Intervarsity.

---

* http://www.scripture-engagement.org

Chapter 24

ENGAGING PEOPLE WITH SCRIPTURE THROUGH THE VISUAL ARTS

Introduction

Throughout the centuries, visual arts have helped people engage with Scripture. In places where most church members didn't know how to read, the church has used paintings or stained glass windows of biblical scenes as a primary means to communicate the message of the gospel. Art touches people in a way words or songs may not. Christians today can use art in various ways to help people engage visually with Scripture, and they don't need to be artists or film producers to do so.

Walls can speak!

One day, Pastor Simon received an invitation to send a couple of church leaders to a special Scripture engagement seminar where they would learn about many different ways of communicating the Scriptures. After a lot of discussion, they all agreed to send one of the deacons, Yuh, and his wife Mary, the leader of the women's work.

Yuh and Mary arrived at the meeting place and found people there from many different churches, including Keti, a leader from the Catholic church in the village next to theirs. After they had all introduced themselves, the facilitators explained that they were going to explore various ways of communicating the stories of the Bible. The first day they were going to look at how to use art. Yuh was horrified! He said, 'When I was at school, the teachers always told me the pictures I drew were awful! There is no way I can draw a picture of a Bible scene!' Mary was a little happier with the idea because she had enjoyed drawing at school.

The leaders explained that it didn't matter whether a person thought he or she could draw or not. There were many different ways of using art, and everyone could do something. For the first exercise, they gave everyone a leaf, a piece of paper, and a pencil and said, 'Look carefully at this leaf for five minutes! Then start to draw it exactly as it is. The first thing in learning how to draw is to look!' Everyone tried this exercise, and then looked at each other's work. They all agreed that Keti's was very good.

Later in the day the participants found a verse that was especially meaningful to them and learned to write it in big, clear letters next to the leaf in their drawing. When Yuh and Mary finally went home, they looked at the walls of their church with new eyes and had many ideas about how they could communicate Scripture through art.

1) Do you think you can draw, or did a teacher tell you that you were no good at art?

2) What are different types of art that could be used in a church building?

3) What could be used outside a church?

Report the answers to questions 2 and 3 back to the large group and list them on the board. (Add any items from the list below that have not been mentioned.)

Art that can be used in church, include:

- art without words—paintings, murals, sculpture
- art with words—posters, banners, Bible pictures, wall paintings
- visual recorded media—filmstrips, videos, films

1. Visual arts in Scripture

In the Bible, God used visual images to communicate with the Israelites. They were told exactly how to construct the tabernacle. Its different parts communicated different messages. For instance, the beautiful curtain dividing off the Holy of Holies showed the holiness of God. Moses was told to find craftsmen who had been given artistic gifts by God to do this work.

[1] *Then the LORD said to Moses,* [2] *'See, I have chosen Bezalel son of Uri, the son of Hur, of the tribe of Judah,* [3] *and I have filled him with the Spirit of God, with skill, ability and knowledge in all kinds of crafts* [4] *to make artistic designs for work in gold, silver and bronze,* [5] *to cut and set stones, to work in wood, and to engage in all kinds of craftsmanship.* [6] *Moreover, I have appointed Oholiab son of Ahisamach, of the tribe of Dan, to help him. Also I have given skill to all the craftsmen to make everything I have commanded you'* (Exodus 31:1–6).

2. Producing and using visual arts

Many kinds of visual art are easy to create. Some are for temporary use, while others are more permanent.

A. Posters

A poster is a big piece of paper or card stock with a text and artwork. Posters can be hung on the wall of a church or a house. It's quite easy to make a Scripture poster. Choose a short verse or part of a verse and write the words in large letters on a piece of paper or card stock. Add a drawing or design that fits the theme of the verse. If you like, glue things on the poster, for example, dried grasses or seeds. Take one session to make these during Scripture engagement seminars.

B. Calendars

In many areas, calendars are very popular. A calendar with Bible verses keeps Scripture in view all year long. If the verses are in the mother tongue, the calendar can be good publicity for mother-tongue Scriptures.

There are many ways of making a calendar. You can have one large picture with twelve smaller tear-off sheets each showing a month and its text, or you can have a page for each month with its own picture and text. The texts can be Scripture verses or proverbs from Scripture with a relevant proverb from your own culture. To have the calendars ready for sale in December, you need to start working on them in August.

C. Banners

Banners are made of cloth or woven mats and have a verse or part of a verse of Scripture and some sort of art work. They are more durable than posters. Some communities use banners when they parade around town to praise God with songs, instruments, and dance as a witness to people there.

Making banners with a group of people can be fun. Here is the process.

1. Pray together for God to guide you to a Scripture passage. It should have less than eight words. You may need to shorten the text for the banner. Think of where the banner will hang and decide on the language(s) that would be most appropriate for that place.

2. Cut the letters of the text out of some fabric or felt that contrasts with the colour of the background. Make the letters big enough to be read easily from across a room.

3. Put the text on the background and see if it looks good and is easy to read.

4. Decide on the decorations. Objects such as rice, maize, millet, cow peas, dried flowers, small remnants of cloth, ribbon, or cord can make the banner more interesting. Let each person work on a separate part.

5. Assemble the banner. Lay out all the parts to check that they will all fit, and then sew, glue, or paint the words on the banner. In some cases, you might write the letters on the banner using a wide felt pen. Make a hem at the top of the banner but leave an opening at each end. Put a stick through the hem and use it to hang up the banner.

6. Find out if people understand what you were hoping to communicate by your banner, especially if you are using symbols to represent things. Make any changes that are necessary to get your message across clearly.

D. Paintings

A painting attracts people's interest and can remind them of biblical truths. It can also serve as a focus for meditation. For example, the Dutch author Henri Nouwen meditated a long time on a picture that showed the return of the prodigal son and then wrote his reflections in a book that has blessed many people.

If a church is engaged in Bible storying, a series of pictures hung around the church showing God's plan of salvation would help people remember the main stories. A set of nine illustrations could include:

the creation of the world	the fall of man
Noah and the flood	the birth of Jesus
Jesus calming the sea	Jesus casting out the Gadarene demons
the Crucifixion	the Resurrection
the Great Commission	

Some paintings have a Scripture verse as a caption. If the verse is in the mother tongue, it helps raise the prestige of the language.

 Ask each participant and staff member to make a poster or a banner, or to sketch a picture that can be painted on a church wall. These should illustrate a Bible story, have a Bible text on it, or in some way help people engage with Scripture.

E. Bible story illustrations

Read this paragraph written by a person working in Asia:

One day a local partner and I were in a village meeting people and giving out tracts. We gave out about twenty and decided to return in a week or two to gauge the response. When we went back, no one could remember the nineteen tracts that were all text. However numerous families in the village had read the one tract with illustrations and could describe its message. Based on this information, we began to develop Bible stories and booklets that only used words to describe the illustrations. The number of people who read these tracts skyrocketed.

People are far more likely to read Bible stories or Bible portions with pictures than those without them. Many types of Bible pictures are available so find out what kind of picture is best understood by local people. One set that is readily available is called *Look and Live*, produced by Gospel Recording Network. They can be bought in many countries.

Illustrations need to be sensitive and accurate. Two areas of concern are:

- Followers of Islam may find illustrations in books containing Scripture offensive. They consider that a holy book should only contain text. Often they accept illustrations in Bible stories, but be sure that people in the illustrations are well clothed, particularly prophets like Abraham.

- If the picture is illustrating a historical event from the Bible, it should be as accurate as possible in terms of the countryside, houses, and so on. It isn't historically correct to portray Jesus as though he came from Africa and lived in a mud hut. It is equally incorrect to have pictures of Jesus with white skin, blue eyes and fair hair! Jesus was born in the Middle East and would have had a light brown skin and dark hair.

Look at a variety of Bible story pictures: some line drawings, some in colour and some cartoons. Ask the group to discuss which they think would be the most suitable in their area for adults, youth, and children.

• • • • • •   *Try out all audio-visual methods with a small audience before using them on a large scale.*

F. Videos and films

Christian films and videos can be great evangelistic tools, as they draw interested crowds. They can also help Christians learn certain important Scriptural truths much more rapidly than if they just hear or read Scripture.

There are a number of videos and films that portray parts of the Bible. Perhaps the best known is the *Jesus Film* produced by Campus Crusade. This uses parts of Luke's Gospel to show the life of Jesus. It is available in many major languages of the world and increasingly in minority languages. Many people become Christians after seeing the film. Viewers who are already Christians benefit by getting a much better idea of what life in

Israel was like. It also helps people realize that Israel is a real country on this earth.

Preparing the *Jesus Film* in your language requires a commitment of time. You also need to have a translation of Luke's Gospel in your language that has been checked by a consultant. Once you have it, follow these steps.

1. Contact your country's *Jesus Film* director to begin the process.

2. Translate the script of the film. This involves getting the number of syllables of the script in your language to match those spoken on the film, if that is possible. You can use different beginnings and the endings for areas where Islam is strong or where there is very little understanding of Christianity.

3. Select people gifted at reading the language to record the script. Rehearse the readings until everyone can read their part well with expression.

4. Plan on taking ten to fourteen days to do the recording and using between seventeen and twenty-five people. *Jesus Film* staff take care of the technology, mixing music and sounds with the voices and getting it all on film.

5. After the film is done, do a test showing of it with a small group and watch their reactions. Ask them about what they have seen. Occasionally, a group of people may seriously misunderstand a part of the film. If this happens, either you can add a special introduction, or not show the film in the area because it is not suitable.

6. Arrange to show the film. This involves obtaining the equipment and contacting the leaders of the village. If the film is used for evangelism, the church needs to have a plan for following up on people who commit their lives to Christ. One ministry that is effective for this is Faith Comes by Hearing. This ministry records the New Testament in various electronic formats such as CDs, MP3s, and podcasts, and organizes people into groups to listen to the Scripture and discuss it.

7. If people are not used to watching films, explain that the film is not reality and that actors are playing the various parts. It may be good to show another short film, like a nature film, before beginning to show the *Jesus Film*. This allows the audience to get used to watching the moving images and to concentrate by the time they see the more important film.

8. Have a book or booklet of passages from Luke to sell at the showing of the film, if possible. The film may motivate non-literate people to learn to read and the books or booklets can reinforce the message.

G. Television

Making TV programmes requires expertise and funds, but if these can be obtained, it is well worth the trouble. There are many possibilities for such a programme including drama groups acting out Bible stories, teams competing in a Bible quiz, or music groups singing Scripture in song. Many religious TV programmes consist of someone preaching a sermon, and this can be boring. If possible, make a programme that is so interesting it attracts non-Christians.

Assignments

1. Which of the methods presented in this chapter are presently used in your church? Which of the others would you like to introduce? Why?

2. Scripture videos can be a very helpful tool, but they may cause problems as well. Describe two possible problems.

3. Compare the advantages and disadvantages of the following ways of communicating the gospel: radio drama, storying, banners or posters, booklets, and a live drama.

*Readings**

Barboza, Francis Peter. 1990. *Christianity in the Indian Dance Forms.* Delhi, India: Sri Satguru Publications.

Bird, Craig. 1991. 'Ministering through Media: Le Combat Speaks to Fears.' *Notes on Scripture in Use and Language Programs* 27:36–39.

Corbitt, J. Nathan. 1992. 'Soften your Media To Put Community in Communication.' *Notes on Scripture in Use and Language Programs* 31:9–15.

Benn, Keith. 1992. 'Scripture in Use: The Bontoc Experience.' *Notes on Literature in Use and Language Programs* 31:29–60.

Bowman, Jim. 1989. 'How the Jesus Movie Is Promoting Scripture Use.' *Notes on Literature in Use and Language Programs* 20:3–6.

---

* http://www.scripture-engagement.org

McKinnies, Shaw. 2004. 'Video Literacy! How the Limbum Literacy VCD Has Made an Unexpected Splash.' *Scripture in Use Today* 9: 20–24.

Myers, Bryant. 1994. 'What Message Did They Receive?' *Notes on Literature in Use and Language Programs* 41:1–5.

Nouwen, Henri. 1994. *Return of the Prodigal Son: A Story of Homecoming.* Garden City, NY: Doubleday.

Peterson, Michelle. 2002. 'Things I Wish We Had Known Before the Jesus Film/ Radio Recording Team Came.' *Scripture in Use Today* 5:11–14.

Shannon, Al. 2004. 'Jesus Video or Luke Video, What's the Difference?' *Scripture in Use Today* 10:14–17.

Stillings, Irene. 2002. 'Art and Scripture Use.' *Scripture in Use Today* 5:24–26.

Weber, Hans-Ruedi. 1996. *The Book that Reads Me: A Handbook for Bible Study Enablers*, pp 37–47. Geneva, Switzerland: WCC.

Welser, Marcia. 2001. 'Use of the Jesus Film.' *Scripture in Use Today* 3:11–13.

Useful website

http://www.jesusfilm.org Find out if the *Jesus Film* has been recorded in your language and download it free of charge.

Literacy

Chapter 25

MOTHER-TONGUE READING AND WRITING FOR LITERATES

Introduction

Many people who speak a minority language already know how to read in a majority language. These people are a key resource for helping a community to use their mother-tongue Scriptures.* Often they can learn to read their own language very quickly, and can then read Scripture in church services and lead Bible studies. They can also learn how to teach others to read. This chapter explains how to help these key people become fluent readers.

Not enough readers!

Pastor Simon was reading Palapala quite well now, but few others in the church could read the language. When he wasn't present at a meeting, there was rarely anyone to read the Palapala Scriptures and people went right back to reading in Kisanu. He realized that he should be teaching people to read, but it seemed like a huge task that would take months.

---

* Teaching literates to read their language can be done in a Scripture engagement seminar if the writing system resembles that of the majority language. If it is very different, you may need to hold a separate seminar devoted to learning to read and write in the mother tongue. If this is the case, the first Scripture engagement seminar can concentrate on oral methods of communicating the message of the Bible.

Pastor Zoki happened to be in the village attending his uncle's funeral, so he took the opportunity to visit Pastor Simon. After visiting for some time, Pastor Simon said, 'Zoki, you're my friend and a very wise man. Can you help me? I want to use Palapala in my church services, but very few people know how to read it. I don't see how I can possibly begin teaching literacy classes. It will take months for people to learn to read and write in Palapala, and I'm already too busy. I don't know what to do!'

Zoki smiled. He knew exactly what Pastor Simon could do. He said, 'It's true, this is a big challenge. You need to break it down into parts. I know that many of your church members already read in Kisanu. The differences between Kisanu and Palapala aren't that great. Within a short time, these people could be reading Palapala fluently and writing it, too. Then they can teach the others. What is more, if you start by teaching the illiterates to read Palapala, the educated people will probably decide reading Palapala is only for those with little education. Start at the top and everyone will want to learn'.

Pastor Simon felt a ray of hope. 'That's a great idea. Why didn't I think of that? It's good to have good friends like you'. They went on talking, and Zoki explained more about how to prepare materials for such a reading class.

1) If you speak a minority language, have you learned to read it? If so, how did you learn?

2) What percentage of your congregation already knows how to read the majority language?

3) If literate people in your church speak a minority language and want to learn to read it, how would they go about it?

1. Making a transfer guide

Teaching people who are literate in the majority language to read and write in their own language involves two main skills:

- Helping them learn letters and tone marks that do not exist in the majority language, or how to pronounce letters that are pronounced differently in the majority language.

- Teaching any necessary conventions connected with the writing system, such as where to divide words and when and how to mark tone.

> List the alphabet of your language and that of the majority language of your area and compare them.

- Are there any letters that only occur in your language?
- Are there any letters that have different sounds in your language?
- Are there other symbols used in your language?

The best way to teach this material is by using a transition guide. This is a book that has a series of lessons covering the differences between the local language and the majority language. For example, the first lesson may cover the sounds and letters that are the same in the two languages, such as ʹk, p, t, aʹ. The second lesson might introduce an implosive b written with ʹb and contrasted with a normal 'b'. The next lesson might teach the letter combinations 'kp' and 'gb' and so on.

Each lesson should have lists of words that compare the sounds and letters being taught. There should also be illustrations of some of the words. The exercises should be laid out in such a way that the student can write in the correct answer. For example, this is an exercise teaching the difference between ʹ'b' and 'b' and 'd' and ʹ'd'.

Fill in the missing letters with b, 'b, d, or 'd.

1. _ _ _ili	4. _ _ _ako	7. _ _ o
trap	sadness	wait
2. _ _ _u	5. _ _afa	8. _ _ _okolo
ten	fix	behind
3. _ olo	6. _ _ _ _ua	9. _ _ _ete
war	goat	palm tree

The lesson should also have a short story that uses many words with the letter or tone being taught in that lesson. This can be followed by an exercise that gives the participants sentences to translate that are based on the story. At the end of the book there may be any or all of the following for extra reading practice: a test, a model letter, a story, riddles or proverbs, a short Scripture passage, or a word list.

If the lessons are being taught during a seminar, give assignments each day. The first page of each lesson in the transition guide might be done in class, and the second page as an assignment to complete before the next morning. At the beginning of the next class, check the answers. A transition guide can be used in various types of seminars and by individuals who are well motivated to learn.

1) If a transfer guide is available in your language, is it used? Could it be used more? Does it need to be improved in any way?

2) If there is not a transfer guide, who could help produce one?

2. Teaching people to read and write their language

Do you think it's important for people to be able to write their language in addition to being able to read it? Why? Add any of the following points that were not mentioned by the group.

It helps people to be able to write their own language because:

- learning to write reinforces reading and improves reading fluency.
- where church services have been entirely in a major language, if leaders switch to the mother tongue, they will need to be able to write such things as the announcements and sermon notes.
- once people realize that their language can be written, it raises its status.

Although people learn to read more rapidly than they learn to write, teaching writing along with reading from the start helps people learn both skills better. This is especially true for people who learn best by oral means. After the participants learn to read each lesson, dictate some words or texts for the participants to write down. For example, for the lesson on "b' dictate five words with "b' and some with 'b'. Correct these words and then give another five words. People need lots of examples before they will be able to write the language confidently and correctly.

It usually takes more than one seminar to teach people to write their language well. During the first seminar in an area, you can only teach the essential parts of the writing system. With each successive seminar, increase the difficulty of the writing tasks. Help them to begin to write their language by giving them useful assignments, for example:

- to write a letter
- to write the order of a church service
- to write announcements to be given in church
- to write exercises on the more difficult parts of the writing system, such as tone marks
- to write folk tales, riddles, or songs
- to write exercises on punctuation
- to write about their experiences
- to write a story they make up (creative writing)
- to produce a newspaper or a newsletter as a group

If a number of people who come to the first seminar are able to read and write the language, put them in an advanced group. To identify those who belong in the advanced group on the first morning, give a quick test such as reading a paragraph or taking a dictation of ten difficult words.

3. Teaching people to read aloud well

One of the main reasons churches do not use newly translated Scriptures in services is that pastors are afraid that they will not be able to read them aloud properly. They need a way to practise reading aloud that will not shame them publicly. Holding seminars that are open only to church leaders can provide good opportunities for such practice.

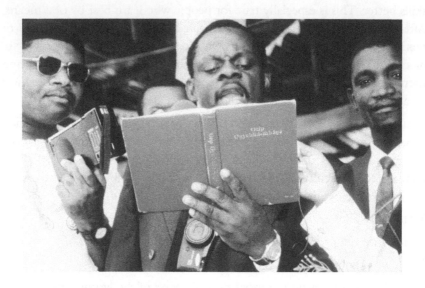

A. Beginning to read aloud

If you are running a Scripture engagement seminar for church leaders who have not learned to read their language, the first teaching session should be designed to give them confidence that it is possible to read the mother tongue. To do this, have a speaker of the language demonstrate briefly (ten minutes maximum) the symbols in the writing system that the participants need to know. For example, these could be unfamiliar vowels, tone marks, ways of writing nasalization, two sorts of 'b's or 'd's. Only teach the things that are essential for reading the language at this point. For example, if tone marks are not critical for reading the language, leave them until later in the seminar.

After this demonstration, divide the participants into small groups so that everyone has a chance to read aloud. Put slower readers in one group and faster readers in another. If older pastors typically read more slowly than younger ones, or if they would lose face by making mistakes in front of them, keep the two age groups apart. Give them an easy, well-known folk story and have everyone read a sentence in turn. Usually they are willing to try in this situation. If they are afraid to get started, read the first part together as a group to build their confidence.

Observe the groups and move any one who should be in a different group, unless this would embarrass them. Follow the folk story with an easy passage from Mark, such as a healing miracle of Jesus, or an easy narrative passage from the Old Testament. You may want to produce a leaflet of these stories and exercises for wider use. If a lot of people are reading the language for the first time, hold sessions like this twice a day, using more difficult materials each time.

If any participants are finding reading difficult, have a fluent reader in each group read aloud for about twenty minutes while the others follow in their books. Then have one person read a phrase and all the participants read it together after him or her. Supply more easy reading materials before moving on to Scripture passages.

B. Speed reading

Once most of the participants can read their language without much difficulty, do some exercises in speed-reading to improve their ability to see more of the sentence at a time. This will enable them to read aloud well. As they learn to read faster, be sure they continue to understand what they're reading. The following exercises will help them to learn this.

> **1)** Prepare a series of sentences for the participants to read. The first few sentences should have only five or six words; the later ones should be longer and have a number of parts divided by commas. If all the participants share the same mother tongue, prepare the sentences in it. If they speak different languages, prepare the sentences in a language that everyone understands. The language used isn't critical, since the skills they learn can be applied to reading in any language. Here are some examples of sentences in English:
> - The man went to the market.
> - The old man went to the market quickly.
> - The dog chased the cat all round the streets of the town.
> - The woman who arrived yesterday was the one I saw in the market earlier today.
> - When you go to your field, don't forget to take your hoe, your basket, your machete and some water to drink.
> - If it doesn't rain this afternoon, I think I will go to the market with my three children, but if it does rain, I will stay home and make some bread.
>
> **2)** Write each sentence on the board or on a transparency before the session begins, but don't let anyone see them. If

you use an overhead projector, cover the transparency to block out the words. If you use a blackboard, ask the participants to close their eyes while you write the sentence on the board.

3) Tell the participants that they will be shown a sentence for a few seconds, and they are to try to see all the words they can in chunks or as a group of words rather read one word at a time. Ask them to try to not move their lips while reading. Then let them see the sentence, just long enough for about half the participants to read it. Cover or erase the sentence and have everyone write down what they saw. When they have finished writing, have everyone look at the sentence again. As you move to longer sentences, most of the participants will improve their speed and no longer mouth the words.

1) Another way to help people learn to read faster with comprehension is to give a copy of a paragraph in the language to each participant. Start with the papers face down. When it's time to start, have them turn over their page and read the paragraph as fast as possible. When they finish, have them turn the paper back over and signal that they have finished. Note down their name and the time that they took. After everyone has finished, read out comprehension questions on the passage and have everyone write down the answers. Correct the answers together, being careful not to shame the slower readers. At the end, tell each student how long he or she took to read the passage. Their papers show them what their comprehension scores are.

2) The next time use a different paragraph and encourage everyone to try to do better. Once most of the participants are reading their language fluently, the time has come for a session on how to read well in public.

• • • • • • *Reading Scripture aloud well takes practice.*

4. Reading Scripture in public

When Scripture is read publicly, people should be able to follow it easily. To read well, it's important to practise reading the passage out loud at least four times. Practise reading the passage to your family or to a friend. Learn how to pronounce difficult names or terms so you don't stumble on them. Think about the meaning of the text and let God speak to you through it. If you don't believe or understand what you are reading, you will communicate this without intending to. Before the service, put a bookmark in your Bible to mark the passage so you can easily find it.

At the service, arrive early and get the order of the service. If you're nervous, breathe deeply to relax. Go up to the front slowly and read slowly, paying special attention to enunciate clearly. If you feel you are reading too slowly, you're probably doing it just right. Project your voice so that those furthest away can hear. Look up to establish eye contact with the congregation and to see if they are following. If you are using a microphone, keep your mouth about two inches away from it. If you are closer, your voice will be distorted and harsh.

Some people begin stuttering when they read in public. Research has shown that if stutterers can stop stuttering in their mother tongue, they will also stop stuttering in other languages. On the other hand, if they learn not to stutter in the majority language, it does not seem to help them in other languages. To help stutterers, encourage them to take deep breaths between sentences and to practise singing first what they want to say in public later.

Use easy passages to practice reading. Here are some from Mark:

Mark 1:21–39	Mark 9:14–29
Mark 3:7–12	Mark 10:46–52
Mark 5:1–20	Mark 12:41–44
Mark 8:1–9	Mark 16:1–8

Here are some easy passages elsewhere from the New Testament:

Matthew 2:1–12	Acts 12:4–11
Matthew 8:23–27	Acts 16:16–34
Matthew 18:22–35	Acts 23:12–22

Luke 10:25–37	Acts 28:1–6
Luke 15:11–32	Ephesians 6:1–4
John 2:1–10	Hebrews 13:1–6
John 8:1–11	James 2:1–4
John 11:17–43	Revelation 22:12–17

Here are some easy passages from the Old Testament:

Genesis 24:10–26	1 Samuel 3:1–10
Genesis 37:1–11	Esther 1–10
Joshua 2:1–7	Job 1:1–12
Judges 16:23–30	Ecclesiastes 3:1–8

1) Assign one of the following examples of bad reading to each small group and ask them to demonstrate it:

  a. Reading too fast or too slow.

  b. Reading too softly or shouting.

  c. Reading with no expression.

  d. Reading in words not phrases, paying no attention to the punctuation or the meaning.

  e. Stopping at the end of the line, even mid-sentence.

  f. Hesitating over the words.

  g. Backtracking-rereading phrases or words.

2) Divide into groups of four and practise reading Mark 1:21–28. First read it aloud together. Then have each person read it to the rest. The group should help each person to improve his reading. After fifteen-twenty minutes, tell everyone to come back together and ask for volunteers who think they can read the passage really well. Listen to two or three people.

Assignments

1. Make up a speed reading exercise in your language and try it out on a group of people.

2. What do you think are the most important points to remember when reading aloud in public?

3. If reading and writing in the mother-tongue is a problem in your area, what could you do to teach literates to read and write it well? Make a list of steps to follow.

Readings[*]

Marsch, Angelika. 1995. 'It's All a Question of Practise! A Scripture-in-use Project in the Central Andes of Peru.' *Notes on Literature in Use and Language Programs* 46:48–55.

Kutsch Lojenga, Constance. 1989. 'Transition Primers.' *Notes on Literacy* 60:31–35.

Loveland, Nancy Jean. 1992. 'Transition Literacy Workshops in the Peruvian Andes.' *Notes on Literacy* 18(1):33–40.

Remple, Robin. 1998. 'Transition Primer Manual for Trainers and Teachers.' *Notes on Literacy* 24(3):18–47.

Trudell, Barbara. 1995. 'Making Readers Literate: Transition Literacy in Sub-Saharan Africa.' *Notes on Literacy* 21(3):47–58.

Walters, Leah. 1986. 'A Back Transition Primer: National Language to Vernacular.' *Notes on Literacy* 48:22–27.

---

[*] http://www.scripture-engagement.org

Chapter 26

BASIC LITERACY AND SCRIPTURE

Introduction

Adults who don't know how to read sometimes feel that it would be impossible for them to learn, but this isn't the case. Learning to read can take months, but it is worth the effort. One of the strongest motivations found amongst Christians in adult literacy classes is to be able to read the Bible. This chapter talks about how Scripture can be a part of a literacy programme.

Pastor Simon's literacy classes

Pastor Simon had successfully helped start classes for educated people in his church to read Palapala and after a few weeks many of them were reading fluently. A few months later a Christian organization came to help start literacy classes in Palapala for those who couldn't read at all. After the classes had been going for about three years, Pastor Simon was at a meeting of all the pastors in the northern part of Sanatu.

One of the subjects the pastors discussed was how to get good literacy programmes in the churches so that more people could read the Bible. While they were together, Pastor Simon heard various tales of woe from his fellow pastors. Pastor Baji from an area in the south said, 'We've started literacy classes two or three times. The first week we had 25 students, but after three or four weeks only two or three people come. They find it so hard learning to read in English'.

Pastor Mambo had a different problem. He said, 'An organisation came into our area and started literacy classes. They teach people to read in our language, but the materials they read are all about cotton production. Some of the women in my church have gone to the classes, but they get bored after a while'.

Pastor Mark had yet another problem. 'A new organisation has come into our region and started some special sort of literacy classes. Some of our church members go to them. They thoroughly enjoy the classes, which consist of long discussions about matters that touch the local community. The problem is that none of them ever actually learn to read!'

When Pastor Simon heard all of this, he began to be happy about the literacy classes in his church, even though they were always having small problems, like a lazy teacher who often didn't come to teach. He told the other pastors, 'We have literacy classes in the church three times a week. The students begin by learning to read and write in Palapala, then in the later classes they go on to learn to read and write Kisanu, and the most advanced class is learning to read English. Anybody can come to the classes, whether they come to our church or not. In fact, the advanced class is held in the Catholic Church. Each of the classes has some Bible reading, because we find that many of our students want to learn to read in order to read the Bible, but we make sure they have plenty of other things to read as well'.

1) Have you had any of the problems expressed by these pastors?

2) Have you had different problems with literacy programmes that were not mentioned?

3) What solutions has Pastor Simon found to the problems stated by the others?

4) Would any of these solutions be helpful in your area?

1. Types of basic mother-tongue literacy programmes

There are two main types of literacy programmes: community-based and church-based. A community-based programme may be organized by the government, the local community leaders, or another organisation. It often meets in a local school. A church-based literacy programme is organized by a church or a group of churches, sometimes with help from other organisations.

Church-based literacy programmes should include Scripture reading in all their classes. This not only helps church members to use Scripture, but also reinforces their motivation for joining literacy classes. The leaders of these programmes should encourage Christians and non-Christians alike to come and learn to read. Non-Christians may well become Christians through hearing and reading the Scriptures for themselves, but they shouldn't be pressured to do so.

Scripture can be used at all levels of a basic literacy program. If the literacy classes consist of people from different church denominations, it is very important that the study of the Scriptures is non-sectarian. Here are some things to bear in mind when organizing such classes:

- Give church leaders an opportunity to study the materials before the classes begin so that they agree with what is being taught.
- Avoid divisive subjects, such as baptism or the end times.
- Instruct literacy teachers to encourage students to stay in their church rather than join another!

Even if the classes are not church-based, it may be possible to have a Scripture component in the programme, but this needs to be researched carefully before it is even suggested. If it is not possible to include Scripture as an integral part of the programme, it might be possible to arrange optional sessions for reading Scripture.

2. Stages in a literacy programme

There are four stages in a literacy programme. After people who don't know how to read finish the programme they will be at the point of being able to read fluently. At the same time, they will learn to write their language.

Depending on the difficulty of the language and the dedication of the participants, it can take people between one and two years to complete all of the stages.

Stage 1: Pre-reading and basic primer stage

In Stage 1 of a literacy programme, students will not be able to read the translated Scriptures, so the teacher should begin each lesson by reading a short passage of Scripture aloud and the class can pray and sing together. This opening part should not take more than fifteen minutes. It is not the time for a sermon.

A primer is the main reading material for this stage. Some primers are based on Scripture. The first lesson may have 'Jesus' as one of the key words. By the sixth lesson, people will be reading short, simple Bible stories, for example, one about Jesus healing a person. The advantage of this sort of primer is that Christians who join a reading class to read the Bible immediately feel that their goal is in sight. Another advantage is that non-Christians may come to Christ. There are some disadvantages, however. The first few lessons of any primer are challenging to write, as only a limited number of letters can be used. Scripture-based primers limit the number of letters even more, as the stories have to be from the Bible. This may result in unnatural or uninteresting stories. In addition, these primers can only be used in church-based programs. Another primer has to be prepared if there is also a community-based literacy program. Non-Christians may find the approach overly aggressive, and so reject both the message and the chance to learn to read.

Other primers teach reading by using stories based on familiar themes from the language group. People master the primer before they begin reading Scripture. These primers are easier to develop and can be used in all kinds of programmes, but may be less appealing to Christians who want to read the Bible.

A combination of these two types of primers is possible. The first lessons can concentrate on finding the best words to teach the most frequent letters and helping the students read meaningful material as quickly as possible. By the time the students have mastered about half of the primer, the lessons can begin to include Christian concepts. By the last quarter of the primer, the lessons can have simple adapted Bible stories as some of the reading material.

Other combinations are also possible. A programme known as Literacy for Life was developed in Ghana. It takes a primer without Scripture content and adds Bible studies for each lesson based on the key word. For example, if the key word is 'well' in a story on drawing water, the story might be about Jesus meeting the Samaritan woman at the well. In the first stages of the literacy programme, the teacher reads this material to the students. Later, the students read it for themselves.

> *Scripture can be used at all levels of a basic literacy program.*

1) In your situation, what kind of primer do you think would serve your community best? Why?

2) Which kind of primer is used at present?

3) Would an approach such as Literacy for Life help you?

Stage 2: Post-primer

Students at the beginning of Stage 2 need small booklets of simple Bible stories. Each story should contain no more than four to six new words. Choose stories that build on the vocabulary learned in Stage 1. Prepare exercises on these new words before you teach the story. The *New Readers' Series* of Bible booklets published by the United Bible Societies are suitable in the second part of this stage. By the end of this stage, students should understand the idea of a chapter and a verse and be able to look these up in a book like Mark's Gospel.

By the middle of Stage 2, students are ready to receive a New Testament if it is available. If not, they should receive at least a gospel or a book of the Old Testament, such as Genesis. The average student at this stage will be able to make a reasonable attempt to read any narrative passage in the

Bible but will still find teaching material, such as the epistles, difficult to read.

During this stage, it should be possible to teach students how to do Bible studies. One way to do this is to prepare workbooks of twelve Bible studies on simple passages in the New Testament or on one book of the Old Testament. Each study should have a series of questions for students to answer, and lines on which they can write their answers. Each lesson should also have a verse to memorize. Teachers lead the study, but they don't tell the students the answers. Instead, they help the students to find the answers in the Bible passage. (See Chapter 11.)

Some passages that may be good for beginning Bible studies from the New Testament are:

- Matthew 1:18–25   Birth of Jesus
- Matthew 4:1–11   Satan tempts Jesus
- Matthew 6:5–15   Jesus teaches about prayer
- Mark 1:29–39   Jesus heals people
- Mark 6:35–44   Jesus feeds 5,000 people
- Luke 8:4–15   The parable of the sower
- Luke 10:29–37   The parable of the good Samaritan
- Luke 19:1–10   Jesus and Zacchaeus
- John 5:1–9   Jesus heals a paralytic
- John 20:24–31   Jesus and Thomas
- Acts 1:6–11   Jesus returns to heaven
- Acts 16:16–34   Paul and Silas in prison

1) Does your church have classes for people who are only partially literate?

2) What Bible stories would you recommend they read?

3) Do they need more materials at different levels of difficulty, from easy-to-read to difficult?

4) Who could prepare these materials?

Stage 3: Adult education

By Stage 3, students are fluent readers and can do many types of Bible studies and activities suggested in this manual. For example, you could prepare a booklet of helpful passages of Scripture for good news encounters, as suggested in Chapter 17, or a booklet on relevant themes, as suggested in Chapters 9, 12 and 13.

If more than one denomination is working in the literacy programme, circulate a draft version of any Bible study books among the church leaders to be sure that everyone agrees with the content.

If the whole Bible is available, have the students learn the order of the books of the Old Testament at this stage.

Stage 4: Advanced adult education

By Stage 4, students should have a Bible if it exists in their language, and they should have acquired a habit of reading and studying it. During this last stage, it is important that the class is able to do their Bible study with minimal help from the teacher. They should study some of the harder books of the Bible, choosing those that are particularly relevant to the problems they are confronting. For example, if there is a lot of misunderstanding of the Christian's power over Satan, Ephesians is a good book to study. If the whole Bible is available, they should study one of the minor prophets.

3. A well-rounded programme

Literacy programmes aim to give a broad education to students so that they can use their literacy skills in everyday life and go on learning for the rest of their lives. A programme should have many parts to it: learning to read and write, writing letters, learning how to balance a budget, using arithmetic in every day tasks, knowing something about the wider world through geography and history, and so forth. If the literacy programme draws its material solely from Scripture, it will not result in a well-educated person.

Assignments

1. Does your church have a literacy programme? If so, describe how Scripture is used in it.

2. Is more than one church involved in your literacy programme? If so, what topics do you need to avoid to make the classes acceptable to all?

3. If you were planning a Bible study book for Stage 4 students, which book of the Bible would you like them to study and why?

4. Imagine that a number of non-Christians who are semi-literate have just joined Stage 2 in a church-based literacy programme. Make a list of easy passages in the NT that you would like them to study. Prepare six questions for the first study.

5. A large church where everyone speaks the same minority language has about 100 students in literacy classes. The pastor continues to read from the majority language Bible every Sunday.

   a) Why might the pastor be doing this?

   b) What problems will this cause?

   c) What can be done about it?

*Readings**

Herbert, Pat. 2006. 'Literacy for Life.' *Scripture in Use Today* 13:24–30.

Hill, Margaret. 2003. 'Scripture Impact and Literacy.' *Scripture in Use Today* 7:8–10.

—. 1995. 'Ngbaka Adult Literacy Program in Northwestern Zaire.' *Notes on Literacy* 21(4):38–55.

Levinsohn, Stephen. 1982. 'Literacy and Scripture Materials in a Bilingual Environment.' *Notes on Scripture Use* 3:24–25.

---

*   http://www.scripture-engagement.org

Passing It On

Fasting Fr Om

Chapter 27

RESEARCH, MARKETING, AND DISTRIBUTION

Introduction

One test of relevance of a Scripture product is the degree to which people voluntarily use it. For people to use it, they need to know that it is available, find it attractive and be able to get hold of a copy. Research can help us know whether people are currently using Scripture, how they are using it, what kinds of Scripture products they are using, and in which languages and media. This can help us evaluate needs and interests and develop marketing and distribution programmes that will improve Scripture engagement. This chapter explores these issues.

Where are the Bibles?

The Southern Anglican diocese of Bingola had just declared the coming year to be the Year of the Bible. Every parish was asked to make plans as to how they would help their church members read, listen to and study the Bible in a language they could understand well. This got off to a good start with a special dedication service.

Bishop Joseph decided to visit all the parishes in February to find out how things were going. Three weeks later, he returned home after travelling many miles and talking a great deal. He was warmly welcomed home by his wife and three children. That evening after his bath and a good meal he relaxed in the house and started to tell his wife about the trip. 'I visited thirty-five churches', he said, 'and they all know about the Year of the Bible. But what is actually happening on the ground is very different from church to church. I counted five churches where the Scriptures are read in languages that most of the congregation don't understand. Another ten churches have no programme to help their ordinary church members study the Bible, and only five are offering Scripture in audio form for those who can't read. I'm not sure exactly what the problem is. I feel discouraged'. His wife said, 'My dear, you need a good night's sleep then maybe you will be able to pray and think about it'.

The next day as the bishop was sitting in his office and praying for guidance, he thought about reports he had heard of a certain Pastor Simon from Sanatu, who had helped a number of churches engage with Scriptures in various local languages. 'Perhaps I should invite him here', he thought. After negotiations, Pastor Simon's denomination lent him to the Anglican Church for three months. Pastor Simon started travelling around and assessing the situation. After a couple of weeks he returned to discuss his findings with the bishop and a group of pastors. After some preliminary discussion, Pastor Simon stood by a blackboard and wrote three words on it: research, marketing, and distribution.

He explained each one, giving examples from the churches he had visited, being careful not to say which church it was! 'First', he said, 'You need to do some research. One church I visited had no idea at all how many members were able to read the Bible or the language they would prefer to read it in. The New Testament had just been published in that region, but no one could tell me how many copies had been sold or whether they were in use in the churches. Getting information from anyone was like groping around in the fog!

'Secondly, in some places there is a marketing problem. I met one poor pastor trying to sell some Bibles that were in tiny print. I watched the people in his church open the Bible, take one look at the words, put it back on the table, and immediately walk away. Then in another place I found a pastor selling Bible study books. They really would have been very useful for Bible studies, but unfortunately they had been published with a picture on the cover that looked like something you find in a children's colouring book! People looked at the cover and wouldn't even pick it up!'

Finally he addressed the issue of distribution. 'You all know about the new revised version of the Likali Bible that was published a year ago? Everywhere I went people asked me where they could buy them. People were still using old tattered Likali Bibles with half the pages falling out! I was curious what had happened, and finally managed to track down all the stock in a church office. I asked the man in charge there why they were stored away when people were asking to buy them. He told me, "No one had told us how much to sell them for, or what we do with the money."'

1) Share any experiences you have had of Bibles or Scripture portions being marketed in the wrong way. For example, they may have a cover that no one liked.

2) Where would you go if you wanted to buy a Bible, New Testament or Scripture portions in:

　　a. English?

　　b. the majority language in your area, if not English?

　　c. your mother tongue?

1. Why do research?

In the course of daily life, we all do research. For example, if we want to buy a bike, we look at the options and decide which one is best. When working in Scripture engagement, we should also do research so we can know which strategies are the most effective.

What are some good and bad reasons for doing research? (Sample answers, p 305)

In the 1980s, the Ghana Evangelical Commission researched whether there was a church in each of the ethnic groups of Ghana. Everyone assumed that all the groups in Ghana had been reached with the gospel. To their great surprise, they found that one people group didn't have any Christian witness at all. When they discovered this, a church sent missionaries to the area.

A language group in Côte d'Ivoire had the New Testament in their language but it was not being used by individuals or churches in the area. When some church leaders were asked about this, it became clear that they didn't even know that the New Testament existed in their language. If there had been attempts to tell people about it, they were not adequate.

Imagine that you want to start producing and marketing a new soft drink called Fantastic Fruit Flavour, or FFF for short. What would you need to find out before you started?

Make a list. Add any of the following points if they have not been mentioned.

- Find out about present sales of soft drinks.
- Find out what type of soft drink people like.
- Decide where the distribution points will be.
- Research the type of label that will appeal to people.
- Research the price people would pay for the product.
- Find out what size and shape bottle appeals the most to the general population.

2. Researching Scripture use

Church leaders need to know whether the people in their churches are receiving enough spiritual food to grow in their faith. Two ways of assessing Scripture use are: 1) to monitor the distribution of Scripture products, and 2) to find out how the Scripture products are being used.

A. Monitoring the distribution of Scripture products

To monitor the distribution of Scripture products, make an inventory of the Scripture products you have prepared for your audience. Include printed, audio and video products. Below is an example of a form. Copy out the form without the numbers into a notebook or on a computer spreadsheet. Leave enough blank spaces to record all your information.

Scripture Products Inventory			Date:	
Title	Date printed	Number printed	Total number sold	Number in stock
Luke (printed)	2004	1500	700	800
Transfer primer	1999	1000	899	101
Luke (audio)	2004			

When you have completed the inventory, take some time to think about the information. Discuss these questions:

1. Which products have sold quickly? Why do you think they did?

2. Which products have not sold quickly? Why do you think they didn't?

3. Which products should be reprinted?

4. What kind of Scripture products should you invest in next?

After six months, do the inventory again and see if the situation has changed. If sales have increased, this would most likely indicate that people are becoming more interested in reading or listening to Scripture.

B. Finding out how Scripture products are being used

People may have a copy of a Bible, but they need to be using it regularly to grow in their faith. To find out who is using which Scripture products in which contexts, languages and media, fill out the following form for each church in your language area. Involve church leaders or their designates in collecting this information.

Researcher's name:	Date:
Church name:	
Location:	
Mother tongue of local church leaders:	
Are local church leaders able to speak the main mother tongue of the congregation?	

Mother tongues represented in congregation. Indicate the approximate percentage of the people that speak them—for example, Palapala, 50 per cent :

Approximate percentage of congregation that is able to read in any language:

Approximate percentage of congregation that is able to read in their mother tongue:

List all of the meetings of the church and find out what Scripture products are used at each one. The title of the product will indicate its language and media. If Bible storying groups are meeting, include these in the list and write 'oral stories' in the second column.

Event	Title of Scripture product used
Mass	
Catechism	
Sunday school	
Women's meeting	
Bible studies	
(add others)	

Gather information on these events in all of the churches in the target area. This may include both urban and rural churches. If there are too many churches to visit them all, write the names of the churches on slips of paper and divide them into two piles, one for urban churches and one for rural. Mix up the papers in each pile and take some slips from each, selecting a number proportional to the number of churches in each group. For example, if the Methodists have forty rural churches and ten urban ones, pick at least ten slips from the pile of rural churches and at least three slips from the pile of urban churches. By picking slips this way, you're far less likely to go only to the churches that are using Scriptures well or the ones with which you're already familiar.

After gathering the information, compile it for each kind of church (Catholic, Baptist, etc.), keeping the results from urban and rural churches separate. Analyze it and look for a pattern in the way the churches use Scripture. For example, eight of the ten churches may use mother-tongue hymnals, but not use mother-tongue Scriptures; or the Catholic churches may use mother-tongue Scriptures for Scripture reading, but the Protestant churches may not.

After analyzing the information, meet with the church leaders and report on the findings. Discuss the following questions being careful to do so in a way that does not shame any church or church leader.

1. How much Scripture are the churches using?

2. In what contexts are they using Scripture?

3. Which churches are using Scripture in the language(s) spoken by most of the congregation?

4. In what contexts are they using mother-tongue Scripture?

5. Which Scripture products are being used?

6. If aural or video products are available, are churches using more aural and video or more printed Scripture products?

With this information in hand, think about the kinds of Scripture engagement activities that seem to be most effective, and what can be done to increase Scripture use where it is weak. Agree together on the best strategies to use. After you have tried these new strategies for a period of time, collect information again and see if there has been any increase in the amount of Scripture churches are using.

1) In a certain group of rural Baptist churches, research showed that in every congregation, over 80 per cent of the people spoke Wezi, but the churches only used Wezi for the announcements and songs. Most of the Baptist pastors there were not Wezi speakers. What Scripture engagement activities could you recommend to the senior pastor of the area?

2) In an urban group of Assemblies of God churches, research showed that all the churches were multi-lingual and multi-cultural but that there were two sizable groups of monolinguals in every church, one that spoke Wezi, the other Bamama. The main services were all held in English. What Scripture engagement activities could you recommend?

3. Marketing

Research may show that some or all of the mother-tongue Scripture products are not being used by most people. This may well be a marketing problem.

A. The appearance of the product

Hold up samples of a variety of attractive and unattractive Scripture products. Describe the product and intended audience.

1) Do you think this product would be appealing to the intended audience?

2) Why or why not?

People judge a book by its cover. They decide what kind of product it is: a Bible, a children's book, only for Christians, for women, and so forth. They decide whether it looks interesting enough to pick up and look inside. If the cover looks shabby, dull, uninteresting or is simply a colour that people don't like, they are unlikely to buy it. Businesses spend a lot of money making the packaging of their goods attractive. For something as important as Scripture products, we need to put effort into packaging as well.

If people find the pages of Scripture products filled with text in a very small font from one edge to the other, they may well set the product aside, especially if they are not used to reading or reading in that language. Leave plenty of blank space around the text, and if culturally acceptable, include illustrations.

People also make quick judgements about aural and visual products. They need to hear a voice that they enjoy listening to and trust. With videos, viewers decide in about three minutes whether they want to watch the whole thing or turn it off, so those first minutes need to capture their attention. With both videos and audio products, the labels on the covers are also very important. Test what people perceive to be attractive and interesting.

B. Advertising the product

Before people can use a product, they need to know that it exists. Develop a plan for advertising the available Scripture products widely and in all parts of the community. Mass media is helpful at this stage.

> What are some ways to advertise Scripture products?
>
> (Add any points below that have not been mentioned.)

Scripture products can be advertised through the following means:

- local radio stations
- television programmes that give the news of each ethnic group in the country
- billboards
- flyers or brochures
- announcements and/or banners at church conferences and pastors' meetings.
- arranging dedications of New Testaments or other Scripture products
- church announcements
- town criers

> **1)** What communication channels are available in your community to advertise your Scripture products?
>
> **2)** What parts of the community are reached by each one?
>
> **3)** What costs would be involved with each one, both in terms of money and effort necessary to prepare the advertisement?
>
> **4)** Which channels do you think would be most effective to use?
>
> **5)** What efforts have you made to market Scripture products? Which have been successful?

C. The appropriateness of the product

The content of Scripture products needs to attract the audience's attention. Some products may not be used because they don't meet a need the audience feels it has. Sometimes a very small thing can keep people from using a product. For example, they may find an illustration offensive, or they may wrongly assume that the Scripture product is only intended for one church, or it may cost more than they are willing to spend, and so forth. In other cases, audio and video products may be in a form they aren't able to use due to lack of machines or power. Find out why a product isn't being used and determine if changes can be made to correct the problem. If the product can't be salvaged, use what you learn about your audience to design more relevant products in the future.

4. Distribution channels

The most carefully prepared book or recording is of no use if it remains in a storeroom. Distributing and selling Scripture products depends on successful distribution networks and money management.

A. Distribution networks

The way products can be distributed successfully will differ from one community to another. Find out how things are distributed successfully in your community and reflect on the distribution of your Scripture products.

1) What sells well in your area? CocaCola? Baseball hats? Cell phones? Lottery tickets?

2) Why does it sell well?

3) Who sells it?

4) Where is it sold?

5) When is it sold?

6) Are there places where books are sold?

7) Are there places where CDs, DVDs, and videos are sold?

8) How is the money from these sales managed?

In many communities, Scripture products can be distributed in bookshops, mission offices, church offices, markets, shops, and at conferences, church services, or meetings. In some communities, colporteurs sell Scripture products door-to-door with great success. They buy the products at a reduced cost and are able to share God's word with people and make a small profit for their efforts.

> *The most carefully prepared book or recording is of no use if it remains in a storeroom!*

B. Money management

Printing and recording Scripture products cost money, and this money must be managed properly.

No reprint for the Ikari

The Ikari language committee were very happy when the Bible was finally published in their language. The stock of Bibles was put in their care and they were told that when all the copies were sold, that money would be used to pay for the next printing. The committee appointed a treasurer to keep track of the money. Things got off to a good start at the dedication of the Bible as many people bought a copy. Many of the pastors asked if they could have copies of the Bible to sell in their churches, so, soon after the dedication, the committee sent boxes of Bibles to pastors throughout the language community.

The committee kept some boxes of the Bibles, and as time went on, they gave out free copies to friends, visiting officials and pastors. Some of the boxes were kept in a small, damp room, and before long the termites began eating them. Gradually some money started to trickle in from the boxes given to pastors, but no one had a list of those who had actually taken Bibles. Without any record of where the Bibles had gone, there was no way to keep track of the money.

One of the committee members was trying hard to get the money in from the sales, and every time he met pastors who had received some to sell, he asked if they had sold any. Most said that they had given the copies to people and they were still waiting for the money. This went on for some months until all the copies had been distributed except those that had been eaten by termites. People started to ask for a reprint as the original printing had been insufficient for all the people who wanted one. When the committee met again to discuss this and hear a report of the money available, the treasurer was absent. After some time they found out that his wife had been ill, and he had used the Bible money to take her to the hospital. No reprint was done for many years, and many Ikari people are still without Bibles.

1) How did distribution affect Scripture engagement?

2) How could this unhappy ending have been avoided?

3) What are some ways to distribute Scripture products successfully?

4) Discuss responses to the third question in the large group. (Add any points not already mentioned.)

Policies for distributing Scripture products can include:

- The best policy may be no cash, no book! This needs to even include pastors!

- A sustainable financial system may need outside funding to print the first publication. After that, money from the sales of that product must be used to pay for reprinting.

- Accountability is needed for any type of finances. It is often best that two people control the cash. This could involve a cash box with two locks. Many communities have ways of ensuring that money is not misused.

- Books or other media must be stored in a place that protects them from theft, termites, water and mould.

Assignments

1. Choose two Scripture products available in your area, one product that you know sells well and one that is difficult to sell. List some of the reasons for the differences.

2. Who should make decisions about the appearance of Scripture products? What process should be used to make these decisions? This includes cover colour, type of illustrations, and so forth.

Readings*

Collins, Wes. 1984. 'Selling Books from a Bookstore.' *Notes on Scripture Use* 8:35–36.

Hill, Harriet. 2000. 'How to Know When Scripture Use is Succeeding', *Notes on Sociolinguistics* 5(2):81–87.

Lauber, Ed. 1993. 'SIU and Funding the Translation Program.' *Notes on Scripture Use and Language Programs* 37:15–21.

McKinney, Carol V. 2000. *Globe Trotting in Sandals: A Field Guide to Cultural Research*. Dallas, TX: SIL.

Porter, Doris. 1993. 'Area-centered Promotion-distribution: The Concept and Some Suggestions for Guidelines.' *Notes on Scripture Use and Language Programs* 37:32–35.

Showalter, Catherine J. 1990. 'Getting What You Ask For: A Study Of Sociolinguistic Survey Questionnaires.' In Bergman, T. G., ed. *Survey reference manual*. Dallas, TX: SIL.

Søgaard, Viggo. 1996. *Research in Church and Mission*. Pasadena, CA: William Carey.

Useful website

http://www.davidccook.com/international/ccmipartners2/ David C Cook's online magazine for Christian publishers. A treasure trove of information!

---

* http://www.scripture-engagement.org

Chapter 28

HOW TO BRING ABOUT CHANGE

Introduction

This book is full of ideas about changes you can bring to your community to help them engage more with Scripture. It particularly addresses the issue of helping people use newly translated Scriptures. To introduce these changes successfully, it's helpful to understand how people adopt changes and what makes them resist change.

Good enough for our fathers, good enough for me!

One afternoon Pastor Simon was sitting talking with the local Catholic catechist, Lambo. They were talking about the way that the new Palapala Scriptures were really helping their Christians to understand the Bible. As they talked, Pastor Simon thought about one of his deacons called Ngulu Mba. He told Lambo, 'Ngulu refuses to buy a Palapala New Testament. He always has his Kisanu Bible with him, and if he is leading the service, we go back to using Kisanu for almost everything except the announcements. I asked him why he doesn't want to use the Palapala translation, and he had various reasons. One of them was that he thinks that it will cause disunity in the church. Another one was that he needs the

266

Kisanu for the Old Testament and doesn't like carrying two books. But really I think he just doesn't want to change!'

Lambo replied, 'If you only have one leader in your church who feels like that, you are lucky! I have a whole group of church leaders that don't want anything at all to change. Not only do they find it hard to use the new translation, but they even resist changes like having the morning service at a different time! One of them said to me, "What was good for our fathers is good for me".'

They discussed this and thought about other changes that had come into their community. 'Remember when they first introduced the idea of planting beans between the corn?' said Pastor Simon. 'Some people accepted those free seeds and started planting beans right away. Other people started doing it once they saw that the first group were enjoying the beans, and that the corn was growing better. Other people waited a couple of years but then they eventually planted beans as well. There are still a few people who won't touch a bean! You know old papa Gambo? He is still saying that the beans are some foreign plot to poison us all!'

'Yes', said Lambo, 'Do you remember that organization that tried to introduce oxen for ploughing? That never worked because no one really could imagine taming those big cows, and no one could show us how to do it'.

They discussed the whole problem of bringing about change and decided they needed to know more about it. Lambo said, 'After all, becoming a Christian brings a big change to people's lives, so maybe some people who won't listen to the gospel are actually just resisting change'.

1) What types of change have come to your community?
2) How have people reacted to them?

1. Is change good or bad?

People have one of three basic attitudes towards change.

A. Change is bad

Some people think change is bad. They think that if anything in a culture changes, the society will fall apart. This type of person thinks cultures are like car engines: you can't just take one part out and put a different part in its place, because then the engine won't work any more. They want to preserve the past.

Sometimes people cling to their traditions for fear that they will lose their identity. For example, the French feel that if their language changes or accepts words from other languages, they will lose part of their heritage.

B. Change is inevitable

Change is all around us and some people see change as inevitable. If agriculture and farming were the same now as they were three hundred years ago, Africa would not have any pineapples, mangoes, corn, cassava, goats or chickens, and Europe would not have potatoes, tea or coffee. When people find that their neighbours have something that they think might be useful to them, they borrow it. Cultures also change in response to significant events, like war, tsunamis, disease, and conquest. Where there is life, there is change.

With globalization, people say that the world is getting smaller. This means that what happens in one part of the world affects people in another part of the world much more quickly than before. Whether we want it or not, even remote villages in developing countries are affected by the wider world.

C. Change is good

Some people see change as a good thing because they believe it helps people. All cultures suffer from the effects of sin. None is perfect. They need to change so that they become all God intended them to be. For example, in some cultures getting drunk is the norm. This leads to problems, such as alcoholism, unemployment, poverty, divorce, abuse, and so forth. The gospel brings change. When people become Christians, they may stop getting drunk, and gradually their way of life may improve. They may develop other ways to have a good time with friends that are less destructive.

Even good practices in a culture can be corrupted by sin. For example, God told Moses to hold up a bronze snake so that those who had been bitten by poisonous snakes would be healed. This was right and God's will for them. However by the reign of King Hezekiah the people were worshipping this bronze snake and so he destroyed it (2 Kings 18:4). Something good became bad.

Good practices in a culture can also become obsolete. For example, men's neckties were intended to keep them warm in very cold climates. Buildings and vehicles are often heated now, and in tropical climates men have no need to try to keep warm, so the reason for wearing ties has become obsolete in many places. Men are gradually wearing them less.

On the board, list some changes you see around you to illustrate each of the following statements:
- Change can be bad.
- Change comes whether we want it or not.
- Change can be good.

2. Determining the need

If you intend to introduce a change in a community, you are a change agent. You may have some ideas about the kinds of changes that might be helpful, but you need to do research in the community to find out if your ideas are correct. This research can involve:

- understanding the culture
- discussing with people, getting their opinions
- observing what is going on in the community, including observing other development organizations that are working in the area
- observing what is going on in the larger world that will affect the community, for example, AIDS, war, and so forth

The goal of this research is to understand the felt needs of people. Another goal is to understand real needs that the community may not be aware they have, such as their need for Christ, AIDS education, and so forth. Change will only be accepted if it responds to a need in the community.

If you asked a young man and an older woman in a typical village in your area what they felt they needed, what do you think they would say?

3. Levels of difficulty

Some changes are more difficult to introduce than others.

* Changes in beliefs and values (what is considered right and wrong) are the most difficult to introduce. For example, Kenyan Pentecostal Christians believe very strongly that alcohol is evil. Other people believe strongly that female excision is good and necessary.

* Changes in activities are less difficult to introduce. For example, queuing to buy bus tickets.

* Changes in technology are the easiest to introduce. For example, using plastic buckets instead of clay pots.

Because things are interrelated in a culture, any change in one area may affect other areas. For example, if people believe that water comes from a deity in the river, using a well would require them to change that belief. They may fear offending the deity and being punished. Getting the water would no longer require the long walk to the river, and this would affect who got water, when, and how. They would also need to learn the new technology of using a bucket on a rope or a pump instead of simply skimming water out of the river.

Things may also fall into different categories in different cultures. For example, farming methods are on the level of technology and activity in the West, but in many traditional cultures, strong religious beliefs surround farming, such as the belief that divinities or ancestors are in charge of the earth's fertility. When people resist a simple technological change that would provide obvious benefits, it may be due to their underlying beliefs. For example, in Democratic Republic of Congo, a development mission wanted to introduce a new type of tree that produced fruit that had high protein and vitamin content. One ethnic group accepted the saplings with joy and soon the trees were growing all over the area. The neighbouring group with the same climate and soil took some saplings but they all died in no time. The second group didn't take care of the newly planted trees because they believed that if you planted a fruit tree, you would die before you could eat the fruit.

When you begin getting ideas about changes that might improve life, test them with several small pilot projects. It's impossible to predict which changes will be adopted and which will be rejected. Pilot projects are the only way to find out. Once you know which things are accepted, you can promote them more widely.

From the beginning, think through how the change could be sustained long term when the change agent is no longer investing resources and energy into the process. The more the local people can do with their existing resources, the more likely the change is to spread throughout the community and be sustained. Finding ways for local communities to sustain their own programmes takes a lot more creative thought and hard work than simply finding an outside donor, but it is well worth the effort.

4. Increasing the appeal of change

As Christians we are all change agents. We want people to turn to Christ and to let him change their lives. How can we increase the appeal of new things, whether this is turning to Christ, using the mother-tongue Scriptures, or any other new thing? Here are some characteristics that make change more appealing:

- Imaginable: people have to be able to imagine themselves adopting the new thing. For example, taking a pastor to see how a multi-lingual church functions will help him to imagine the possibility for his church.

- Advantageous: the advantages of the change should be greater than the pain of making the change. If there is no advantage that makes sense to people, they probably won't choose to adopt the change. Advantages are not only material benefits. Prestige and power provide surprisingly strong motivation.

- Compatible: the innovation must fit (or be made to fit) into existing values and experiences. This may mean emphasizing different aspects of the change with different groups. For example, you might present literacy in a church setting as helping people to read God's word.

When speaking about the same literacy programme to a university, you could present it as developing the country's languages.

- Simple: keep the new idea as simple as possible. There are three kinds of knowledge: awareness knowledge, user knowledge, and theoretical knowledge. At this stage, people only need to be aware of the change. Keeping the message simple may be difficult because what seems simple to you might seem very complex to your audience. Explain the change you're promoting to someone from your intended audience to get feedback. Keep working on the message until your explanation seems simple to them.

- Sample-able: if people can try out the new thing, they are more likely to adopt it. For example, people are more likely to buy a Bible in their language if they can first sample a small brochure with some key passages from it. If people can try out the new thing without having to abandon their present practice, the chances of them adopting it also increase.

- Positive: changes that prevent something bad from happening are more difficult to introduce than those that result in immediate positive differences. One implication of this is to introduce things in a positive way whenever possible. For example, rather than saying that people should boil water so that they don't become ill, say boiling water makes you very healthy.

- Incentives: people can be motivated to change if rewards are given to those who adopt the change or penalties to those who do not. This kind of motivation will only work in the short term, however. Eventually, the change needs to spread on its own merits.

1) Choose one change you would all like to see come to your community.

2) Choose three of the above ways to increase the appeal of this change, and discuss how this could be done.

5. Stages of change

Change occurs in stages, not all at once. If you understand these stages, it will help you know how to introduce change successfully. The change agent's involvement in the process is different at each stage.

A. Knowledge stage

People cannot adopt changes they don't know about. Letting them know about the change is the first step. This may involve radio, newspaper, television, flyers, billboards, town criers, and so forth. Mass media is the best way to get the information out to the widest possible audience.

When people hear about a new thing for the first time, the information has to be simple and clear. For example, if you're trying to get the pastors in your community involved in a translation committee, don't tell them about all the 15 steps involved in getting a translation ready for publication. Give them a summary, the big picture. Too much information can overwhelm them and they will stop listening.

The information also has to catch people's attention and do so in such a way that they go on thinking about it. This is referred to as making your change 'sticky'. There is always too much going on around us to pay attention to everything, so we have to choose what we give our attention to. Find out what grabs your audience's attention. People often pay attention to those they respect. If respected people in the community have adopted the change you're proposing, publicize this in the mass media.

B. Persuasion stage

Once people know about a change, they need to be persuaded to adopt it. This requires personal interaction. They need to be able to ask questions and get answers about exactly how the change will affect their lives. Feelings become more important than facts. If someone they know and trust recommends the change, they are much more likely to adopt it.

C. Decision stage

At this point, the change agent needs to leave people alone to decide whether they want to adopt the change. If a change agent pressures people to accept a change, they may decide to do it just to please him or her. Later, they will not follow through on their decision.

D. Implementation stage

As people adopt a change, the change agent needs to be on hand to help solve any problems that might arise. Many changes have been abandoned because one small piece of equipment or one small bit of knowledge was lacking. For example, a project in Democratic Republic of Congo was set up to teach people how to make reading glasses. This went well for a few months until a clip on the side of one of the tools broke off. No one knew how to mend it or how to use another method, and the whole project stopped until someone with the right knowledge came and solved the problem.

Often people adjust a new thing to make it fit their situation better. For example, one community adopted the change of planting beans in rows between their corn plants. After a while, they found it was easier to plant the beans in patches rather than in rows. Now almost everyone does this. When people adjust a change to fit their situation, it is a good sign because it shows they have personalized it and made it their own.

As a change agent, you need to be able to recognize the adjustments that will help or at least not ruin the change you're introducing, and the things that will ruin it. Be flexible enough to encourage the former and discerning enough to spot the latter!

When a change has become a part of the routine, it is adopted. The change agent is no longer needed on a full-time basis.

E. Confirmation stage

Whenever people adopt a change, it upsets the way things are done. Like a stone that is dropped into a pond, change causes a ripple effect. This can make people feel insecure because life isn't as predictable as it was before. For example, when women attend literacy classes in the evenings, their other chores may go undone, and this may cause trouble in their marriages. Or they may find new self-confidence and defend themselves against abuse they had always accepted.

If tensions become too great, people may give up and go back to their old ways. For example, literacy classes may be tried for a year and then abandoned. During the confirmation stage, the change agent needs to make occasional visits to encourage people and help them solve unexpected problems.

Discuss a change that has happened recently in your community, for example the introduction of mother-tongue Scriptures.

1) Which stage are you at in the stages of change given above?

2) What do you need to do to arrive at the confirmation stage, if you are not there already?

6. Kinds of adopters

In any society, some people are adventurous and others cautious. They don't all adopt a change at the same time.

1) Think of a change that most of the participants have been exposed to. Some suggestions are: buying or using a mobile phone, using a computer, or a new agricultural innovation. Ask them to arrange themselves in a line according to the year that they adopted this change. At one end of the line there will be those who adopted it first and at the other end, those who adopted it last, or not at all. Then divide the line into the five sections below. The first three per cent of the group are the innovators, the next 13 per cent the early adopters, and so forth. Do this in a way that doesn't cause embarrassment.

First 3 per cent	Innovators
Next 13 per cent	Early adopters
Next 34 per cent	Early majority
Next 34 per cent	Late majority
Last 16 per cent	Laggards

2) Now tell them about the typical characteristics of each group, as explained below.

A. Innovators

Innovators are people who are known to be risk takers, willing to try anything. Others don't follow them because many of the things they're excited about never work out. They are often on the fringes of a community. If you are trying to introduce a change, don't concentrate on this group.

B. Early adopters

Early adopters are progressive. They are able to make a decision to try out something new more quickly and take more risks than others in the community, but they're more sensible than the innovators, and so they make good role models. They have more connections with the outside world, so they are exposed to new ideas more quickly and more often than others. They are often better educated and richer than average.

Change agents should focus their attention on the early adopters, and more precisely on the opinion leaders who are in this category. These are the few people who influence the opinions of others. They are not necessarily in formal leadership roles, but the eyes of the community are on them, watching to see if they will adopt or reject the change.

C. Early majority

The early majority are slightly more conservative than the early adopters. When people in this group see those they trust adopting a change, they began to feel that they could adopt it, too.

Often a change has to be adapted in some way to make it appealing to the early majority. For example, the early adopters may be willing to meet five nights per week for literacy classes, but the early majority may only be interested if the classes meet two nights per week. Certain people sense what would appeal to others and are good at 'translating' the change in a way others will accept. Try to identify these 'translators'.

When 25 per cent of the people have accepted a change, then what is called 'the tipping point' has been reached. From then on, the change will continue to filter through the society largely on its own momentum. For example, a literacy programme in Democratic Republic of Congo started with fourteen students. During the first six years it grew steadily, totalling about 5,000 students at the end of the sixth year. Suddenly for a combination of reasons, the next year it grew to 25,000 students!* At this point, the programme had taken on a momentum of its own that nothing could stop.

---

* Some of the reasons for this growth were that the Ngbaka realized that the classes were the equivalent of primary school, two volunteers publicized the schools throughout the area, and the government schools were no longer functioning.

D. Late majority

The late majority are more cautious. When they see the positive effect the change has had on those who adopted it, they are willing to accept the change, too. By the time the change has reached this group, it will be accepted by most of the community without any further work from the change agent.

E. Laggards

Laggards are people who are very slow to adopt change, if they do at all. Change agents should not worry about this group. There will always be some, and they don't have much influence on the larger group.

1) Among Jesus' disciples, who do you think was an opinion leader? Give evidence for your opinion, especially from the time of Christ's death and resurrection.

2) Who do you think was part of the late majority? Give evidence.

7. Important gifted people

We have already seen that the early adopters are important people in the change process. Other people with certain character qualities are also important in the change process. We refer to them as connectors, information specialists, and salespeople. Identify these people and focus your energy on getting them on board!

A. Connectors

Some people are naturally good at connecting with many different people in and out of their communities. Because they know so many people, they hear of new ideas and spread them far and wide. Information travels best by word of mouth. If the connectors are involved in the change you're proposing, it will spread rapidly.

B. Information specialists

Information specialists are people who enjoy collecting information and sharing it with others. They are databanks of knowledge and remember facts correctly. When they recommend something, people listen. People trust them and go to them for information. Be sure they know the facts about the change you are proposing.

C. Salespeople

Salespeople can convince people to do things. These are generally optimistic, energetic, likeable people who have good social skills. If you can convince them of the change you're proposing, they will sell it to the masses.

1) Identify people in your group who are early adaptors, connectors, information specialists, and salespeople.

2) How can you interest these people in the changes you want to bring about?

Assignments

1. Write a short description of different ways two ethnic groups you know have responded to change.

2. Think about a change you would like to introduce to a community. Give the three most important things you have learned from this chapter that will help you introduce it better.

3. If you are working in a community where witchcraft is common, discuss how witchcraft accusations can work against people accepting change.

*Readings**

Bradshaw, Bruce. 1993. *Bridging the Gap: Evangelism, Development and Shalom.* Monrovia, CA: MARC.

—. 2002. *Change across Cultures.* Grand Rapids, MI: Baker.

Carlson, Joyce. 1995. *The Stranger's Eyes: Best of Ethno-Info.* H. Hill and J. Arensen, eds. Nairobi: SIL Africa Area, pp 159–163.

Crickmore, Mary. 'Change—How it Happens, How To Understand and Promote it'. Unpublished manuscript.

Cromartie, Michael. 2000. 'How To Infect a Culture.' *Christianity Today* 8-7:64–66.

Elkins, Richard E. 1995. 'Conversion or Acculturation?' *Notes on Literature Use and Language Programs* 46:1–13.

Gladwell, Malcolm. 2000. *The Tipping Point: How Little Things Can Make a Big Difference.* NY: Little, Brown and Co.

Godin, Seth. 2001. *Unleashing the Ideavirus.* New York, NY: Hyperion.

Johnson, Scott and James D. Ludema. 1997. *Partnering to Build and Measure Organizational Capacity.* Grand Rapids, MI: Christian Reformed World Relief Committee.

Johnson, Spensor. 1998. 'Who Moved my Cheese?' New York, NY: G.P. Putnam's Sons.

Rogers, Everett M. 1983. *Diffusion of Innovations.* New York, NY: Macmillan.

---

* http://www.scripture-engagement.org

Chapter 29

PREPARING FOR SCRIPTURE ENGAGEMENT SEMINARS

Introduction

Scripture engagement seminars have been discussed and described throughout this book. They are one of the best ways of helping church leaders to translate the Bible into action in church and personal life. This chapter discusses some of the practical details of running these seminars.

Pastor Simon passes it on

One year, Pastor Simon was asked to go to a central Scripture engagement seminar to be held in Retali, the capital of the country. He was excited at the opportunity, though he wasn't looking forward to the journey by public transport over some very bad roads. One of the Palapala Catholic priests was also invited to the seminar. Happily for Pastor Simon, Father James could use a mission car so they were able to travel together in much more comfort.

Right from start, they discovered that the emphasis of the seminar was on teaching what they learned to church leaders back home. They learned more about how to reach people who were not only resistant to following Christ but also uninterested in learning how to read. They listened with interest to presenters who talked about using songs, stories, recordings, radio, and films to reach such people. They spent most afternoon sessions improving their Bible storying skills.

On the last day of the seminar, participants worked in language groups to plan the seminars and other activities that they hoped to have when they got home. Pastor Simon and Father James sat down together. After praying for wisdom, they discussed who should be invited to the seminars, which subjects they would choose to teach and how they could finance the event. Before the closing meeting, each language group had the chance to present their plans.

On the way home, Pastor Simon said, 'There still seems to be a lot of things to decide. Where do we start?' Father James replied, 'I think we need to form a small group of people to help arrange this. We should be involving the other churches in the area, and I'm sure the Palapala Old Testament translators will want to help'.

After about two weeks, they were able to get a small representative group together and discuss a possible seminar for church leaders to help them use the Palapala New Testament. In addition, they agreed that everyone would be interested in learning about oral ways of telling people about Christ. Then they needed to agree on where it would be, who would teach, when they would hold it, and other practical details. They found that this couldn't all be decided in one meeting and that other people needed to be consulted.

Finally after a couple of months, the plans were made for a seminar in three months' time. Pastor Simon thought about it all night and wondered, 'What if no one comes?' He needn't have worried! Fifty church leaders came from five different kinds of churches. They really enjoyed learning together. At the end, they left very happy to have new skills and with new confidence in their abilities to help people engage with the Palapala Scriptures.

1) Do church leaders from different kinds of churches in your area come together for other kinds of seminars? If not, will there be a problem in getting them to come together?

2) If there is a problem in getting leaders from different kinds of churches together, can you think of any solutions that will help to overcome it?

1. Overview of a Scripture engagement seminar

A seminar may last from a day to two weeks. Each day is usually made up of four or five sessions. As you plan the first seminar, keep in mind that it will be the first of a series. Change takes time! During a seminar, there are two sorts of sessions:

- those in which the participants work in small groups for the whole time, for example, when they are learning to write the language.

- those in which the subject is introduced by a short lecture with discussion in the large group, followed by smaller groups or by individuals working to put what they learned into practice. For example, a talk on Bible studies may be followed by the groups doing a Bible study on a specific passage. Or a talk on studying topics in Scripture may be followed by each person studying a topic and filling in answers on a sheet.

If participants have the chance to discuss and to put new information into practice, they are far more likely to remember it and apply it to their lives. So each session should include some exercises and discussion groups. Plan these first, and then plan to teach only what is necessary to prepare the participants for the exercises or discussion. Try to stay with the ten minute rule: no one should teach for more than ten minutes at a time without having exercises, discussions, or questions.

• • • • • •   *People learn much more by doing than by only hearing!*

2. Preparing for Scripture engagement seminars

There are a number of things to do before the start of a Scripture engagement seminar. They are listed here in the approximate order in which they need to be done.

A. Form a planning committee

To hold a Scripture engagement seminar, you'll need a planning committee. This committee prepares for and makes decisions about the seminar. It should consist of three to six people. Top church leaders from the churches that are expected to attend the seminar should be on this committee, as well as people who have already attended a Scripture engagement seminar. This group should discuss the ways people are presently engaging with Scripture in the churches and the barriers to that engagement. They should also discuss ways they hope to break through those barriers during the seminar.

B. Practical arrangements

The first issues that the planning committee needs to address are practical ones:

- Location: if the seminar is for one language only, a village setting may be more hospitable and less distracting than a city.
- Timing: check that there are no conflicts with the dates of other conferences and events.
- Length: typically local courses last from three to six days.
- Food and lodging: work out who will arrange food and lodging, and how the finances will be managed.
- Timetable: decide when the programme will start and stop each day. This depends on local conditions and customs.

C. Choose the participants

The participants invited to come should be people in leadership roles in the church and should include the pastors and priests. A suitable number for one of these courses is somewhere between twenty and sixty people. Once the committee decides how many churches to involve, it can calculate how many people each church may send. For example, if the course is meant for a church region that has 45 churches, each church should be asked to send only the main leader, so as not to make the group too large. If too many people want to come to the seminar, it will be difficult to keep it participatory. Arrange to have another seminar later so you can include everyone.

⚬ ⚬ ⚬ ⚬ ⚬ ⚬   *Always aim to train trainers of others!*

D. Choose and train the leaders

Once you know how many participants to expect, you will know how many leaders you need to help with the training. There should be one leader for each group of six to eight participants. If this is the first seminar in which you are promoting written mother-tongue Scripture, you may need more leaders as people are likely to need help to read their mother tongue. One member of the planning committee should serve as the overall organizer with the other members serving as small group leaders.

Group leaders should be people who are well respected and have good Bible knowledge. If you are using written Scriptures, they should be able to read their mother tongue fluently. To find these people look among the top church leaders, members of a translation team, reviewers, school teachers, missionaries, and so forth.

Decide who will train the small group leaders and draw up a programme for this. Different members of the planning committee can take it in turn to teach. Include the following in the training:

- If reading and writing will be part of the seminar, check that each person can read and write the language correctly. If necessary, give spelling lessons.

- Go over all the sessions, explaining what will be done in the small groups and how to lead them.

- If there is time, and if the leaders can read English, read through parts of this book and discuss it.

- Decide who is going to give each talk, and let them practise the talk in front of the other leaders.

- Pray and sing together.

This type of leadership training is especially necessary when you run your first seminar. Later on, it may be possible to do the training in a short session just before the seminar begins.

E. Content of the course

To plan the content of the course, the committee needs to decide which subjects are most important in the churches at the time. Your seminar should be lively and stimulating and give the participants several new tools to use in their churches. They should go home wanting to come back to future seminars.

It takes about half a day to teach a chapter of this book, so in a seminar of three days do not try to cover more than six subjects at the most. If time needs to be spent practising reading and writing the local language, then choose fewer subjects. Don't give your participants mental indigestion! Break up the daily schedules into one-hour or one-and-a-half-hour blocks. Often it's possible to have three sessions before the noon meal and two sessions in the afternoon. Begin the day with a thirty-minute devotional time and take time for singing during the day. If possible, use a variety of local music.

Aim to have variety in the programme each day of your seminar. Follow a session that requires a lot of concentration with something easier. Have sessions in which participants are learning something new followed by sessions in which they practise what they have learned. Include enough time to practise new skills for the participants to master them. For example, teach about Bible studies on passages during one seminar and introduce Bible studies on themes at the next.

It may be possible to meet in the evenings, particularly if everyone is housed at the same place. The evening sessions should not require great concentration and should be fun! Here are some suggestions:

- Show a film, filmstrip or video, on such subjects as *How the Bible Came to Us* (a United Bible Society production), the *Jesus Film* (Chapter 24), videos of life in Israel today, and so on.
- Share, learn, and record new Scripture songs.
- Pray and share together.
- Have the participants present skits or dramas they developed.

The workshop should end with a closing ceremony. This can be a time to invite others in the community or local churches to see what has been learned. The workshop participants can share their Bible studies, songs, dramas, and testimonies of what they learned. Awarding certificates to the participants can be a joyous time after many days of hard work.

●●●●●● *The details of the seminar schedule and timetable all depend on the local situation.*

3. Preparing the materials

Once the programme is settled, draw up a list of all the materials that must be translated and made available to the participants. These could include the following:

- all the Scriptures that are available in the language, in printed and recorded media
- a hymn book or a sheet of hymns
- certificates for the end of the course
- a writing manual or a series of exercises to teach writing
- if liturgical churches are involved, the passages for the next group of Sundays including Old Testament passages, if possible
- if learning to read the mother tongue is a goal, easy reading material such as folk stories
- invitations to the closing ceremony
- computers or equipment to record stories and songs
- large sheets of paper for posters, markers, glue, and tape to hang posters on the wall

In addition, other materials will be needed according to the subjects that have been chosen for the programme. Once a list of all the necessary materials has been prepared, the next step is to be sure you have all of the materials in the appropriate language. If the seminar is promoting mother-tongue Scripture, this may involve translating materials that do not already exist in the language. This takes time. The people who do this should have already received training in translation principles. If you need help, contact a Bible translation agency in your area.

Certificates need to be prepared in advance in the appropriate language. They could look something like this.

Scripture Engagement Seminar

_____NAME_____

has attended a Scripture engagement seminar held at

_____LOCATION_____

from ___BEGINNING DATE___ to ___ENDING DATE___

and is able to

___INSERT MAIN TEACHING GOAL OF WORKSHOP___

in _____LANGUAGE_____ and is able to teach this

to others.

Signed _____   Date _____

SEMINAR DIRECTOR

---

4. Assembling the materials

The materials for the seminar need to be assembled in a way that they can be distributed quickly to the participants. The best way to do this is to put them in plastic bags to be sold during the first session on the first day. If some Scripture has just been published, include it in the bag. If not, sell it separately to those who do not have it. In some countries it is very helpful to include a pencil and a small exercise book.

In addition to the bags for the participants, other things also need to be ready:

- chalk
- blackboard(s)
- cloth to clean the blackboard
- prizes for the competitions, where appropriate
- answer sheets for the leaders, where needed
- programmes for the leaders
- a register book or sheet for the participants to write down their names and any other information about themselves that is needed

5. Preparing for follow-up Scripture engagement seminars

Plan for a follow-up seminar to happen about a year after the first one. Only invite those to the follow-up who have put what they learned into practice. (Knowing this will happen can motivate participants to hold local seminars within the year.)

When you make the timetable for the follow-up seminar, include time for participants to report on how they have put ideas from the previous course into practice. Some may have some good ideas to share with the group. They may also have problems that need to be discussed.

Remember that some participants will be there for the first time and others will have already attended a seminar. For some sessions, you may need to schedule beginner and advanced classes at the same time. For other subjects, it is good to have everyone together. Those who have heard the presentation before may benefit from hearing it again or they may be able to help teach part of the session.

Each seminar should include fresh material and approaches. Basic subjects, such as Bible studies and reading aloud well, should be taught at every seminar until they are completely mastered, but these subjects can be taught in slightly different ways. For example, if the first course had Bible studies on Mark, the second course might have Bible studies on James. It should not be necessary to repeat any sessions in exactly the same form.

If church leaders can attend a seminar every twelve to fifteen months, this will almost certainly increase their ability to help people in their churches to engage with Scripture. Courses need to continue until the majority of church leaders and church members are using Scriptures in appropriate languages and media in all aspects of their lives.

These courses require a lot of work, but you will find it is worth the effort when you see men, women and children studying God's word in a language they understand well and applying it to their lives.

Make tentative plans for a Scripture engagement seminar for your area. Think about these questions as you make your plan:

1) If you were planning a Scripture engagement seminar in your home area, who do you think should be members of the decision-making group?

2) Who would you invite to the seminar as participants?

3) When would you hold it?

4) How long would it last?

5) What chapters would you teach?

6) How would you arrange for the participants to be housed and fed? How is this done for other types of training in your area?

Assignments

1. There are two ways to change the ideas and practices of church leaders: one is by holding a seminar for them, the other is by giving them the same information individually or in written form. Give at least three reasons why the seminar is more likely to be successful than giving the information individually or in writing.

2. You can teach a topic either by using discussion and exercises or by a lecture. Which do you think is the better and why?

3. How many courses would have to be held in your area to enable all church leaders to participate without needing to travel more than twenty miles (thirty-two kilometres)?

Readings[*]

McKinnies, Kimberly. 2004. 'Helpful Hints for Holding Scripture Impact Seminars.' *Scripture in Use Today* 10:34–36.

Benn, Keith. 2002. 'A Philosophy of Scripture in Use.' *Scripture in Use Today* 4:2–8.

Grebe, Karl. 2003. 'A Typical Single Local Language Seminar for Pastors.' *Scripture in Use Today* 7:16–18.

Stallsmith, Glenn. 2003. 'A Report of the Worldview Scripture Use Workshop.' *Scripture in Use Today* 6:24–27.

Vella, Jane. 2000. *Taking Learning to Task: Creative Strategies for Teaching Adults.* San Francisco, CA: Jossey-Bass.

---

[*]   http://www.scripture-engagement.org

Appendix 1

GOOD NEWS FOR MUSLIMS

Certain things in the Bible are especially attractive to Muslims. This appendix provides key biblical themes, important questions from the gospels, and important characteristics of Jesus.

Key Biblical Themes

There are a number of biblical themes which Muslims find attractive. These themes are good news to them and create interest in the Scriptures.

1. God's goodness, love, reliability, and care for his servants.	These qualities are demonstrated in the stories of Abraham, Joseph, the Exodus, Daniel, Jesus, and the Apostles, among others.
2. God's guidance of history towards good ends as he works through events to oppose evil, to train his servants in righteousness and truth, and to fulfil his good purposes for his people.	This is clearly seen in the stories of Abraham, Joseph, Moses, Ruth, David, Jonah, Daniel, Job, and in Revelation.
3. The portrait of Jesus himself: his kindness, devotion, wisdom, power, and ongoing reign as saviour and king.	Jesus is presented in all of the Gospels, but Luke is the one that is used the most to introduce Muslims to Jesus.
4. The love and forgiveness exhibited by true followers of Jesus.	This can be seen in stories from the Acts of the Apostles and in the lives of true disciples that people meet today. A similar theme is present in the life of Joseph.

5. The offer of personal forgiveness and acceptance by God.	This is presented in the Gospels and in Acts.
6. The offer of assured and complete salvation from hell and acceptance into God's kingdom.	This is foretold in Isaiah 53, and it comes out in the Gospels, particularly in Matthew 11:27–29 and Luke 7:36–50; 10:20; 12:32; 23:42–43; John 3:14–16; 11:25–27; and 20:31.
7. The offer of a personal relationship with the Lord, fully realized in the next life.	Matthew 18:20; 28:20; John 14:16–20; Acts 18:10; Revelation 21–22.
8. The offer of inner cleansing and renewal through God's Holy Spirit.	These are presented in segments of the Gospels, Acts, and epistles.
9. The offer and example of grace to live a godly life through the strengthening and guidance of the Holy Spirit.	This is described in the Acts of the Apostles and in some of the epistles.
10. Power to resist and repel Satan and evil spirits in Jesus' name.	This is found in the Gospels (for example, Luke 10:17–20), Acts, James, 1 Peter.

Important questions in the Gospels to ponder

- Luke 5:21 'Who can forgive sins, but God alone?'
- Luke 7:49 'Who is this, who even forgives sins?'
- Luke 8:25 'Who is this? He commands even the winds and the water, and they obey him.'
- Mark 6:2 'Where did this man get these things? they asked. What's this wisdom that has been given him, that he even does miracles!'
- Mark 10:18 'Why do you call me good? Jesus answered. No-one is good—except God alone.'
- Luke 24:26 'Did not the Christ have to suffer these things and then enter into his glory?'

Important characteristics of Jesus to ponder

- Jesus declared that he came from God.
- Jesus creates matter from nothing.

- Jesus controls the forces of nature.
- Jesus proclaims he is lord of all and has all power on heaven and earth.
- Jesus issues commandments on his own authority.
- Jesus knows the thoughts and hearts of people.
- Jesus sits on the throne of God in glory.
- Jesus sends and commands his angels.
- Jesus judges the nations.
- Jesus forgives sins.
- Jesus bestows eternal life.
- Jesus condemns people to hell.
- Jesus receives and accepts worship.
- Jesus receives and accepts prayer.
- Jesus receives and accepts being addressed as God.

Appendix 2

RESEARCHING SONG STYLES

Each culture has its own music. To begin finding out about your culture's music, choose one kind of song from your language group and answer the following questions.

1. At what events, for what occasions, and under what circumstances is this kind of song sung?

2. At what times of the day or what seasons of the year are these songs sung?

3. Where are they typically sung?

4. Do you know where and when this kind of song originated?

5. Are there still people who compose new songs in this style?

6. Why are these kinds of songs sung? What emotions are expressed?

7. Who typically sings these kinds of songs? (Women? Men? Children? Adults? Everybody? Specialists only?)

8. What instruments typically accompany these kinds of songs? How many? Who plays them? (Men or women, adults or children, anyone or specialists?)

9. Does performing this music require special clothing?

10. Does performing this music require other special objects? (a machete, magical objects, and so forth.)

11. How do people feel during the performance?

12. Is there dancing with these kinds of songs? How many dancers? Are they men, women, adults, children, or specialists?

13. Are there observers? How many? Who?

14. How are these songs composed? (Spontaneously? Improvised? With pencil and paper? While dreaming/ thinking under a tree? Other?) Who composes them?

15. What social or religious connotations, positive or negative, are associated with these kinds of songs? (Sorcery? Immoral acts? Initiations? Virtuous acts? Amusement? Neutral? Youth only? Drunkenness? Other?)

16. Considering the positive, negative, and neutral associations in the question above, would it be appropriate to adapt this genre of song to biblical texts for use in the church? Why or why not?

17. Has this kind of song style already been adapted to Bible texts currently sung in the church?

18. How do people learn this kind of song? In what contexts? Was it different before? What changed?

Appendix 3

DRAMAS ON THEMES

These dramas are intended to communicate biblical messages in a culturally appropriate format. They should be adapted to the local culture.

Ingratitude

A rich businessman, Mamadou, welcomes a needy stranger to live with him. Another stranger arrives, then another, and Mamadou accepts that they stay with him, too. He takes care of them, but they don't help him or his family out. He is so hospitable that he eventually welcomes ten strangers in need. Mamadou then loses his business and can no longer help them. Rather than returning the favour now that Mamadou is in need, eight of the guests insult him and only two help out and show themselves to be true friends.

Mamadou's friend Seydou comes to visit and asks him why he is sad. Mamadou tells his story; he is frustrated that eight of his guests have proved unfaithful friends and have even insulted him. Seydou tells Mamadou that even Nabila Isa (Jesus) experienced ingratitude. Seydou tells Mamadou the story of how Jesus healed ten lepers (Luke 17:11–19). Nine of them were not thankful. Mamadou realizes that he, too, has been unthankful for what Jesus has done for him. Mamadou decides to continue to do good as he is able. This story ends with a song: Ten lepers were healed, ten lepers were cleansed; only one came back to say thank you. Leprosy is not the only terrible disease; so is sin. And you, after Jesus forgave you your sins, what have you said to Him? Have you been thankful to Him?'

Only one sacrifice

A family performs a chicken sacrifice for a family member who is ill but the person still dies. Their teenage son begins to question the value of these sacrifices. The family discusses the importance of sacrifice. The teenage son talks to a Christian friend who explains the Jewish Passover sacrifice from Exodus. He also explains that Jesus' sacrifice is like the Passover lamb. It is the only sacrifice necessary to make peace with God. He explains from Hebrews how Jesus' sacrifice has made other sacrifices unnecessary. The young man prays to receive Christ. The community accuses him of going against their traditions. The village sorcerer puts a spell on him to kill him, but nothing adverse happens. The people are surprised and talk amongst themselves how Jesus is more powerful than the village sorcerer.

The greedy man

An old rich man is very greedy. He has two wives and five children. Because of his greed he doesn't trust anyone. He doesn't even like to spend money on his own wives' and children's needs. He hides his vast wealth in holes in the ground which he guards anxiously. His friends talk about him behind his back, how he won't even spend money on himself for his own enjoyment. His family is suffering and they complain about him behind his back, too.

He visits a friend who tells him the story of the rich fool (Luke 12:13–21). He comes home and asks forgiveness from his wives and gives them the money they need for food. They are very surprised at his sudden generosity and ask what has brought about this change. He tells them what he has learned. His children talk on the road about how their father has changed. The narrator ends with Hebrews 13:5, 'Keep your lives free from the love of money and be content with what you have, because God has said, "Never will I leave you; never will I forsake you".'

Appendix 4

RECORDING SCRIPTURE AND DRAMAS

Introduction

In Chapter 23, we discussed the various types of dramas that are possible and how to develop them. The quality of a Scripture recording can make people want to listen to it or it can put them off completely. Good recordings can be made locally with very simple technology. This chapter tells you how.

Preparing for recording

Before recording, the actors should come together and rehearse the script. Speak as though you are speaking to one person or one family, even though you are aiming to communicate to a large group.

The art of the radio actor is reading without sounding like you're reading. Here are some suggestions to help prepare your reading well:

1. Read your script two or three times to familiarize yourself with the whole story and all the characters.

2. Take a pencil or marker and underline or tick all the lines your character speaks. Write yourself notes about where to talk louder or softer, show an emotion, or a reaction.

3. Read the line to yourself and then look up and say it to someone. Or, ask a friend to read your line to you and repeat it after them with the right expression.

4. Make sure you understand what you are reading. If you don't, you won't sound believable. Think about how this scene is contributing to the story. What does this character want in this scene? How is he working at getting it?

5. If there is something in the text you would like to change, make a note in the margin. Then, at a pause, ask the others if they agree. The only thing that cannot be changed is the translated text of the word of God, although this may be interrupted with questions and explanations. If it is interrupted, the narrator needs to say something like 'so God's word continues . . .' when it resumes. This helps the audience know which parts of the drama are God's word.

6. Imagine you are the person you are playing. Live in their shoes. Think about his or her character and mannerisms, temperament, likes and dislikes, strengths and weaknesses. Much of this will be evident in the story from your script. You can complete it with your own character traits or those of someone you know well.

7. Find the emotion needed for each scene. At this time is this person happy? Sad? Angry? Suffering? Stunned? Avoid speaking in a monotone unless you want your character to be boring. Vary your volume, speed, and emotion. Even though the audience will not see your gestures, feel free to use them. Your listeners will be able to tell from your voice that you are using your hands properly when you speak. A programme is interesting if the speakers are enthusiastic. If the performers are not involved in the programme, you can't expect the listener to feel involved either.

8. Listen to the person speaking to you and say mmmm or m-hm or hm! These small reactions keep you in the scene in the listeners' minds.

9. Sound effects can liven up a recording and make it more real. Look through the script to decide what sound effects might be appropriate (rain, a car door slamming, a rooster crowing, and so forth). Figure out how you can make these sounds.

10. Ask others to critique your acting. You will learn more from others than from evaluating yourself. You can always learn something from feedback, but remember that you can't please all the people all the time. Stay balanced when thinking about the critiques you receive.

1) In groups of six, think of a three to five minute drama. Decide on a theme and develop it through a story line, involving conflict of some sort.

2) Decide who will act each part.

3) Without any rehearsal, perform this for the large group.

4) The group gives feedback on what they found to be believable, and what they would have liked to have seen more of.

Recording the programme

You will need a quiet room to record in. To get rid of echoes while you record, make everything in the room which is made out of metal or cement soft by covering it with cushions, rugs, wood, fabric, or mats.

Most computers are able to make excellent recordings. These recordings are easy to edit with free programs available on the internet, such as Audacity or Cool Edit.* A simple microphone can be used and passed between the actors, or you may be able to use several mikes that are all plugged into the computer or recorder.

When you are recording the script, the following will help you produce a good quality recording:

• Sit opposite those you are talking to and look at them often. This will help you sound more natural.

• Read your line quickly and silently and hold it in your mind. Look up and say it to the person you are talking to with the right expression and intonation.

• Stay close to your mike, but don't touch it. Be careful not to breathe heavily into your mike. Try to breathe quietly unless your character is tired or in pain. Hold the mike a bit to one side of your mouth so 'p' and 'b' don't make a loud puffy noise. If you back away from your mike, you will sound further away from the person you are talking to. Turn the pages of your script during the moments when you are not being recorded, or else the noise will be heard.

• Pronounce all your words clearly rather than swallowing them. The listener can't ask you to repeat anything he or she hasn't understood.

---

* Audacity is a free program available at **http://audacity.sourceforge.net**.

- Take a drink of water when your mouth is dry. Take breaks when you get tired. If the group is making a lot of errors, take a break. Go outside and walk around, or take a drink or eat a snack and try again later.

- Replay and listen to each scene as soon as you have recorded it. Re-record any lines that you're not happy with. If there are many changes, you may want to redo a whole section.

> Find a computer or other machine that can record and a mike.
>
> In groups of six, practise reading the story of the rich young fool (Mark 10:17–30). Have one person be the narrator, another the rich young fool, another Jesus, another Peter, and others some of the other disciples.
>
> **1)** Practise until you feel you are ready. Try to 'put your face in your voice'.
>
> **2)** Record your drama.
>
> **3)** Play it for the large group. Ask for feedback.

Editing and distributing your recording

After recording, someone with technical skills should listen to it and remove any undesirable sounds. If you have access to a computer, this can be easily done with simple, free programs.

Give each recording you make a number and a name. Make copies of the recordings to distribute. Keep a chart of which recordings you have given to whom, so you know what other recordings they may want next.

Assignments

1. Choose one passage of Scripture that God has used to speak to you in the past. Practise reading it and then record it very carefully. After you have recorded the passage, record yourself explaining why you have chosen that passage.

2. Make up a programme for a ten-minute radio broadcast. Say why you have chosen the subject, and how you would get people to help you make the recording.

Appendix 5

ANSWERS

Some answers, page 25

For example, Acts 8:30–35, 2 Timothy 3:16–17, Deuteronomy 6:6–7.

Sample answers, page 40

Question	Original meaning	Underlying principle	Application
1. John 13:14–15	Gentile slaves or women would wash guests feet to welcome them hospitably. Jewish men, even if they were slaves, would never be expected to perform this task.	Leaders should humble themselves to the point of assuming the role of a slave to serve one another	?
2. Exodus 23:19	Perhaps a protest against a Canaanite pagan ritual (NIV Study Bible).	Don't join in the worship practices of pagans.	?
3. 1 Timothy 2:8; 1 Kings 8:22	This was the usual Jewish position of praising God.	Praise God and pray in a culturally appropriate way.	?

4. Leviticus 19:13	Farm workers were poor and had no cash reserves. They were counting on getting paid at the end of the day to be able to eat. Employers needed to provide for the needs of their workers in a timely manner.	Be sure that the needs of those who work for you are met in a timely manner.	?

Sample answers, page 83

If witchcraft didn't exist, the world would be perfect: only very old people would die and there would be no illness, sterility, or misfortune.	Genesis 3
Spirits and spiritual forces are more powerful than humans.	Genesis 1:28–30 Psalm 8:4–8
Evil is stronger than good.	1 John 5:4–5
Misfortune is due to others, not due to any fault of my own. For example, if I drive while I'm drunk, crash my car, and kill a passenger, it's because someone was working witchcraft on me, not because of my drunk driving	1 John 1:8–10 Galatians 6:7–8
People need to protect themselves from spiritual attack.	1 John 5:18 Psalm 121
A person can become a soul-eating witch without wanting to and can do evil without knowing it.	James 4:7 1 Peter 5:8–9
It is right and necessary to take vengeance against those who harm family members.	Romans 12:17–19

Answers, page 93

The Herodians supported the colonial Roman government. The Pharisees considered anyone who supported it to be a traitor to their faith in God.

Answers, page 103

Joshua 1:8; 2 Timothy 2:15, and other passages.

Answers, page 120

1. What do the letters in the word AIDS stand for?
   A: Acquired—you get it
   I: Immune—the system that protects your body from disease
   D: Deficiency—you are missing something
   S: Syndrome—a group of symptoms

2. What does it mean to be HIV positive?
   HIV stands for Human Immune-deficiency Virus. If you are HIV positive, it means the HIV virus is already in your body.

3. What way do most people get AIDS?
   through having sex with an infected person

4. What is the second most common way?
   a mother giving it to her baby through childbirth

5. Is there a cure for this disease?
   No! Anti-retroviral drugs can slow its progress, however.

6. Can you get AIDS in the following ways?
   a. Hugging a person with AIDS: *NO*
   b. Sharing the same razor blade with a person who has AIDS: *YES*
   c. Using the same toilet as a person who has AIDS: *NO*
   d. Having sex with a person who has AIDS: *YES*
   e. Through an injection using a used needle: *YES*
   f. Sharing food with a person with AIDS: *NO*
   g. Through receiving a blood transfusion: *YES*
   h. Kissing a person who has AIDS on a cheek: *NO*
   i. Drinking out of the same cup at communion: *NO*
   j. Treating the open sores of a person with AIDS: *YES*
   k. By insect bites: *NO*

7. How can you tell if you have AIDS?
   by having a blood test.

8. How can a person with AIDS live longer?
   by eating good food especially fruit and vegetables
   by having medicine for other illnesses, like malaria
   by being loved and cared for
   If anti-retroviral drugs are available, they will help.

9. If a married couple find one is HIV positive and one is not, how can they avoid the healthy one becoming infected?

either by not having sex at all
or by using a condom every time they have sex

Answers, page 255

Possible answers: Good—to understand the situation, to be able to take appropriate action. Bad—to prove someone hasn't done well or is wrong.

The Africa Bible Commentary

A ONE-volume Bible Commentary by 70 African Scholars

General Editor: Tokunboh Adeyemo

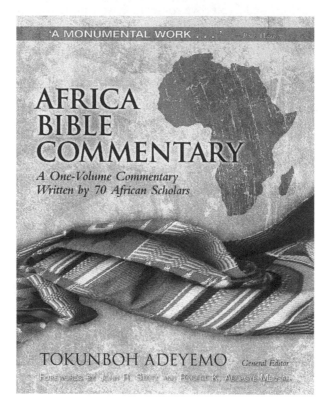

ISBN 978-9966-805-78-2

Published by WordAlive Publishers, Nairobi, Kenya

www.wordalivepublishers.com

"A publishing landmark ... its foundation is biblical, its perspective African ... I intend to use it myself in order to gain insight into the Word of God."

John R. Stott

CPSIA information can be obtained
at www.ICGtesting.com
Printed in the USA
LVHW031945111219
640174LV00013B/1038/P